11+ Maths

For the CEM test

It's no secret that the CEM 11+ test can be seriously tricky. But don't worry — this CGP Practice Book will give children a brilliant headstart on their test preparation.

In the first few sections, they can practise answering questions on one topic at a time. Then, when they're ready for more realistic 11+ practice, give the Assessment Tests a try.

It's all set at just the right level for Ages 8-9, so it's perfect for building their confidence. And with detailed answers included in a pull-out booklet, marking is a breeze!

How to access your free Online Edition

This book includes a free Online Edition to read on your PC, Mac or tablet. You'll just need to go to **cgpbooks.co.uk/extras** and enter this code:

0900 6797 8186 9015

By the way, this code only works for one person. If somebody else has used this book before you, they might have already claimed the Online Edition.

Practice Book – Ages 8-9

with Assessment Tests

How to use this Practice Book

This book is divided into two parts — themed question practice and assessment tests.
There are answers and detailed explanations in the pull-out section at the end of the book.

Themed question practice

- Each page contains practice questions divided by topic. Use these pages to work out your child's strengths and the areas they find tricky. The questions get harder down each page.
- Your child can use the smiley face tick boxes to evaluate how confident they feel with each topic.

Assessment tests

- The second half of the book contains six assessment tests, each with a mix of question types from the first half of the book. They take a similar form to the maths sections of the real test.
- You can print off multiple-choice answer sheets from cgpbooks.co.uk/11plus/answer-sheets, so your child can practise taking the tests as if they're sitting the real thing.
- Use the printable answer sheets if you want your child to do each test more than once.
- If you want to give your child timed practice, give them a time limit of 23 minutes for each test, and ask them to work as quickly and carefully as they can.
- Your child should aim for a mark of around 85% (33 questions correct) in each test.
  If they score less than this, use their results to work out the areas they need more practice on.
- If they haven't managed to finish the test in time, they need to work on increasing their speed, whereas if they have made a lot of mistakes, they need to work more carefully.
- Keep track of your child's scores using the progress chart on the inside back cover of the book.

Published by CGP

Editors:
Joe Brazier, Shaun Harrogate, Sophie Scott

Contributors:
Sue Foord, John Hawkins, Julie Hunt, Katrina Saville

With thanks to Paul Jordin and Rachel Murray for the proofreading.

Please note that CGP is not associated with CEM in any way.
This book does not include any official questions and is not endorsed by CEM.

ISBN: 978 1 78908 145 9
Printed by Elanders Ltd, Newcastle upon Tyne
Clipart from Corel®

Based on the classic CGP style created by Richard Parsons.

Text, design, layout and original illustrations © Coordination Group Publications Ltd. (CGP) 2018
All rights reserved.

Photocopying this book is not permitted, even if you have a CLA licence.
Extra copies are available from CGP with next day delivery • 0800 1712 712 • www.cgpbooks.co.uk

Contents

Section One — Working with Numbers

Place Value 2
Rounding Up and Down 4
Addition 6
Subtraction 8
Multiplying and Dividing by 10 and 100 10
Multiplication 11
Division 13
Mixed Calculations 15

Section Two — Number Knowledge

Types of Number 16
Factors and Multiples 17
Fractions 18
More on Fractions 19
Fractions and Decimals 20

Section Three — Number Problems

Number Sequences 21
Word Problems 23

Section Four — Data Handling

Data Tables 25
Displaying Data 27

Section Five — Shape and Space

Angles 29
2D Shapes 30
2D Shapes — Perimeter and Area 31
Symmetry 32
3D Shapes 33
Shape Problems 34
Coordinates 35

Section Six — Units and Measures

Units 36
Time 37

Section Seven — Mixed Problems

Mixed Problems 39

Assessment Tests

Assessment Test 1 41
Assessment Test 2 46
Assessment Test 3 51
Assessment Test 4 56
Assessment Test 5 61
Assessment Test 6 66

Tick off the check box for each topic as you go along.

Section One — Working with Numbers

Place Value

For each row of numbers below, circle the number that is the smallest.

1. A 165   B 95   C 120   D 180   E (50)
2. A 3000   B (890)   C 2450   D 1900   E 980
3. A 120   B 174   C 131   D (114)   E 128
4. A (1230)   B 3420   C 2030   D 1440   E 2620
5. A 4.2   B 2.7   C 3.1   D 3.5   E (2.4)

What number is the arrow pointing to on each of these number lines?

6. [number line 10 to 20, arrow at 14]   14
7. [number line 0 to 20, arrow at 6]   06
8. [number line 45 to 95, arrow at 80]   80
9. [number line 14 to 24, arrow at 19]   19
10. [number line 30 to 80, arrow at 65] 65

/ 10

Does the 7 in each of the following numbers stand for hundreds, tens, units, tenths or hundredths? Circle the correct answer.

11. 710   A (Hundreds)   B Tens   C Units   D Tenths   E Hundredths
12. 627.4   A Hundreds   B Tens   C (Units)   D Tenths   E Hundredths
13. 7.36   A Hundreds   B Tens   C Units   D (Tenths)   E Hundredths
14. 26.71   A Hundreds   B (Tens)   C Units   D Tenths   E Hundredths
15. 14.27   A Hundreds   B Tens   C (Units)   D Tenths   E Hundredths

/ 5

Place Value

16. Josephine timed how long each member of her family spent brushing their teeth. She recorded the results in this table. Who brushed their teeth in the shortest time? Circle the correct answer.

    A Dad   (C) John   E Karen
    B Mum   D Natalie

Name	Time (seconds)
Dad	138
Mum	146
John	108
Nat	155
Karen	114

17. The heights of 5 children are 1.21 m, 1.12 m, 1.20 m, 1.02 m and 1.10 m. What is the height of the shortest person? **1.02** m

18. Circle the number which is closest to 1000.

    A 996.7   B 1004.1   C 1002.9   D 996.3   (E) 997.5

Mr and Mrs Pearson are looking at flights for their holiday. The table shows five different airlines and how much luggage they allow per person.

19. Mr Pearson's luggage weighs 20.08 kg. How many of these airlines would let him take his luggage on the plane? **3**

20. Mrs Pearson's luggage weighs 20.15 kg. How many of these airlines would let her take her luggage on the plane? **2**

Airline	Maximum luggage weight (kg)
Air Kings	20.2
Fast Flights	19.95
Fly by Night	20.14
Pronto Planes	20.4
Speedy Jet	20.05

21. Rearrange the digits in 2753 to make the largest number possible. **7532**

22. 6 is exactly halfway between one of these pairs of numbers. Circle the correct pair.

    A 5.7 and 6.7   B 5.6 and 6.4   C 5.7 and 6.1   (D) 5.5 and 6.8   E 5.3 and 6.6

23. Which of these pairs of numbers are the same distance from 19? Circle the correct answer.

    (A) 12 and 24   B 17 and 22   C 16 and 21   D 15 and 23   E 14 and 25

24. Circle the number that is exactly halfway between 2.4 and 3.8.

    A 3.0   B 3.2   C 2.9   D 2.6   (E) 3.1

Rounding Up and Down

Round the following numbers to the nearest 10.

1. 71   60
2. 349
3. 407
4. 1536
5. 3092

Round 1295.61 to:

6. the nearest 100.
7. the nearest tenth.
8. the nearest 10.
9. the nearest whole number.

Circle the correct answer to show whether these numbers have been rounded to the nearest 10, 100 or 1000:

10. 25 rounded to 30.   A 10   B 100   C 1000
11. 381 rounded to 400.   A 10   B 100   C 1000
12. 615 rounded to 620.   A 10   B 100   C 1000
13. 1247 rounded to 1000.   A 10   B 100   C 1000
14. 517.4 rounded to 500.   A 10   B 100   C 1000

15. Anya has £6.27 in her purse. What is £6.27 rounded to the nearest pound?   £

16. There are 212 fish in an aquarium. How many fish are there to the nearest 10?

17. The path around Mo's garden is 1265 cm. Round this length to the nearest 10 cm.   cm

Section One — Working with Numbers

Rounding Up and Down

18. Jan runs a market stall. She decides to round all of her prices to the nearest 10p. Which two items will now be cheaper? Circle the correct answer.

    A potatoes and cauliflower
    B tomatoes and runner beans
    C cabbage and tomatoes
    D runner beans and cauliflower
    E cabbage and cauliflower

Item	Price
Potatoes	76p
Cauliflower	£1.15
Tomatoes	93p
Runner beans	47p
Cabbage	84p

19. The mass of a book is 159.53 g. What is this mass rounded to the nearest whole number of grams? ☐☐☐ g

20. 3264 people attended a rugby match. How many is this to the nearest 100? ☐☐☐☐

21. Ben's dad has a mass of 78.49 kg. What is his mass rounded to the nearest 0.1 kg? ☐☐.☐ kg

22. The town of Thelston has a population of 6000, rounded to the nearest 1000. Circle the number that could not be the actual number of people in Thelston.
    A 5621   B 5495   C 6497   D 6010   E 6318

23. Which of these is equal to 650? Circle the correct answer.
    A 626.5 to the nearest 10
    B 6490 to the nearest 100
    C 657.2 to the nearest 10
    D 650.7 to the nearest whole number
    E 646.1 to the nearest 10

Josie and Martina are measuring how tall they are in centimetres.

24. Josie is 147.5 cm tall and Martina is 145.3 cm tall. They both round their height to the nearest 10 cm. Which statement is true? Circle the correct answer.
    A Josie's rounded height is greater than Martina's rounded height.
    B Martina and Josie have the same rounded height.
    C Josie's height is rounded to 148 cm.
    D Martina's height is rounded to 140 cm.
    E Martina's height is rounded to 100 cm.

25. What is Josie's height rounded to the nearest cm? ☐☐☐ cm

Addition

Write down the answer to each calculation.

1. 33 + 9 = `42`
2. 23 + 47 = `70`
3. 85 + 16 = `101`
4. 65 + 48 = `114`

Write down the answer to each calculation.

5. 211 + 54 = `265`
6. 38 + 340 = `378`
7. 685 + 19 = `704`
8. 507 + 182 = `689`

What is the total cost of buying the following items?

Hat	£2.20
Scarf	£7.40
Shirt	£12.30
Jumper	£15.50
Jacket	£22.50

9. A jacket and a hat.   £ `24.70`
10. A scarf and a jumper.   £ `22.90`
11. A scarf and a jacket.   £ `29.90`
12. A shirt and a scarf.   £ `19.70`
13. A jumper and a shirt.   £ `27.80`

/ 13

14. 191 adults and 216 children went to a school concert. How many people went to the concert in total?   `407`

15. Mr Black grows two melons with masses 320 g and 446 g. What is the total mass of the melons?   `766` g

16. Jane buys garden ornaments with masses 315 g and 350 g. What is the total mass of the ornaments?   `665` g

/ 3

Section One — Working with Numbers

Addition

17. Two planks of wood measuring 133 cm and 327 cm are laid end to end. What is the total length of the planks? 4 6 0 cm

18. Pete poured 199 ml of lemonade and 178 ml of orange juice into an empty jug. How much liquid was in the jug? 2 4 7 ml

19. What is the total of all of the numbers on this spinner? 3 9

20. 336 Barchester City fans and 582 Dartfield fans were at a football match. How many fans were there altogether? Circle the correct answer.

    A 958   (B) 918   C 988   D 888   E 998

21. John ran two races in 152 seconds and 147 seconds. What was his total time for both races? 2 9 9 seconds

22. Which of these additions equals 90? Circle the correct answer.

    A 71 + 21   (C) 57 + 33   E 43 + 37
    B 45 + 55   D 24 + 56

Mel has 45 tulips in her front garden and 46 tulips in her back garden.

23. How many tulips does Mel have in total? 0 9 1

24. Mel plants another 15 tulips in her front garden and another 29 in her back garden. How many tulips does Mel have in total now? 1 3 5

25. Jake had fish and chips at the café. How much did he spend? £ 3.71

Café Menu	
Chicken	£3.59
Fish	£2.46
Chips	£1.25
Peas	45p

26. A bag contains 25 green marbles, 85 yellow marbles, 54 red marbles and 58 blue marbles. How many marbles are in the bag? 2 2 2

Subtraction

Write down the answer to each calculation.

1. 73 − 12 = 61
2. 69 − 34 = 35
3. 100 − 47 = 53
4. 125 − 77 = 48

Use each of the numbers in the box once to complete the calculations below.

| ~~87~~ ~~126~~ 49 ~~24~~ ~~121~~ |

5. 198 − 72 = 126
6. 249 − 225 = 024
7. 123 − 36 = 087
8. 166 − 121 = 45
9. 71 − 049 = 22

10. John spends 78p.
    How much change will he get from £1?   22 p

11. Alisha spends £3.50.
    How much change will she get from £5?   £ 2.50

12. Kate spends £2.60.
    How much change will she get from £5?   £ 3.60

13. Sita spends £4.30.
    How much change will she get from £10?   £ 6.30

14. Perry spends £7.85.
    How much change will he get from £10?   £ 3.85   /14

15. A pond was filled with 167 litres of water but 45 litres leaked out. How much water was left in the pond?   122 litres

16. There were 132 people in a theatre. 16 people left during the interval. How many people were left in the theatre?   116

17. Terri has 387 points on a computer game but she loses 136 points. What is her final score?   251

/3

Subtraction

Peter is training to run in a 1000 metre race.
His first attempt takes him 215 seconds.

18. After a week of practice, Peter can run 1000 metres 18 seconds faster than his first attempt. How long does it take him to run 1000 metres now? `197` seconds

19. After another 2 weeks of practise, Peter can run 1000 metres in 181 seconds. By how many seconds has he improved on the time he set after one week of training? `016` seconds

20. Which two numbers have a difference of 23? Circle the correct answer.
    - A   32 and 15
    - B   56 and 39
    - C   67 and 24
    - (D) 71 and 48
    - E   43 and 25

21. Mr Samson enters three sunflowers in the local flower show. They are 178 cm, 213 cm and 163 cm tall. What is the difference in height between the shortest sunflower and the tallest sunflower? Circle the correct answer.
    - A 350 cm
    - B 165 cm
    - (C) 50 cm
    - D 43 cm
    - E 52 cm

22. Patrick wants to buy a game costing £10.00. He has saved £6.65. How much more money does he need to save? Circle the correct answer.
    - A £3.45
    - B £4.45
    - C £6.15
    - (D) £3.35
    - E £2.55

23. Bobby inflates 317 balloons for a party. By the end of the party, 38 balloons have popped. How many balloons are left? `279`

Martin delivers milk to five towns in a round trip from Barrowford to Darmouth. The table shows how many bottles he delivers in each town.
He starts with 250 milk bottles.

Location	Number of Bottles
Barrowford	47
Canton	70
Morristone	16
Topsham	64
Darmouth	33

24. How many bottles of milk will Martin have left after delivering to Barrowford? `203`

25. How many bottles of milk will Martin have left after delivering to Morristone? `127`

26. How many bottles of milk will Martin have left over after visiting all five towns? `020`

Multiplying and Dividing by 10 and 100

Complete the calculations below.

1. 70 × 10 = 700
2. 62 × 10 = 620
3. 28 × 100 = 2600
4. 510 ÷ 10 = 501
5. 6000 ÷ 100 = 60

/ 5

6. Farmer Joe's chickens lay 15 eggs every day. How many eggs will they have laid after 10 days? 150

7. Crisps cost 72p per packet. There are 10 packets in every box. What is the price of each box? Give your answer in pence. 720 p

8. Tickets for a school concert cost £10 each. The school sold £6210 worth of tickets. How many tickets were sold? Circle the correct answer.

   A 6210   B 621   C 62100   D 6.21   E 62

9. Jake has a plank of wood that is 500 cm long. He cuts the plank of wood into 10 equal pieces. How many centimetres long is each piece? Circle the correct answer.

   A 500 cm   B 0.5 cm   C 5 cm   D 50 cm   E 5000 cm

10. ___?___ ÷ 10 = 44.
    Circle the missing number in this calculation.
    A 44   B 4   C 4400   D 440   E 140

George, David and Shaun are all chicken farmers. George has 670 chickens.

11. David has 10 times as many chickens as George. How many chickens does David have? 6700

12. Shaun has 100 times fewer chickens than David. How many chickens does Shaun have? 670

/ 7

Section One — Working with Numbers

Multiplication

The cost of some items in a shop are shown below.

Book £5   CD £7   Teddy Bear £6   Football £4

Work out how much each person spends.

1. Mabel buys 5 books. £ 25
2. Mohammed buys 4 CDs. £ 28
3. Phillip buys 6 teddy bears. £ 36
4. Naomi buys 8 footballs. £ 32

Write down the answer to each calculation.

5. 30 × 4 = 120
6. 90 × 5 = 450
7. 6 × 70 = 420
8. 60 × 3 = 180
9. 80 × 5 = 400
10. 15 × 6 = 090
11. 27 × 3 = 081
12. 43 × 5 = 215
13. 36 × 4 = 144
14. 5 × 45 = 270

/ 14

15. Ross buys eight packs of pencils. Each pack contains six pencils. How many pencils does he buy in total? 048

16. ___?___ × 9 = 36
    What is the missing number in this calculation? 04

Carol has a book in which she collects stickers. The book has 24 pages in total.

17. On each page there are 7 stickers. How many stickers are in the book in total? 168

18. Carol removes 2 stickers from every page. How many stickers has Carol removed in total? 120

/ 4

Section One — Working with Numbers

Multiplication

19. Mrs Robinson has a roll of ribbon. She cuts it into seven parts that are 5 m long each. How long was the roll of ribbon? `0 3 5` m

20. A teacher marks 30 test papers. There are nine questions on each paper. What is the total number of questions she marks? `2 7 0`

21. Which of the following calculations is correct? Circle the correct answer.
    - (A) 6 × 7 = 42
    - C 6 × 9 = 63
    - E 7 × 7 = 48
    - B 9 × 8 = 56
    - D 9 × 5 = 50

22. What is the total cost of three DVDs that cost 99p each? Circle the correct answer.
    - A £3.00
    - B £3.03
    - C £2.97
    - (D) £2.91
    - E £3.09

23. A hospital orders 30 boxes of bandages. Each box contains seven bandages. How many bandages does the hospital order? Circle the correct answer.
    - (A) 210
    - B 140
    - C 224
    - D 196
    - E 188

24. One coach can seat 33 people. How many people can four coaches seat? Circle the correct answer.
    - A 106
    - (B) 132
    - C 124
    - D 120
    - E 99

Hannah orders sweets from a sweet shop for her birthday. The table below shows the number of sweets in one packet, and how many of each packet Hannah ordered.

	Number in a packet	Packets ordered
Strawberry Laces	6	8
Lemon Drops	40	5
Chocolate Mice	28	5
Fizzy Whizzers	32	9
Cola Bottles	17	9

25. How many Strawberry Laces has Hannah ordered? `0 4 8`

26. How many Lemon Drops has Hannah ordered? `2 5 0`

27. How many Lemon Drops and Chocolate Mice has Hannah ordered together? `3 9 0`

Division

Write down the answer to each calculation.

1. 16 ÷ 2 = 8
2. 27 ÷ 3 = 9
3. 42 ÷ 6 = 7
4. 36 ÷ 6 = 6
5. 81 ÷ 9 = 9

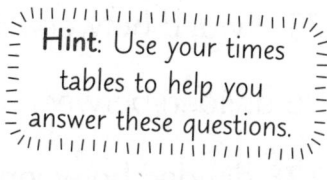

Hint: Use your times tables to help you answer these questions.

Write down the remainder in each calculation.

6. 19 ÷ 2   1
7. 46 ÷ 6   4
8. 69 ÷ 9   6
9. 68 ÷ 5   2
10. 88 ÷ 7   4

/ 10

11. A bookcase has three shelves. Jim divides 69 books equally between the three shelves. How many books are there on each shelf?  23

12. A box of 96 chocolates is divided equally between eight friends. How many chocolates does each friend get? Circle the correct answer.

    A 15   **B** 12   C 9   D 11   E 13

13. Look at the calculations given below. Circle the calculation that is incorrect.

    A   125 ÷ 5 = 25   **C**   58 ÷ 7 = 8   E   121 ÷ 11 = 11
    B   72 ÷ 6 = 12   D   350 ÷ 5 = 70

14. Farmer Giles has 86 eggs. He packs them into boxes of 6. How many full boxes does he have?   14

/ 4

Section One — Working with Numbers

Division

Work out how much money each person will get.

15. £16 divided between 4 people.   £ `04`
16. £75 divided between 5 people.   £ `16`
17. £96 divided between 6 people.   £ `16`
18. £128 divided between 4 people. £ `32`
19. £57 divided between 3 people.   £ `19`

/ 5

20. Which of these numbers can be exactly divided by four?
    Circle the correct answer.

    (A) 50   B 87   (C) 58   D 60   E 73

21. 68 ÷ 9 = __?__ remainder 5

    What is the missing number in this calculation?

22. Phoebe has 79 coins in her coin collection. She places all of the coins in an album. Each page of the album holds seven coins. How many pages will she need to fit all 79 coins in her album? `12`

23. June has 39 brownies. She divides all of the brownies into boxes of 9. She fills as many boxes as possible but has some brownies left over. How many brownies does she have left over? Circle the correct answer.

    A 1   B 2   (C) 3   D 4   E 5

Grace is making necklaces for a craft fair using coloured beads.
She uses 180 beads to make 9 identical necklaces.

24. How many beads are on each necklace? `20`

25. Grace has 108 red beads.
    How many red beads go on each necklace? `12`

26. Grace sells all 9 of her necklaces. She makes £54 in total. How much did each necklace sell for?   £ `06`

/ 7

Section One — Working with Numbers

Mixed Calculations

Complete the calculations in questions 1 to 5.

1. (11 + 17) − 6 = 22
2. (44 ÷ 4) + 3 = 14
3. (7 × 6) − 12 = 30
4. 8 + (12 ÷ 2) = 08 ✗
5. 3 × (12 ÷ 4) = 09

Hint: In these calculations do the bit that's inside the brackets first.

Find the numbers needed to complete the each of the function machines below.

6. 9 → +17 → −3 → ☐☐
7. 4 → +7 → ×6 → ☐☐
8. 81 → ÷9 → +4 → ☐☐

9. 42 → ÷2 → − ☐ → 14
10. 7 → ×4 → ÷ ☐ → 14

/ 10

11. Which calculation has the largest value? Circle the correct answer.

    A   (3 + 5) − (4 × 1)   B   (3 × 5) − (4 + 1)   **C**   (3 + 5) + (4 × 1)

12. Lizzy invites 8 people over for a party. She is making party bags for each guest. Each party bag must contain 3 toys and 12 sweets. Altogether, how many toys and sweets does Lizzy need? Circle the correct answer.

    A 80   **B 120**   C 40   D 105   E 135

13. Jake wants to work out how much it will cost for his family to go to the theatre. They need tickets for 2 adults, 1 student, 3 children and 2 seniors. Circle the option below which will complete this calculation to find the total cost of the tickets:

Ticket Prices	
Adult	£5.10
Child	£3.10
Student	£4.10
Senior	£4.10

    (2 × £5) + (1 × £4) + (3 × £3) + (2 × £4) ___?___

    A + 80p   B − 80p   C − 60 p   D + 60p   E + 10p

/ 3

Section Two — Number Knowledge

Types of Number

For each row of numbers below, circle the lowest value.

1. A 0.7   B 6   C 0.2   **D 1**   E 3
2. **A 2**   B 0.5   **C –1**   D 0   E 4
3. A 3   **B –6**   C 1   D 0   E –2

Complete each statement using a < or > sign.

4. –5 [>] –9   5. –3 [<] 0

Hint: < means 'is less than' and > means 'is greater than'.

6. What is 64 in Roman numerals? Circle the correct answer.
   A CXIV   **B LXIV**   C XLVI   D DXIV   E LXVI

/ 6

7. This table shows the maximum temperature each morning for 5 days.

   What is the difference between the highest and lowest temperatures recorded?

   [5] °C

Day	Temperature (°C)
Monday	–3
Tuesday	0
Wednesday	2
Thursday	–2
Friday	–1

8. Which of these statements is false? Circle the correct answer.
   A 49 + 17 will give an even number.
   B 34 – 18 will give an even number.
   C 17 + 12 will give an odd number.
   D 6 × 6 will give an even number.
   E 19 – 9 will give an odd number.

9. Jacob starts at –26 and subtracts 22. What number does Jacob end up at? [–04]

10. Which number is in the wrong section of this Venn diagram? [04]

    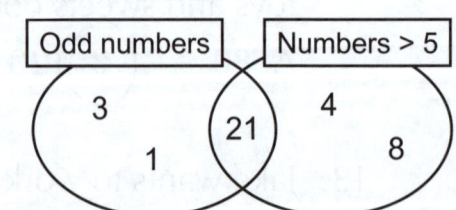

11. Circle the number below that is even and greater than –3.
    A 1   B 7   C –6   **D 2**   E 5

12. Constance thinks of a number. It is the sum of all of the odd numbers between 0 and 10. What is her number? [25]

/ 6

Factors and Multiples

For each row below, write down the next two multiples.

1. Multiples of 3:   3   6

2. Multiples of 7:   7   14

3. Rabin's age is equal to the sum of the first three multiples of 4. How old is Rabin?

4. Circle the number that is not a factor of 48.
   A 8   B 4   C 12   D 6   E 9

5. Circle the number which is a multiple of 6 and 9.
   A 30   B 12   C 18   D 27   E 3

6. There are 36 children at a party. They all split into equal teams to play some games. Which of these cannot be the number of children in each team? Circle the correct answer.
   A 6   B 3   C 4   D 9   E 8

   Hint: The number of children on each team must be a factor of 36.

7. Cathy says that all multiples of 3 are odd numbers.
   Dolly says that all multiples of 4 are even numbers.
   Ellie says that all multiples of 2 are also multiples of 4.
   Which of the statements below is true? Circle the correct answer.

   A Only Ellie is correct.
   B Cathy and Dolly are both correct.
   C Cathy, Dolly and Ellie are all correct.
   D Ellie and Dolly are both correct.
   E Only Dolly is correct.

8. Which set of labels is missing from this sorting table? Circle the correct answer.

	odd numbers	even numbers
?	3, 5	6
?	7	4, 8

   A factors of 15 / not factors of 15
   B multiples of 3 / not multiples of 3
   C less than 6 / 6 or more
   D factors of 30 / not factors of 30
   E less than 5 / 5 or more

9. Circle the set of numbers which contains only multiples of 2 or 5.
   A 2, 10, 13   C 16, 20, 25   E 25, 30, 33
   B 3, 4, 15   D 12, 13, 14

Fractions

A fraction of each of these shapes is shaded.
Write down the letter of the shape that matches each fraction.

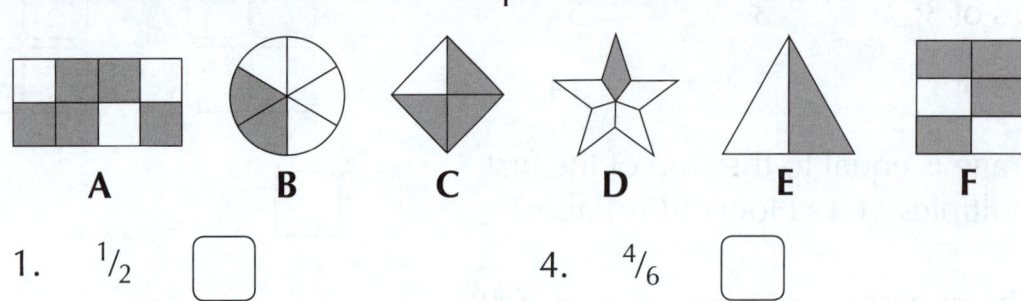

1. ½ ☐
2. ¾ ☐
3. ²⁄₆ ☐
4. ⁴⁄₆ ☐
5. ⅝ ☐
6. ⅕ ☐

/ 6

7. There are 16 sweets in a bag. Lakshmi eats ¼ of the sweets. How many sweets does Lakshmi eat? ☐

8. What fraction of the rectangle is shaded?
   Circle the correct answer.

   A ³⁄₁₂   B ⁵⁄₁₂   C ⁸⁄₁₂   D ⁷⁄₁₂   E ⁶⁄₁₂

   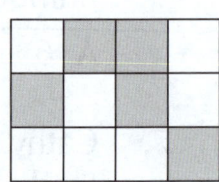

9. Which letter shows where the fraction ¾ should be placed on this number line? Circle the correct answer.

   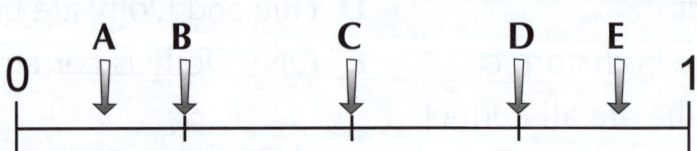

10. A bag of crisps is normally 60p.
    How much do the crisps cost under this special offer? ☐☐ p

    Special Offer
    Crisps are ⅓ of the normal price.

11. ¼ of the circle on the right is shaded. Which of the circles below is also ¼ shaded? Circle the correct answer.

    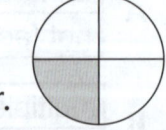

    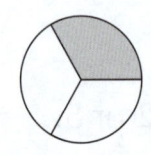 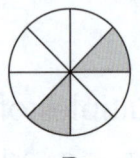 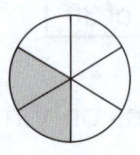 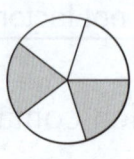 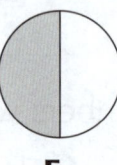
       A   B   C   D   E

    Hint: Fractions with different numerators and denominators can be equal in value.

    / 5

Section Two — Number Knowledge

More on Fractions

What fraction of each shape is shaded?
Write down the letter of the fraction that matches each shape.

A $\frac{1}{2}$ **B** $\frac{1}{4}$ **C** $\frac{1}{5}$ **D** $\frac{3}{4}$ **E** $\frac{1}{3}$

1.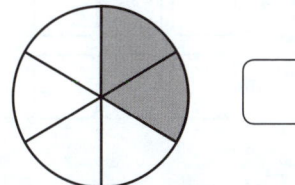

2.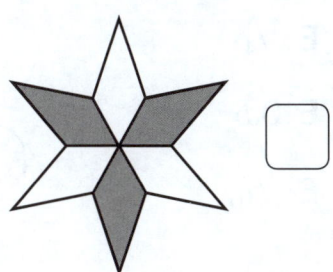

3.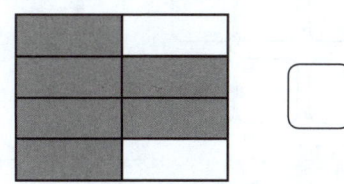

4.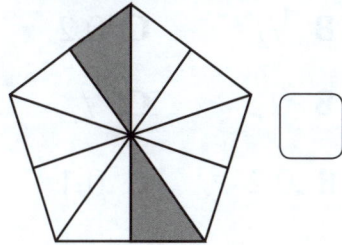

/ 4

5. Circle the fraction below that is equivalent to these fractions: $\frac{1}{5}, \frac{2}{10}, \frac{3}{15}$

   A $\frac{5}{20}$ **B** $\frac{4}{20}$ **C** $\frac{4}{18}$ **D** $\frac{3}{12}$ **E** $\frac{4}{15}$

6. Circle the fraction below that is equivalent to $\frac{1}{3}$.

   A $\frac{1}{6}$ **B** $\frac{3}{9}$ **C** $\frac{3}{6}$ **D** $\frac{6}{9}$ **E** $\frac{3}{18}$

7. Circle the fraction below that is not equivalent to $\frac{2}{12}$.

   A $\frac{4}{24}$ **B** $\frac{1}{6}$ **C** $\frac{1}{3}$ **D** $\frac{3}{18}$ **E** $\frac{10}{60}$

Complete the following:

8. $\frac{3}{5} + \frac{1}{5} = \frac{\Box}{\Box}$

9. $\frac{8}{9} - \frac{4}{9} = \frac{\Box}{\Box}$

10. Clara plants carrots in $\frac{1}{8}$ of her vegetable patch and onions in $\frac{4}{8}$ of it. What fraction of her vegetable patch has she used so far?

11. Beth, Eveline and Ryan are sharing a bar of chocolate. Beth eats $\frac{1}{15}$ of it, Eveline eats $\frac{4}{15}$ and Ryan eats $\frac{2}{15}$ of it. What fraction of the chocolate bar have they eaten in total?

12. In a car park there are red cars, silver cars and white cars only. $\frac{3}{7}$ of the cars are red and $\frac{2}{7}$ are silver. What fraction of the cars are white?

/ 8

Section Two — Number Knowledge

Fractions and Decimals

Write the fractions below as decimals.

1. ½   ☐.☐☐
2. ¼   ☐.☐☐
3. ¹⁄₁₀   ☐.☐☐

4. ¾   ☐.☐☐
5. ⁸⁄₁₀   ☐.☐☐
6. ¹⁰⁄₁₀   ☐.☐☐

Circle the largest value in each row.

7. **A** 0.8 **B** ½ **C** 0.2 **D** 0.75 **E** ¼
8. **A** ⁶⁄₁₀ **B** ¾ **C** ½ **D** 0.4 **E** 0.5
9. **A** ¼ **B** 0.2 **C** 0.1 **D** ¹⁄₁₀ **E** ²⁄₁₀

/ 9

10. ⁷⁄₁₀ of this shape is shaded. What is this value as a decimal?

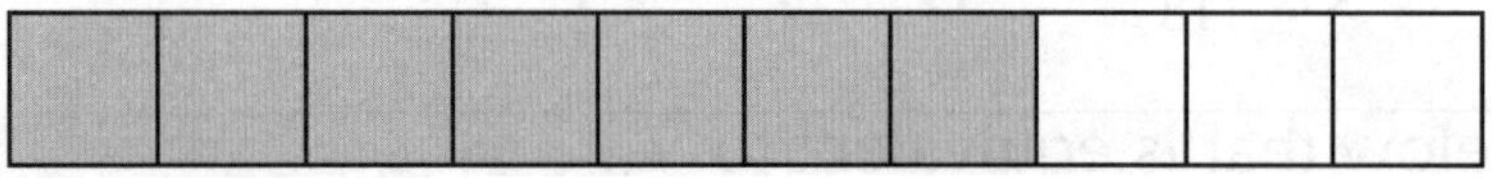

☐.☐☐

11. Joyce shared £1.00 with her two sisters. Annette got £0.10, Elizabeth got £0.50 and Joyce kept £0.40. What fraction of the money did Elizabeth get? Give the fraction in its simplest form.

☐/☐

12. Micah eats ²⁄₄ of a pizza and Rose eats ¼. Which of the following decimals shows the amount of pizza left over? Circle the correct answer.

   A 0.2   **B** 0.5   **C** 0.4   **D** 0.6   **E** 0.25

13. The table shows the amount of a cake eaten by four people. Who ate ³⁄₁₀ of the cake? Circle the correct answer.

   A Kelly   **C** Susan
   B Bethan   **D** Gurpreet

Name	Amount of cake eaten
Kelly	0.1
Bethan	0.35
Susan	0.3
Gurpreet	0.25

14. How many quarters are there in 0.75? ☐

/ 5

Section Three — Number Problems

Number Sequences

Write down the next number in each of the sequences below.

1. 7, 10, 13, 16...
2. 6, 12, 18, 24...
3. 28, 26, 24, 22...
4. 8.5, 9, 9.5, 10...
5. 1, 2, 4, 8...

The students in Year 4 are making number sequences.
What is the 3rd number in each person's sequence?

6. Tariq starts at 2 and counts on in steps of 3.
7. Michelle starts at 8 and counts on in steps of 6.
8. Harpreet starts at 0 and counts on in steps of 0.5.
9. Paul starts at 20 and counts back in steps of 6.
10. Gabrielle starts at 36 and counts back in steps of 5.

Hint: To find the numbers in a sequence, you can draw a number line and use it to help you count on or back.

/ 10

Write down the missing number in each of the sequences below.

11. 5, 10, 15, _?_, 25
12. 9, 13, 17, 21, _?_
13. 52, _?_, 56, 58, 60
14. 45, 42, _?_, 36, 33
15. _?_, 42, 35, 28, 21

16. Klara starts at 18 and counts on in steps of 6.
    Circle the number which will be in her sequence.

    A 34   B 35   C 36   D 37   E 38

/ 6

Number Sequences

17. The diagram shows the tiles on Mr Aston's roof. In each row there is 1 more tile than in the previous row. How many tiles will be on Mr Aston's roof if there are 5 rows?

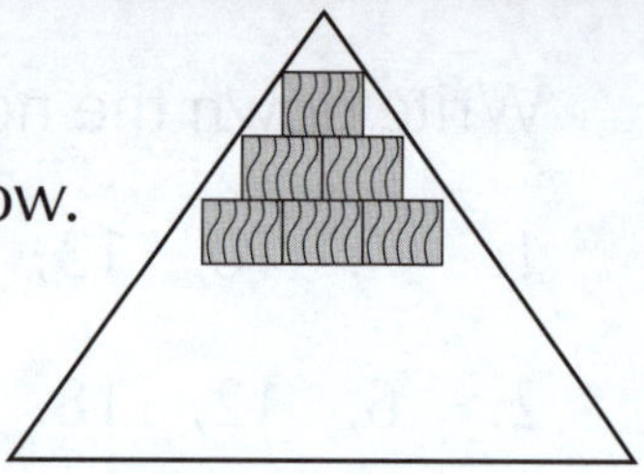

18. Nilesh writes down a sequence starting at 16. He counts back in steps of 3. Circle the number that will not be in his sequence.

    A 7   B 3   C 4   D 1   E 10

19. Caitlin starts at 10 and counts on in steps of 2.5. Circle the number that will be in her sequence.

    A 16.5   B 18   C 17.5   D 14   E 13.5

20. Charlie started at 7 and used the rule "subtract 5" to make a sequence. What is the 4th number in his sequence? Circle the correct answer.

    A –3   B –7   C 2   D –2   E –8

21. Jesper writes a sequence of numbers with the rule:
    To get the next number add the two previous numbers together.
    The first five numbers in the sequence are:
    1, 2, 3, 5, 8
    What is the 7th number in Jesper's sequence?

22. Molly writes a sequence using the rule "add 5". She starts at 2. Circle the number that will be in her sequence.

    A 27   B 28   C 29   D 30   E 31

Gina is using a sequence to plant seeds in some plant pots.

23. She plants 1 seed in the 1st pot, 4 seeds in the 2nd pot, 7 seeds in the 3rd pot and so on. How many seeds she will plant in the 5th pot?

24. What number pot will Gina plant 19 seeds in?

25. Dorothy is painting a bicycle. She needs to give it 4 coats of paint. Each coat of paint takes 8 minutes less than the previous coat. The first coat of paint takes her 40 minutes. How long will the last coat take her? minutes

Word Problems

1. Beth spent £2.50 on two mugs of hot chocolate and one banana milkshake. The banana milkshake cost 50p. How much did each mug of hot chocolate cost?

    £ ☐.☐☐

2. Mr Warren brought 10 boxes of fizzy sweets to a school party. Each box contained 128 fizzy sweets. How many fizzy sweets did Mr Warren bring in total?

    ☐☐☐☐☐

3. Darren bought 4 chews and 1 chocolate mouse from the tuck shop. How much did Darren pay?

    ☐☐☐ p

Tuck Shop Prices	
Chews	8p each
Lollies	10p each
Chocolate mice	12p each
Jelly worms	6p each

4. Waleed paid £20 for six cinema tickets. He received £2 in change. How much did each cinema ticket cost?

    £ ☐.☐☐

5. Jodie wants to buy a jacket that costs £40, but she only has £20. She saves £4 each week until she has enough money to buy the jacket. How many weeks does she need to save for? Circle the correct answer.

    A 5   B 10   C 7   D 4   E 8

6. Callum thinks of a number. He divides it by 4 and ends up with 6. What number did Callum start with? Circle the correct answer.

    A 24   B 18   C 15   D 1.5   E 12

7. William has £10 to spend on his mum's birthday presents. Which of the following would cost exactly £10? Circle the correct answer.

    A 2 scarves and 1 plant.
    B 2 bottles of perfume.
    C 1 bottle of perfume and 2 scarves.
    D 2 plants and 1 scarf.
    E 1 plant and 1 bottle of perfume.

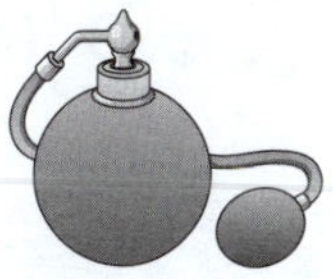

    Plant £5 
    Perfume £7
    Scarf £1.50

8. Nicola's dad has seen exactly 6 times as many football matches as Nicola has. Which of these could be the number of football matches her dad has seen? Circle the correct answer.

    A 32   B 36   C 41   D 28   E 38

Word Problems

9. Mr Bracken paid £15 for 10 litres of petrol for his car. He used 6 litres of petrol to drive to his aunt's house. How much did the petrol for this journey cost? £ ☐☐.☐☐

10. Robin multiplies 3 by 8 and divides the answer by 6. Arjen also starts with 3, but does a different calculation. Both boys get the same answer. Which of these calculations could Arjen have done? Circle the correct answer.

    A   Multiply by 4 then divide by 3.
    B   Multiply by 16 then divide by 2.
    C   Multiply by 4 then divide by 2.
    D   Multiply by 2 then divide by 4.
    E   Multiply by 2 then divide by 3.

11. The table shows the ingredients used to make pasta carbonara for 4 people. How much pasta would be needed for exactly 5 people? ☐☐☐ g

Pasta Carbonara (serves 4)	
Pasta	400 g
Cream	100 ml
Ham	100 g
Shallots	2

12. Mrs Price is making costumes for a play. She can make 3 rabbit costumes and 2 squirrel costumes from 5 metres of fabric. How many metres of fabric will she need to make 9 rabbit costumes and 6 squirrel costumes? ☐☐ m

13. A pack of butter has a mass of 200 g and is 4 cm tall. Penny places packs of butter on top of each other to make a stack that is 12 cm tall. What is the mass of the stack of butter? Circle the correct answer.

    A 800 g   C 12 g   E 48 g
    B 200 g   D 600 g

    Hint: Start by working out the number of packs of butter in the stack.

Martha is buying hair clips from Hair Care, where they cost £1.50 each.

14. How many hair clips can Martha afford to buy from Hair Care with £10? ☐☐

At Super Style, hair clips also cost £1.50 each but if you buy 2 you get 50p off.

15. How many hair clips can Martha afford to buy from Super Style with £10? ☐☐

/ 7

Section Four — Data Handling

Data Tables

Use the school uniform order form to answer these questions.

School Uniform Order Form		
Item	Price (each)	Number Ordered
Shirt	£5.99	3
Trousers	£10.99	1
Jumper	£12.99	1
Shorts	£5.99	2
Blazer	£19.99	1

1. How many shirts have been ordered? ☐☐

2. How much did a jumper cost? £ ☐☐.☐☐

3. Which item has been ordered exactly twice?
   A Shirt   C Jumper   E Blazer
   B Trousers D Shorts

4. What is the most expensive item of uniform?
   A Shirt   B Trousers   C Jumper   D Shorts   E Blazer

5. How much more expensive are trousers than shorts?   £ ☐

/ 5

6. The table shows the number of pets owned by the children in Class D.

Number of pets owned	1	2	3	4	5
Number of children	7	8	3	4	3

   How many children in Class D own two or more pets? ☐☐

The table below shows information about four towns.

7. Which two towns have the same number of shops and the same number of parks? Circle the correct answer.
   A Dellville and Coalton
   B Herdnell and Dellville
   C Coalton and Nolanbeck
   D Dellville and Nolanbeck
   E Herdnell and Nolanbeck

Town	Population	Number of shops	Number of parks
Herdnell	16 500	112	4
Dellville	28 000	136	6
Coalton	35 500	207	6
Nolanbeck	28 000	112	4

8. How many more shops does Dellville have than Nolanbeck? ☐☐

9. The table shows the number of boys and girls in Years 4 and 5 at Westfield School. What is the total number of children in Year 5? ☐☐

	Girls	Boys	Total
Year 4	13	12	25
Year 5	17	14	?

/ 4

Data Tables

10. The table shows the temperature of the water in Tony's bath over a 3 hour period. Between which two times did the temperature fall by 5 °C? Circle the correct answer.

    A 12:00 and 12:30   D 14:00 and 14:30
    B 12:30 and 13:00   E 14:30 and 15:00
    C 13:00 and 13:30

Time	Temperature (°C)
12:00	42
12:30	39
13:00	34
13:30	30
14:00	28
14:30	25
15:00	21

11. 40 children were asked how they travel to school. The results are shown in the table.

	Car	Bus	Bike	Train	Walk
Number of children	8	3	6	2	21

    How many children did not travel to school by car? Circle the correct answer.

    A 26   B 32   C 19   D 8   E 22

Mrs Chung is putting her shopping bill into this table.

12. How many onions did she buy?

13. What was the cost per item of the baked beans she bought? ☐☐☐ p

Item	Number Bought	Cost (per item)	Total Cost
Cereal	2	£2.60	£5.20
Milk	1	£1.90	£1.90
Baked Beans	4	?	£2.80
Onions	?	20p	£1.40

A bakery started to record the number of items it sold in one day in this table.

14. How many cookies did they sell in the afternoon?

15. They sold 30 items altogether in the morning. How many brownies did they sell in the morning?

Item	Number sold		
	Morning	Afternoon	Total
Doughnuts		10	26
Cookies	7		18
Brownies		24	

16. Which item was sold the most over the whole day?

    A Doughnuts   B Cookies   C Brownies

Displaying Data

Mr Potter made this bar chart to show how many tomatoes he picked each day. Use the bar chart to answer questions 1-4.

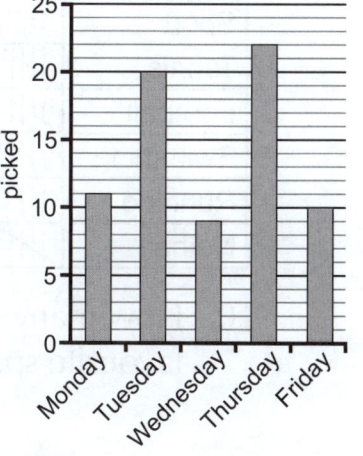

1. On which day did Mr Potter pick the most tomatoes?
   - A Monday
   - B Tuesday
   - C Wednesday
   - D Thursday
   - E Friday

2. On which day were exactly 10 tomatoes picked?
   - A Monday
   - B Tuesday
   - C Wednesday
   - D Thursday
   - E Friday

3. How many tomatoes were picked on Monday?

4. What was the total number of tomatoes picked on Thursday and Friday?

/ 4

5. Shirley made this pictogram to show the different buttons that she found in her drawer. How many red buttons did she find? Circle the correct answer.

   - A 2.5
   - B 12
   - C 4
   - D 3
   - E 10

Button colour	Number of buttons
White	⬤ ⬤ ⬤ ⬤ ⬤
Red	⬤ ⬤ ◖
Black	⬤ ⬤ ⬤ ⬤

   ⬤ = 4 buttons

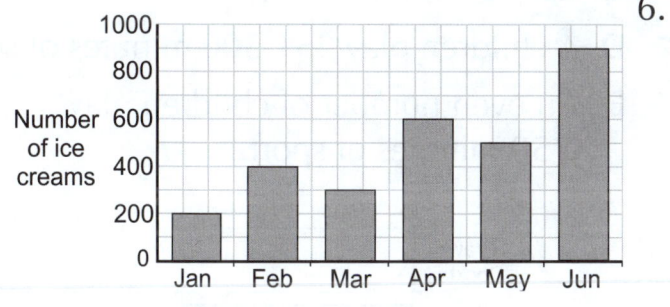

6. The bar chart shows the number of ice creams sold from an ice cream van over six months. In which month were exactly 300 ice creams sold?
   - A January
   - B February
   - C March
   - D April
   - E May
   - F June

7. Alexa counted the number of chickens, ducks and turkeys she saw at a farm. The pictogram shows her results. How many more ducks did she see than turkeys?

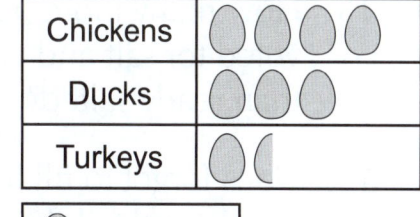

= 6 birds

/ 3

Section Four — Data Handling

Displaying Data

George took a survey in his school. He asked people what their favourite sports were.

Sport	Tally
Tennis	IIII IIII IIII I
Football	IIII IIII IIII II
Swimming	IIII
Running	III
Netball	IIII IIII

8. How many people said tennis was their favourite sport?

9. How many people said running or netball was their favourite sport?

10. How many more people said football was their favourite sport than said swimming?

11. The pictogram shows the number of goals scored by Milton United in their matches. In how many matches did they score 2 or more goals?

⚽ = 8 matches

12. The bar chart shows the amount of sport played each week by a group of children. Which of the following sentences is true? Circle the correct answer.

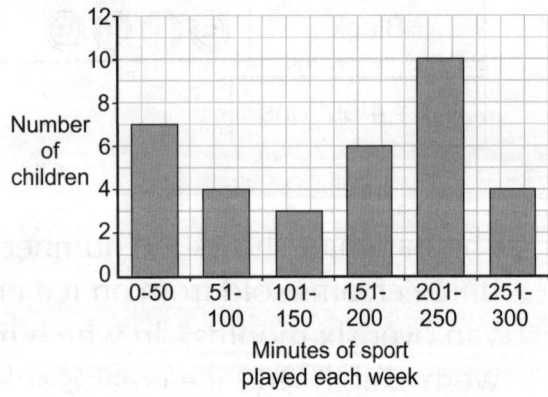

A 5 children play 51-100 minutes of sport.

B 8 children play less than 50 minutes of sport.

C Most of the children play 101-150 minutes of sport.

D 4 children play 251-300 minutes of sport.

E An even number of children play 0-50 minutes of sport.

26 people voted for their favourite crisp flavour. Hans made a bar chart to show the results.

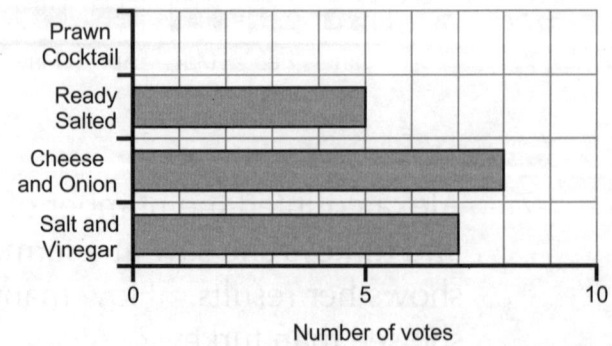

13. How many more people voted for salt and vinegar than ready salted?

14. Hans forgot to fill in the bar for prawn cocktail flavour. How many people voted for prawn cocktail?

/7

Section Four — Data Handling

Section Five — Shape and Space

Angles

Look at the angles below and answer questions 1-4.

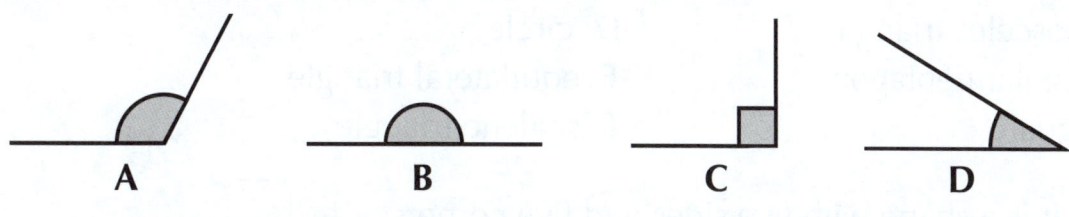

1. Which angle is exactly 90°?

2. Which angle is smaller than 90°?

3. Which angle is exactly 180°?

4. Which angle is bigger than 90° and smaller than 180°?

/ 4

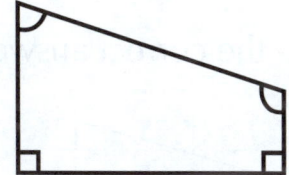

5. How many right angles are there in this shape? Circle the correct answer.

   A 0   B 1   C 2   D 3   E 4

The hour hand on this clock is pointing at 12.

6. What number will the hour hand be pointing at if it turns 90° clockwise?

7. From its original position at 12, what number will the hour hand be pointing at if it turns 180° anti-clockwise?

8. Circle the obtuse angle.

   Hint: An obtuse angle is bigger than 90° but smaller than 180°.

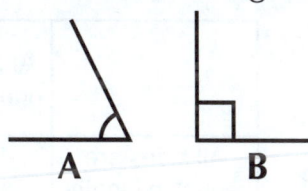 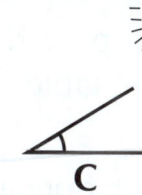 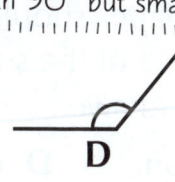 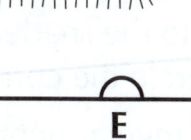

   A   B   C   D   E

9. Josie is facing south. She turns clockwise to face north. How many right angles has she turned through?

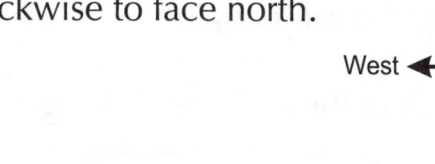

10. Estimate the size of angle *a*. Circle the correct answer.

    A 100°   B 45°   C 180°   D 90°   E 125°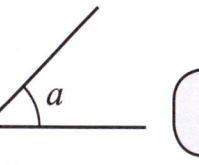

/ 6

2D Shapes

Match each shape below to its description.

A isosceles triangle
B regular pentagon
C square
D circle
E equilateral triangle
F scalene triangle

1. It is a shape with five sides and five corners. ☐
2. It is a shape with no corners. ☐
3. It has three equal sides and three equal angles. ☐
4. It is a triangle with only two equal sides. ☐
5. It has four equal sides and four right angles. ☐

/ 5

6. Which of these shapes is a scalene triangle? Circle the correct answer.

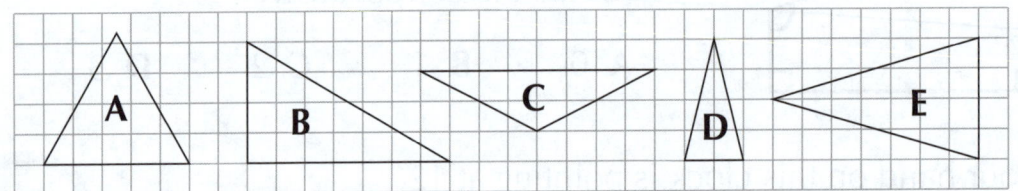

7. Which of these shapes is not a quadrilateral? Circle the correct answer.

 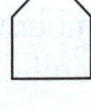   

A   B   C   D   E

8. Which of these shapes should be placed into the shaded box of the sorting table? Circle the correct answer.

   A regular pentagon
   B regular hexagon
   C equilateral triangle
   D regular octagon
   E square

	At least 1 right angle	It does not have right angles
All sides are equal in length		
Not all sides are equal in length		

9. Which of these shapes is irregular? Circle the correct answer.

 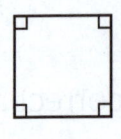 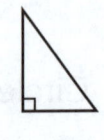  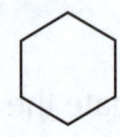

A   B   C   D   E

/ 4

Section Five — Shape and Space

2D Shapes — Perimeter and Area

Indira drew some shapes on squared paper. The area of each square on the paper is 1 cm².

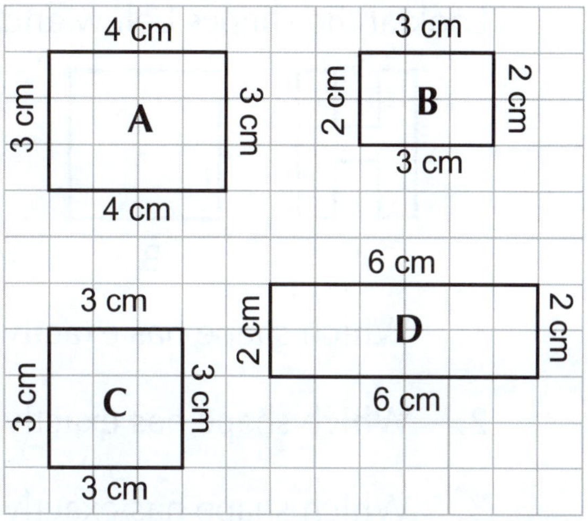

1. What is the perimeter of shape C? ☐☐ cm

2. Which shape has a perimeter of 10 cm? ☐

3. What is the area of shape D? ☐☐ cm²

4. What is the area of shape C? ☐☐ cm²

5. What is the perimeter of shape A? ☐☐ cm

/ 5

6. A hexagon has six sides that are each 4 cm long. What is the perimeter of the hexagon? ☐☐ cm

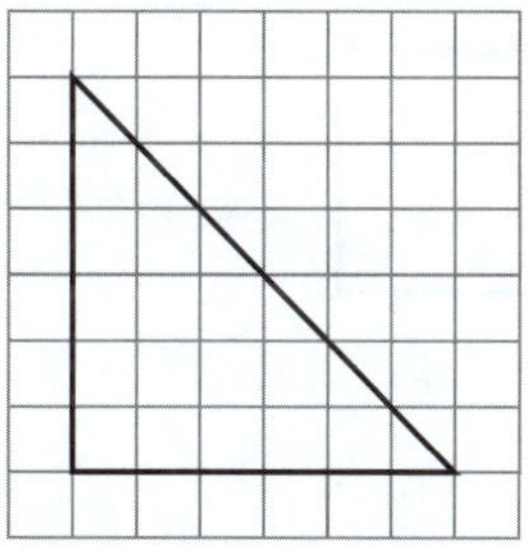

7. Each square on this diagram has an area of 1 cm². What is the area of the triangle? ☐☐ cm²

The shape on the right is made up of two rectangles, labelled A and B.

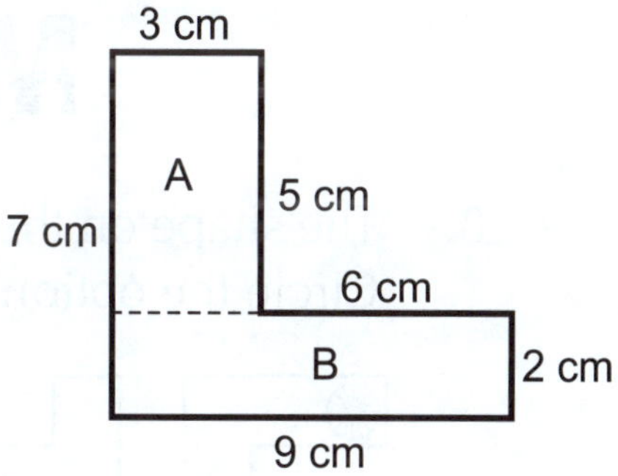

8. What is the perimeter of the whole shape? ☐☐ cm

9. What is the area of the whole shape? Circle the correct answer.

   A 15 cm²   C 30 cm²   E 33 cm²
   B 27 cm²   D 39 cm²

   Hint: The area of a rectangle is found by multiplying its length by width.

Mr Stiles has a rectangular vegetable patch with a perimeter of 28 m. The two longest sides are both 10 m long.

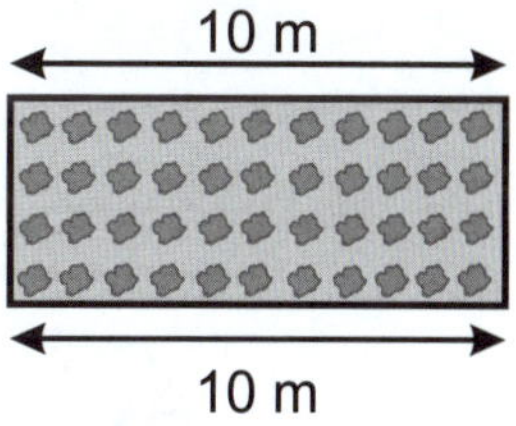

10. What is the width of the vegetable patch? Circle the correct answer.

    A 8 m   B 5 m   C 3 m   D 10 m   E 4 m

11. What is the area of the vegetable patch? ☐☐ m²

/ 6

Symmetry

Look at the shapes below and answer questions 1-5.

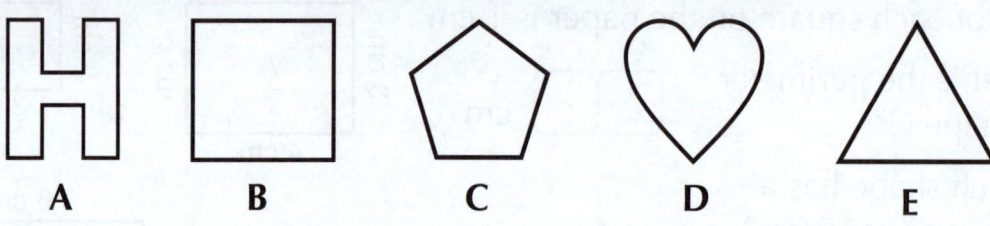

1. Which shape has exactly four lines of symmetry? ☐
2. Which shape has exactly one line of symmetry? ☐
3. Which shape has exactly three lines of symmetry? ☐
4. Which shape has exactly two lines of symmetry? ☐
5. Which shape has exactly five lines of symmetry? ☐

/ 5

6. How many lines of symmetry does this rectangle have? ☐

7. Which of the following letters has no lines of symmetry? Circle the correct answer.

   M   T   D   V   N

8. The shape on the right is reflected in the vertical mirror line. Circle the option which shows the reflection of the shape.

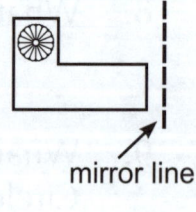

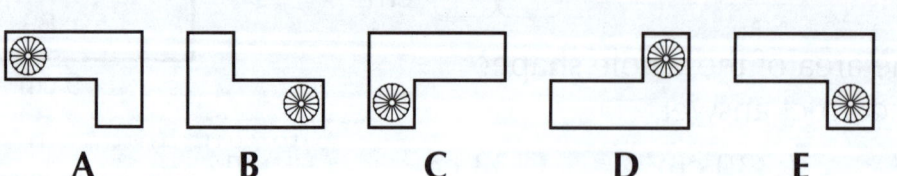

A   B   C   D   E

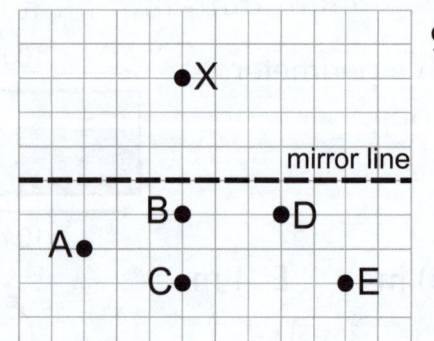

9. Point X is reflected in the horizontal mirror line. Which letter shows the position of its reflection? Circle the correct answer.

   A   B   C   D   E

/ 4

3D Shapes

Match each 3D shape below to its description.

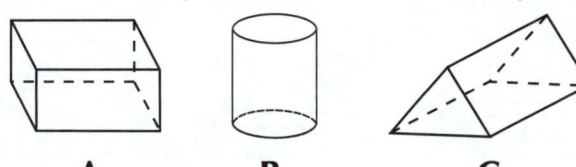
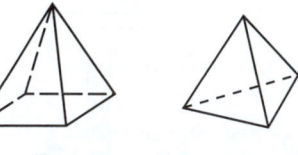

    A   B   C   D   E

1. A shape with 3 faces. ☐
2. A shape with 6 faces and 12 edges. ☐
3. A shape with 4 faces and 6 edges. ☐
4. A shape with 5 faces and 9 edges. ☐
5. A shape with 5 faces and 8 edges. ☐

/ 5

6. Jack is making a gift box. He uses this net.
   Which 3D shape does Jack make? Circle the correct answer.

   A pyramid   **C** cube   **E** sphere
   B cone   **D** cylinder

   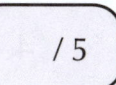

7. Ravi picks a 3D shape at random. It has 7 faces. Which of the following could be Ravi's shape? Circle the correct answer.

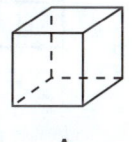
       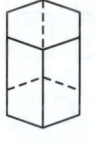
       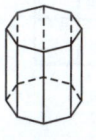
       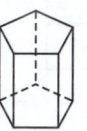

   A   B   C   D   E

8. Rebecca made a 3D shape from this net.
   What shape did she make? Circle the correct answer.

   A cube   **D** triangle-based pyramid
   B quadrilateral   **E** hexagonal prism
   C triangular prism

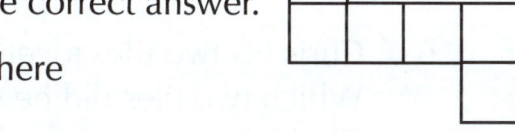

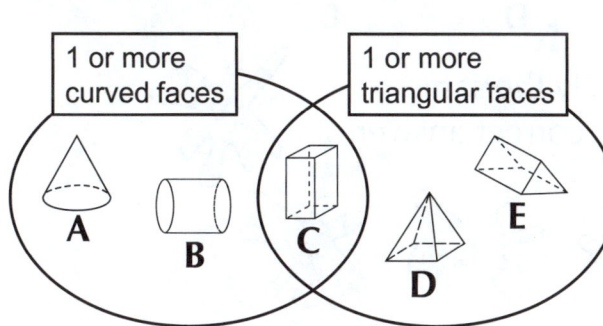

9. Which shape should not be in the Venn diagram? Circle the correct answer.

   A   B   C   D   E

/ 4

Section Five — Shape and Space

Shape Problems

Look at the shapes below and answer questions 1-5.

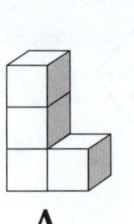 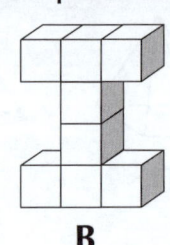 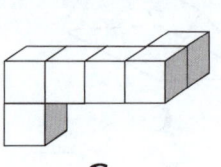 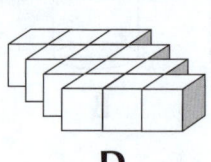 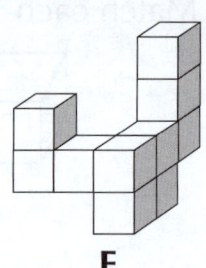

A   B   C   D   E

1. Which shape contains exactly 4 cubes? ☐
2. Which shape contains exactly 6 cubes? ☐
3. Which shape contains exactly 8 cubes? ☐
4. Which shape contains exactly 10 cubes? ☐
5. Which shape contains exactly 12 cubes? ☐

/ 5

6. Chris fits two tiles together to make shape X.
   Which two tiles did he use?
   Circle the correct answer.

X

Hint: You can flip tiles to make shape X.

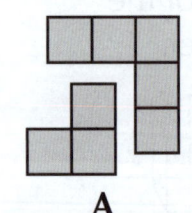 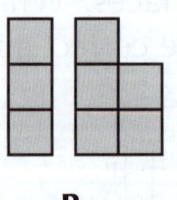 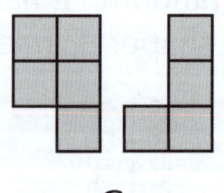 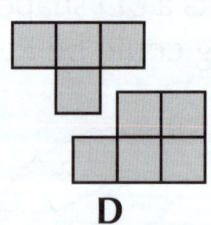 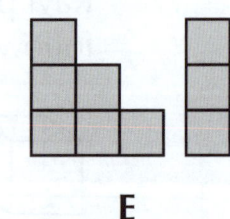

A   B   C   D   E

7. Dominic reflects the shape on the right in the mirror line.
   Which of the following shows the reflected shape?
   Circle the correct answer.

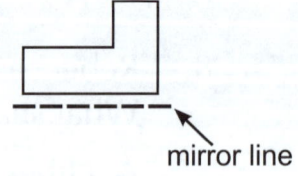

mirror line

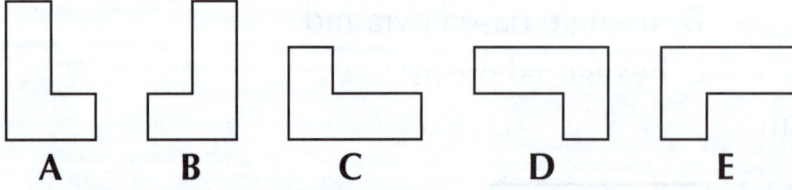

A   B   C   D   E

8. Which of these shapes is exactly the same shape as shape W? Circle the correct answer.

/ 3

Section Five — Shape and Space

Coordinates

Sasha drew some objects on a coordinate grid.
Write down the coordinates of these objects:

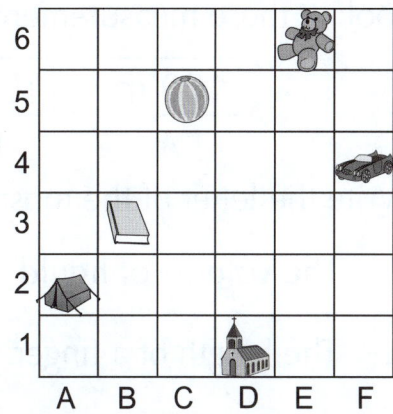

1. the book
2. the tent
3. the bear
4. the church
5. the car

Hint: Write your coordinates with the letter first and then the number.

/ 5

Carlos is drawing shapes on a coordinate grid.

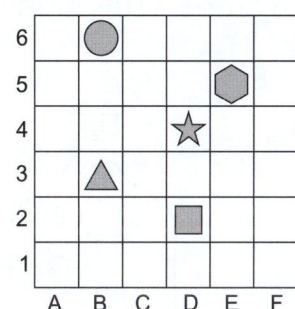

6. What shape has he drawn in the square B3?
   Circle the correct answer.

   A circle   **C** square   **E** triangle
   B star   **D** hexagon

7. What are the coordinates of the shape which is directly north-east of the star?

8. The coordinates of point A are (1, 2).
   What are the coordinates of point B?
   Circle the correct answer.

   A (3, 7)   **C** (3, 9)   **E** (2, 6)
   B (5, 9)   **D** (7, 4)

   Hint: When you're writing coordinates, put the x-axis coordinate first and then the y-axis coordinate.

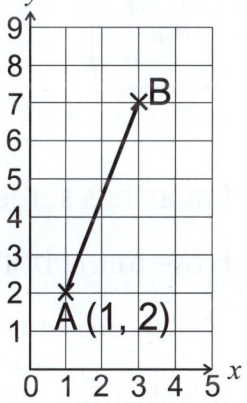

9. Shape B on the grid is a translation of shape A.
   Which of the following describes the translation?
   Circle the correct answer.

   A three squares right, two squares up
   B two squares left, one square up
   C three squares left, one square up
   D three squares left, one square down
   E two squares right, two squares down

/ 4

Section Five — Shape and Space

Section Six — Units and Measures

Units

Look at these measurements.

100 m	100 g	0.3 litres	5 ml	7 cm
A	B	C	D	E

Write the letter of the most likely measurement for:

1. The volume of liquid in a full mug of tea.
2. The length of a finger.
3. The mass of a mobile phone.
4. The volume of medicine in a teaspoonful.
5. The length of a football pitch.

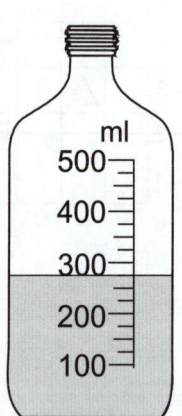

6. How much liquid is in the bottle on the left? ▢▢▢ ml

7. Mrs Patel bought 30 cm of gold chain and 1.5 m of silver chain. How many centimetres of chain did she buy altogether? ▢▢▢ cm

8. Lucas has some 500 ml bottles of cola. He pours them into a 2 litre jug. How many bottles are needed to fill the jug? ▢

9. A baker fills 10 bags with doughnuts. Each bag of doughnuts weighs 350 g. What is the total weight of all the bags? Circle the correct answer.

   A 3.5 kg   B 35 kg   C 350 kg   D 35 g   E 3.5 g

10. Deepak is doing a 10 km run. He has run 9¾ km. How many more metres are left to run? Circle the correct answer.

    A ¼ m   B 25 m   C 250 m   D 750 m   E 300 m

Time

4:50	5:45	5:10	7:30	6:15
A	B	C	D	E

Write the letter of the time above that is the same as:

1. Ten minutes to five. ☐
2. Half past seven. ☐
3. Quarter to six. ☐
4. Half an hour earlier than quarter to seven. ☐
5. Twenty minutes later than ten minutes to five. ☐

6. How many minutes are there in a quarter of an hour? ☐☐ minutes
7. How many days are there in 3 weeks? ☐☐ days
8. How many months are there in half a year? ☐ months

/ 8

Read the clocks below and answer questions 9-12.

9. 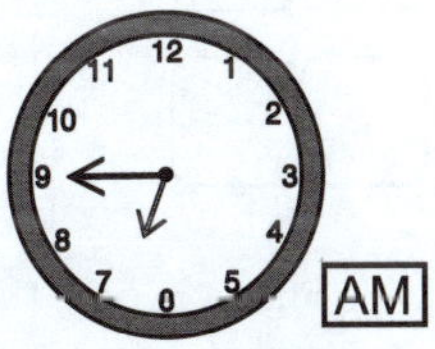 What was the time 45 minutes earlier than the time shown on the clock? ☐☐:☐☐ am

10. 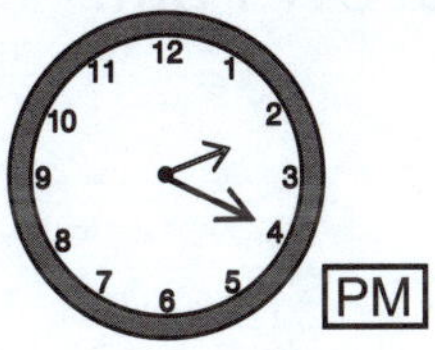 What will the time be 10 minutes later than the time shown on the clock? ☐☐:☐☐ pm

11. 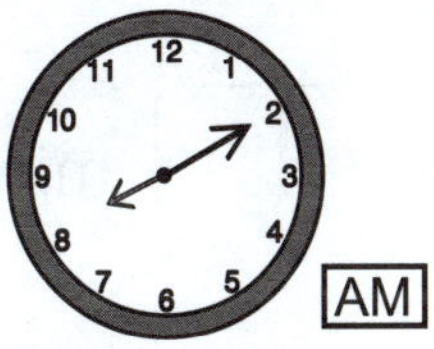 What was the time 20 minutes earlier than the time shown on the clock? ☐☐:☐☐ am

12. 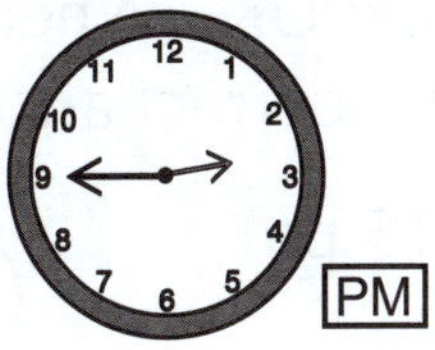 What will the time be 20 minutes later than the time shown on the clock? ☐☐:☐☐ pm

/ 4

Section Six — Units and Measures

Time

This timetable shows the times of buses going from Whitdale to the hospital.

13. How long does the bus from Whitdale to the hospital take? ☐☐ minutes

Whitdale	10:15	10:30	10:45
Thornby	10:25	10:40	10:55
Hospital	10:40	10:55	11:10

14. Sarah needs to be at the hospital at 11:00. What is the latest time that she can catch the bus from Whitdale? Circle the correct answer.

    A 10:15   B 10:30   C 10:45   D 10:40   E 10:55

15. Peter needs to catch the 10:25 bus from Thornby.
    It takes Peter 30 minutes to walk from his house to Thornby bus station.
    What is the latest time Peter should leave his house? ☐☐:☐☐

16. Jo goes on holiday on Tuesday 24th May.
    The last day of her holiday is the 13th June.
    How many weeks was she on holiday for? ☐ weeks

    Hint: Make sure you know how many days there are in each month.

Lokesh starts his homework at 6:45 pm. He finishes it 70 minutes later.

17. What time does he finish his homework? ☐☐:☐☐ pm

18. What is this time on the 24-hour clock? ☐☐:☐☐

Mrs Brown is going to a school concert. The concert starts at 3:15 pm.
It takes her 35 minutes to drive to the school and
5 minutes to park her car and walk to the school.

19. What time must she leave home? ☐☐:☐☐ pm

20. The concert finishes at 6:05 pm.
    How long was the concert? ☐ hours and ☐☐ minutes

21. The time in Sydney, Australia, is 11 hours later than in the UK. When it is 10:15 am in the UK, what time is it in Sydney? Circle the correct answer.

    A 9:15 am   C 10:15 am   E 11:15 pm
    B 11:15 am   D 9:15 pm

Section Seven — Mixed Problems

Mixed Problems

1. Which one of these shapes can be placed in the shaded area of the Venn diagram? Circle the correct answer.

   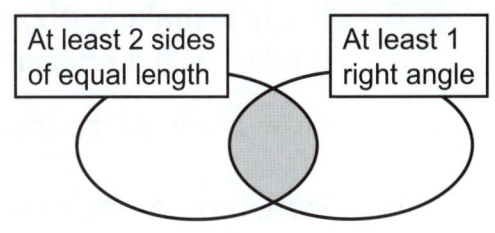

   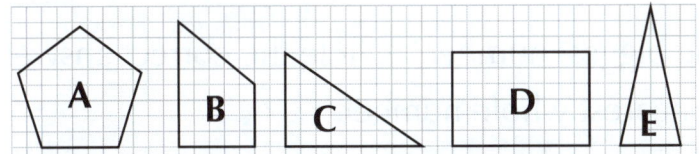

2. Anna worked for 4½ hours on Saturday and 5½ hours on Sunday. She is paid £4.50 for each hour of work. How much money did she earn in total?

   Hint: Start by working out the total number of hours that Anna worked.

   £ ☐☐.☐☐

3. A 500 ml bottle of water costs 40p. How much will it cost to buy 3 litres of water?

   £ ☐.☐☐

4. What fraction of these shapes have at least one line of symmetry? Circle the correct answer.

   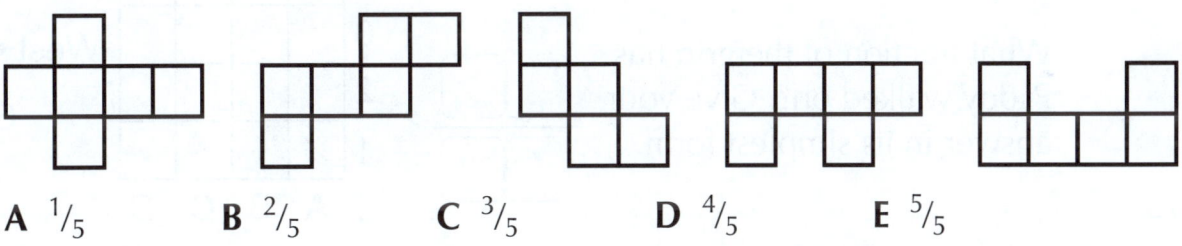

   A ⅕   B ⅖   C ⅗   D ⅘   E ⁵⁄₅

5. Hilda starts washing eight cars at 4:45 pm. It takes her 10 minutes to wash each car. What time will she finish washing the cars? Circle the correct answer.

   A 5:45 pm   B 5:05 pm   C 6:30 pm   D 5:30 pm   E 6:05 pm

6. Lucy runs 8 km in an hour. How many metres does she run in 15 minutes?

   ☐☐☐☐ metres

7. Fran drew the shape on the right and reflected it in the mirror line. What is the total perimeter of the shape and its reflection? Circle the correct answer.

   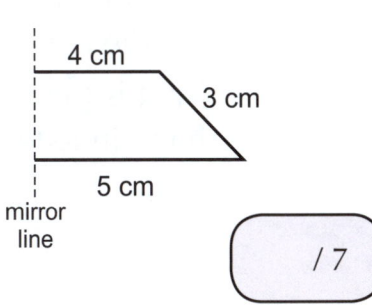

   A 24 cm   C 16 cm   E 20 cm
   B 28 cm   D 12 cm

   /7

Mixed Problems

8. Jenny is making pizza bases.
   It takes 500 g of flour to make enough dough for 3 pizza bases.

   How many pizza bases could she make with 2.5 kg of flour? ☐☐

9. Which of these gives the biggest number? Circle the correct answer.
   A 19.5 rounded to the nearest whole number.
   B $\frac{1}{2}$ of 40
   C 70 − 46
   D A tenth of 200
   E The next number in the following sequence: 7, 11, 15, 19

10. Pierre is buying packs of football stickers to give to his four friends. Packs of football stickers cost 40p and he wants to get 3 packs for each of his friends.

    How much change will Pierre get if he pays with a £5 note? £☐.☐☐

11. Paddy starts on square A1.
    He walks 4 squares north. He then walks 3 squares east and then 3 squares south.

    What fraction of the grid has Paddy walked on? Give your answer in its simplest form. ☐☐/☐☐

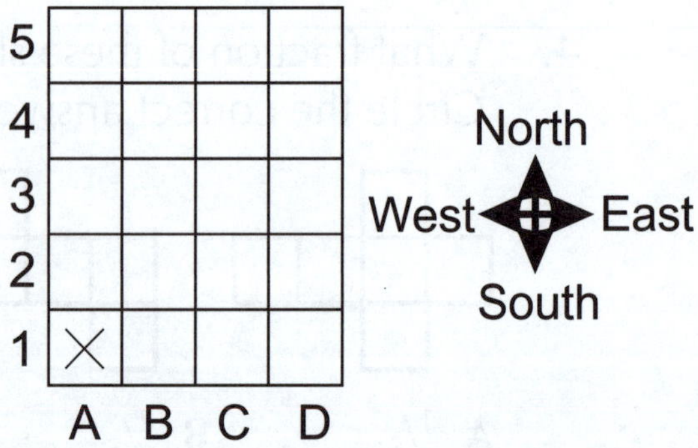

12. This table shows Lucy's last four marks in her weekly maths test.
    Her mark for the whole month is calculated by adding her four weekly marks together, then dividing by 4.

    What was Lucy's mark for the whole month? ☐☐

	Mark
Test 1	13
Test 2	15
Test 3	9
Test 4	11

13. Kyle draws the first three shapes in a sequence. The rule for the sequence is:
    The number of sides increases by 1 each time and the length of each side is always 2 cm.
    What is the perimeter of the fourth shape in Kyle's sequence? ☐☐ cm

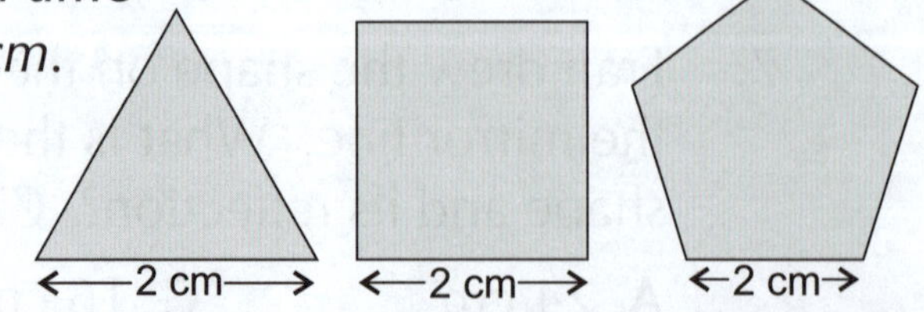

    ←2 cm→ ←2 cm→ ←2 cm→

/ 6

Section Seven — Mixed Problems

Assessment Test 1

The rest of the book contains six assessment tests to help you improve your maths skills. Each test is divided into two parts. Section A is the 'quick maths' section — the questions are more straightforward but with less time available per question. Section B is the 'long maths' section — the questions are more complex, but there's more time to answer them.

For each test, allow 8 minutes to do Section A and 15 minutes to do Section B. Work as quickly and as carefully as you can.

If you want to attempt each test more than once, you will need to print **multiple-choice answer sheets** for these questions from our website — go to cgpbooks.co.uk/11plus/answer-sheets. If you'd prefer to answer them in write-in format, either write your answers in the spaces provided or circle the **correct answer** from the options given.

Section A — Quick Maths
You have **8 minutes** to complete this section.
There are **20 questions** in this section.

1. Max has the following values of coins. How much money does he have?

   £2 £1 5p 2p 2p

   A £3.90 **B** £2.09 **C** £3.09 **D** £3.54 **E** £2.90

2. Pat and Imran are at the Post Office. They walk 2 squares north and 1 square east. Where do they walk to?
   - **A** Leisure Centre
   - **B** Library
   - **C** Supermarket
   - **D** Newsagent
   - **E** Sports Shop

   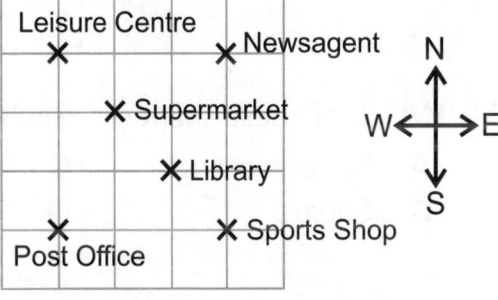

3. A horse weighs 295 kg. What is this weight rounded to the nearest 10 kg?

   A 200 kg **B** 250 kg **C** 280 kg **D** 290 kg **E** 300 kg

4. Hannah records the number of plants in her garden on a pictogram. How many bean plants does she have?

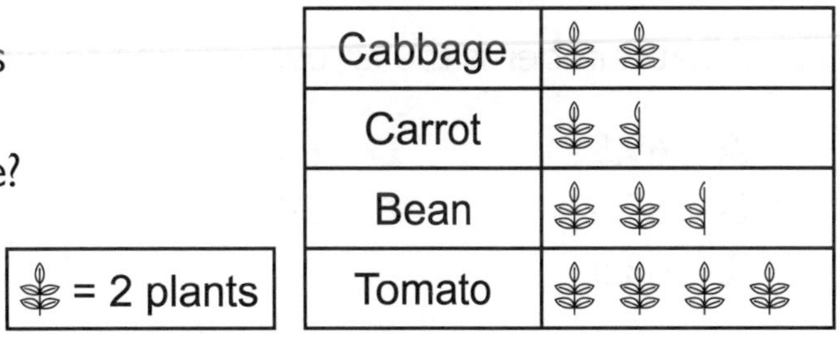

   A 3   **C** 4   **E** 1½
   B 5   **D** 2½

   ❀ = 2 plants

Cabbage	❀ ❀
Carrot	❀ ∮
Bean	❀ ❀ ∮
Tomato	❀ ❀ ❀ ❀

5. How many lines of symmetry does a regular pentagon have?

   A 4 **B** 7 **C** 6 **D** 5 **E** 8

   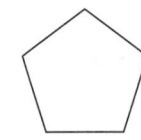

   Carry on to the next question → →

6. Which of these angles is bigger than 90°?

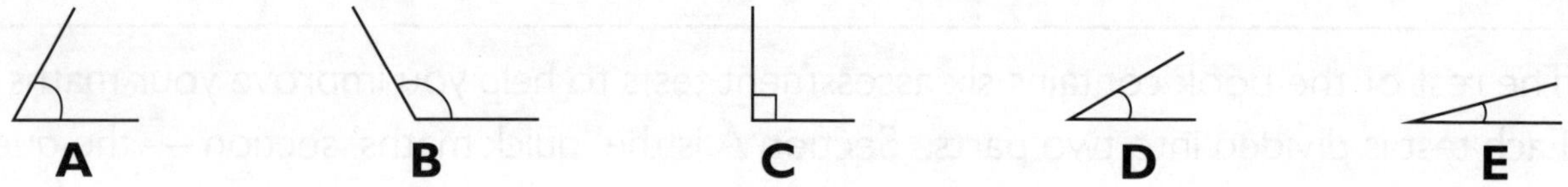

   A   B   C   D   E

7. Julia buys some bags of treats for her dog. There are 8 treats in each bag. She gets 48 treats altogether. How many bags did she buy?

8. What number is shown by the Roman numeral XXXVII?
   A 36   B 27   C 33   D 37   E 26

9. Amber buys 8 packets of Walrus biscuits and has 56 biscuits. Hazel buys 80 packets of Walrus biscuits. How many biscuits does Hazel have?
   A 73   B 490   C 650   D 560   E 87

10. Leo and Robin are both artists. Leo sold a painting for £998 while Robin sold his for £1029. How much more money did Robin's painting sell for than Leo's?
    A £1971   B £31   C £32   D £28   E £2027

11. Which of these shapes is regular?
    A Scalene triangle   C Isosceles triangle   E Right-angled triangle
    B Square   D Rectangle

12. Matilda buys 41 boxes of cookies. Each box contains 8 individual cookies. How many cookies does Matilda have in total?

13. What number is the arrow pointing to on the number line?
    A 69.5   D 68.2
    B 67.5   E 68.9
    C 68.5

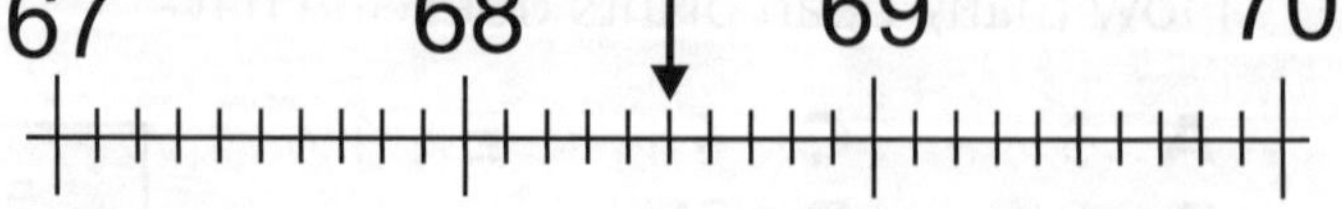

14. John bought 10 identical stamps. They cost £3.60 altogether. How much did each stamp cost?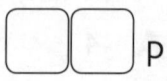

Assessment Test 1

15. Which of these fractions is smallest?

    A ¾   **B** ½   **C** ⅛   **D** ¼   **E** ⅜

16. This diagram shows the length and width of a school playground. What is the perimeter of the playground? ▢▢▢ m

    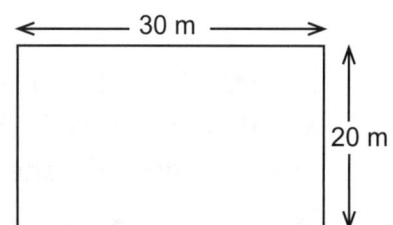

17. Jay receives £2.40 pocket money every week. How many weeks will it take him to save £7.20? ▢▢

18. Tara's shape has 5 faces and 9 edges. Which of the following options could be Tara's shape?

       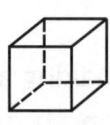 

    A   B   C   D   E

19. 7 + 7 + 7 + 7 = ? × 2

    What is the missing number?

    A 7   **B** 14   **C** 28   **D** 11   **E** 17

20. Jemma makes a chart which shows the hair colour of the children in her year.

    How many more children have brown hair than black hair?

    ▢▢▢

Colour	Number of children
Brown	140
Black	65
Blonde	73
Red	16

    (/ 20)

Section B — Long Maths

You have **15 minutes** to complete this section.
There are **18 questions** in this section.

Suki has a 2 m roll of ribbon. She cuts off 2 pieces of ribbon, each measuring 75 cm.

1. How much ribbon is left on the roll?

   A 1.25 m   **C** 50 m   **E** 0.5 m
   B 0.75 m   **D** 5 m

2. The ribbon is 3 cm wide. What is the area of the ribbon left on the roll? ▢▢▢ cm²

Carry on to the next question → →

Assessment Test 1

3. This chart shows how many children go to different clubs. How many more children go to choir than dance? ☐

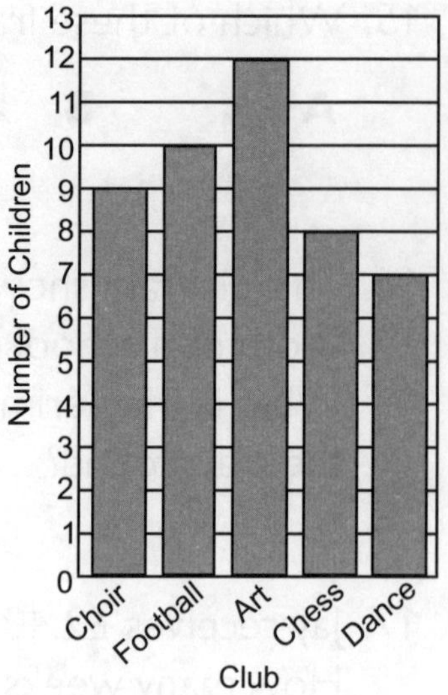

4. Ruth thinks of a number. She multiplies it by 7 and then she adds 1. She ends up with 50. What number did she start with?

   A 5   **B** 8   **C** 6   **D** 7   **E** 9

5. Which of the following pairs of numbers are factors of 36?

   A 4 and 8   **C** 7 and 12   **E** 6 and 7
   B 6 and 9   **D** 5 and 8

Jessica is making a game of pass the parcel. She puts 1 sweet in the first layer, 4 sweets in the second layer, 7 sweets in the third layer and 10 sweets in the fourth layer.

6. How many sweets will be in the 7th layer of the parcel? ☐☐

7. In what number layer will Jessica put 28 sweets? ☐☐

8. In total, Jessica needs 287 sweets to make 14 layers in her parcel. Sweets come in tubes of 20. How many tubes of sweets will Jessica need? ☐☐

In 100 g of bread there is:	
Protein	12 g
Carbohydrate	48 g
Fat	2 g
Fibre	3 g
Salt	1 g

9. Look at the table on the right. How much carbohydrate and protein is there altogether in 150 g of bread?

   A 60 g   **C** 120 g   **E** 62 g
   B 84 g   **D** 90 g

10. Claire has 80 stickers. She gives ½ of them to Luke. Luke then gives ¼ of his stickers to Jenny. How many stickers does Jenny get?

    A 40   **B** 30   **C** 20   **D** 10   **E** 5

11. The diagram on the right shows Daniel's garden. It is made up of a square patio and a lawn. What is the area of the lawn? ☐☐☐ m²

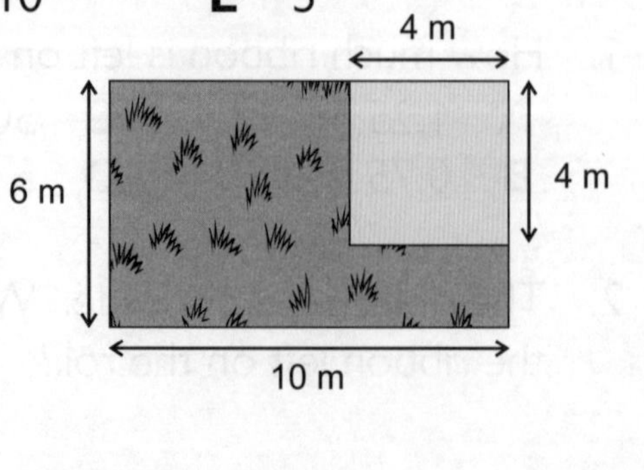

Assessment Test 1

12. Jill recorded the temperature on five mornings. She put her results in this table.
    Between which two days did the temperature change by the greatest amount?

Day	Temperature
Monday	6 °C
Tuesday	3 °C
Wednesday	2 °C
Thursday	−2 °C
Friday	1 °C

    A   Monday and Tuesday
    B   Tuesday and Wednesday
    C   Wednesday and Thursday
    D   Thursday and Friday

Jeremiah has drawn the incomplete Venn diagram shown below.

13. Which of these could be the missing label from Jeremiah's Venn diagram?

    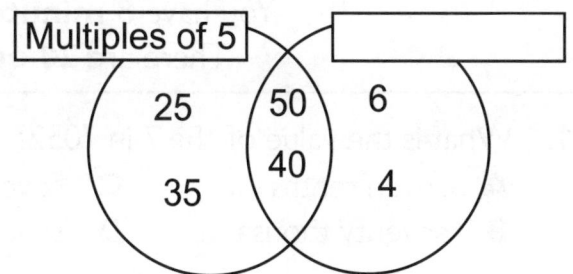

    A   Multiples of 3
    B   Even numbers
    C   Odd numbers
    D   Multiples of 7
    E   Factors of 8

14. Using the missing label from question 13, which of the following sets of numbers could Jeremiah put into the central section of his Venn diagram?

    A   55, 20, 45   C   20, 40, 55   E   20, 30, 10
    B   16, 24, 54   D   20, 35, 10

15. Siti is cycling into town. She leaves home at 1:30 pm. It takes 45 minutes to cycle into town. She spends 1½ hours in town, then it takes 45 minutes to cycle back home. What time does Siti arrive back home?

    ☐ : ☐☐ pm

The picture shows Farmer Jo's pen containing black and white sheep.

16. What fraction of the sheep are white?

    A   ⅚   C   ⁶⁄₁₁   E   ½
    B   ⁵⁄₁₁   D   ⁶⁄₁₃

17. Farmer Jo buys some more sheep so that she has 22 sheep in total.
    The fraction of her sheep that are white is the same as before.
    How many white sheep does she have now?

    ☐☐

18. Farmer Jo shears her sheep. She dyes some of the wool. She dyes ²⁄₉ of the wool red and ⁵⁄₉ of the wool blue. What fraction of the wool has she dyed in total?

    A   ⁵⁄₉   C   ²⁄₉   E   ⁷⁄₉
    B   ³⁄₉   D   ¹⁰⁄₈₁

/ 18

End of Test

Assessment Test 1

Assessment Test 2

Allow 8 minutes to do Section A and 15 minutes to do Section B.
Work as quickly and as carefully as you can.

You can print **multiple-choice answer sheets** for these questions from our website — go to cgpbooks.co.uk/11plus/answer-sheets. If you'd prefer to answer them in write-in format, either write your answers in the spaces provided or circle the **correct answer** from the options given.

Section A — Quick Maths
You have **8 minutes** to complete this section.
There are **20 questions** in this section.

1. What is the value of the 7 in 7052?
   A seven tenths   **C** seven hundred   **E** seventy
   B seventy thousand   **D** seven thousand

2. How many edges does a cube have?
   A 12   **B** 6   **C** 7   **D** 8   **E** 9

   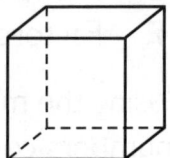

3. Bill shares his pens out equally between 8 pencil cases. He has none left over. How many pens could Bill have had?
   A 12   **B** 63   **C** 72   **D** 84   **E** 94

4. Which of these shapes has a line of symmetry?

   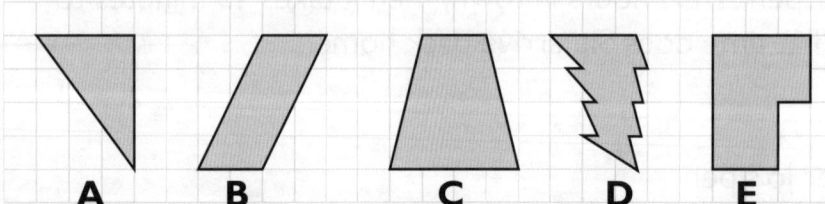

5. Below are the heights, in metres, of 5 different plants in Henry's garden.

   | 0.35 | 1.03 | 1.30 | 0.98 | 0.65 |

   Which of the following options shows the heights in order from smallest to largest?

A	0.35	0.98	0.65	1.30	1.03
B	0.35	0.65	0.98	1.03	1.30
C	1.30	1.03	0.98	0.65	0.35
D	0.35	0.65	0.98	1.30	1.03
E	1.03	1.30	0.98	0.65	0.35

6. £87 is shared equally between three people. How much money do they each receive?

   £ ☐☐

7. Which of these triangles is definitely not an equilateral triangle?

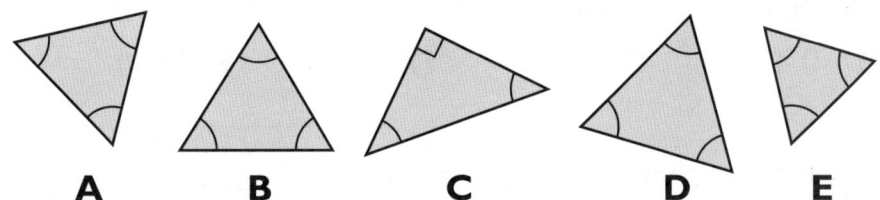

8. Apples come in packs of 6. Ted's class need to buy enough packs so that each child can have one apple. There are 32 children in the class. How many packs of apples will they need?

   A 5   **B** 6   **C** 8   **D** 4   **E** 7

9. Ahmed asked the children in his class to name their favourite type of dog. He put the results in this bar chart. How many children chose the most popular type of dog?

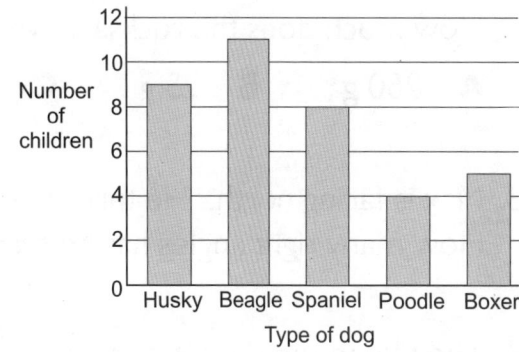

10. A postman collects 5240 letters. What is the number of letters rounded to the nearest hundred?

    A 10 000   **B** 5300   **C** 5270   **D** 5200   **E** 5000

11. Which corner of the pentagon on the right is at point (1, 4)?

    A   **B**   **C**   **D**   **E**

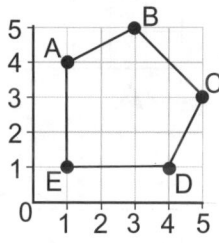

12. Sarah visits her grandma every Sunday. She visits on 12th February. What is the date of the next Sunday she will visit her grandma?

    A 5th February   **C** 17th February   **E** 19th February
    B 12th March   **D** 20th February

13. John records the maximum temperature in Aberdeen each day for a week. He draws this bar chart to show his results. What is the difference between the temperature on Wednesday and on Saturday? ☐☐ °C

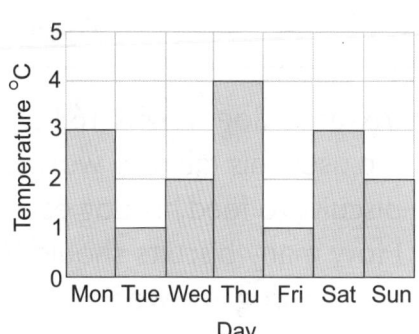

14. $\boxed{60 - 37 = 23}$

    What is 560 − 237?

Carry on to the next question → →

Assessment Test 2

15. Pat is putting parcels in lorries to deliver. He divides 4500 parcels equally between 100 lorries. How many parcels are in each lorry?

    A 400.5   **B** 0.45   **C** 4.5   **D** 45   **E** 450

16. Class 4C counted the vehicles that passed by the window in 1 hour. They put the results in this pictogram. How many buses and motorbikes did they see in total?

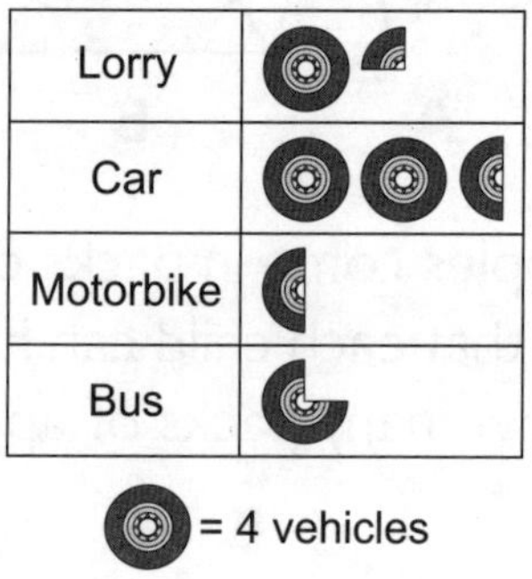

Lorry	
Car	
Motorbike	
Bus	

    = 4 vehicles

17. A rucksack weighs 2½ kilograms. How much does the rucksack weigh in grams?

    A 250 g   **B** 25 g   **C** 2500 g   **D** 2050 g   **E** 2.5 g

18. Max is facing north. He turns until he is facing south. How many right angles has he turned through?

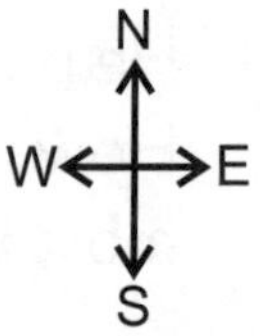

19. The tile on the right is rotated anti-clockwise through 90°. Circle the image that shows how the tile will look after the rotation.

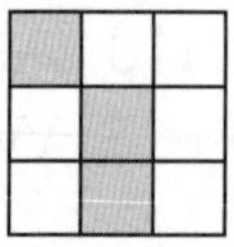

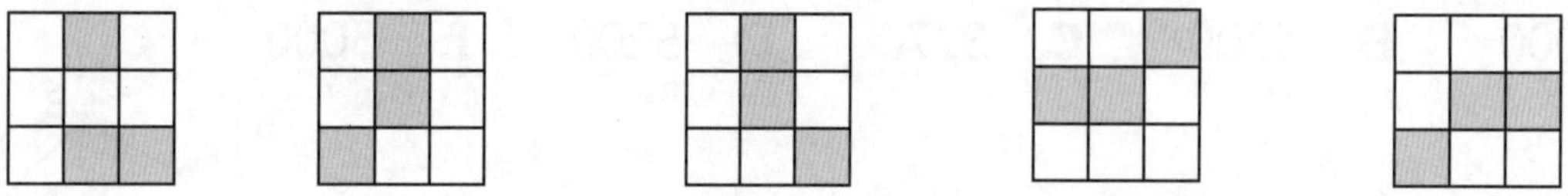

    A   **B**   **C**   **D**   **E**

20. _____ < 4652

    Which of the following numbers could go in the space above?

    A 4731   **B** 4599   **C** 5120   **D** 4655   **E** 6021

    / 20

Section B — Long Maths

You have **15 minutes** to complete this section.
There are **18 questions** in this section.

---

1. Vikram's dog weighs 16 kg. He uses this table to work out how many biscuits to feed his dog each day. How many biscuits should Vikram give his dog in a week?

Dog weight	Number of biscuits a day
Up to 7 kg	1
Up to 15 kg	2
Up to 30 kg	4

    A 14   **C** 15   **E** 28
    B 7   **D** 29

Assessment Test 2

Tom is making a pattern of squares using counters.

```
  •     • •     • • •     • • • •
        • •     • • •     • • • •
                • • •     • • • •
                          • • • •
  1      2        3          4
```

2. How many counters will he need to make the next square in the pattern?

3. How many counters will Tom have used altogether to make the first 5 squares in the pattern?

4. A packet of raisins weighs 65 g.
   What do 6 packets of raisins weigh to the nearest 100 g?

   A 300 g   **B** 400 g   **C** 200 g   **D** 500 g   **E** 390 g

Alex uses some matchsticks to create a model of two cubes.

5. He wants to join another cube to the side of this model. How many additional matchsticks will he need?

6. Each matchstick is 10 cm long. Alex lays all the matchsticks for his finished three-cube model out in a row. How long with this row be? cm

Sophie is having a birthday party. It starts at 4 pm and finishes at 6:30 pm.

7. Exactly halfway through the party the children have the birthday cake. At what time do they have the cake?

   A 5:00 pm   **B** 5:30 pm   **C** 5:15 pm   **D** 5:45 pm   **E** 6:00 pm

8. The first guest leaves the party at 6:30. After that, one guest leaves every two minutes. How many guests will have left after 15 minutes?

9. What is the next number in this sequence?

   13   9   5   1   –3   ?

10. Azra cuts a cake into 20 slices. He gives ¼ of it to his friends and ½ of it to his family. How many slices of cake does Azra have left?

Carry on to the next question → →

Assessment Test 2

11. Noel's family go to the cinema. How much does it cost for 3 children and 2 adults?

    Cinema tickets
    Child £3.50
    Adult £7.50

    £ ☐☐.☐☐

12. A stall sells hot dogs for £1.25 each.
    Dee buys 3 hot dogs and pays with a £10 note.
    How much change does she get?

    A £5.25 **B** £7.52 **C** £6.25 **D** £7.25 **E** £6.50

13. A horse has 250 ml of medicine every day.
    There are 2 litres of medicine in the bottle.
    How many days will the bottle of medicine last for?

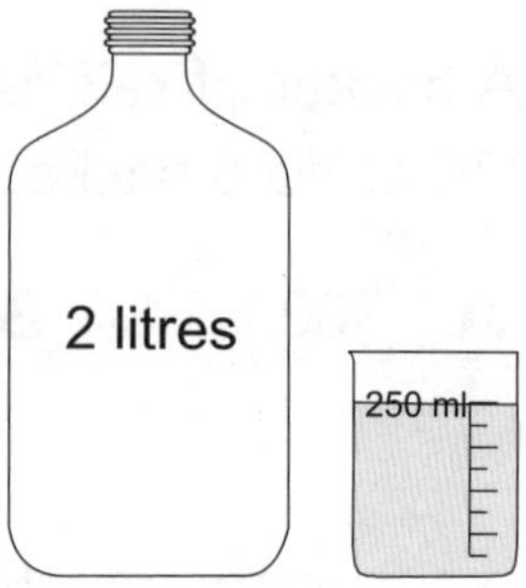

    ☐☐ days

The opening times of Sparrowton Zoo are in the table below.

Opening Times	
Monday	9:00 - 17:00
Tuesday	7:30 - 16:00
Wednesday	9:00 - 16:00
Thursday	8:30 - 16:30
Friday	8:30 - 17:30
Saturday	10:00 - 17:30
Sunday	10:00 - 17:00

14. Which day has the longest opening hours?

    A Monday **D** Thursday **G** Sunday
    B Tuesday **E** Friday
    C Wednesday **F** Saturday

15. Jim goes to the zoo on Tuesday. He arrives 1 hour and 25 minutes after the opening time. When does he arrive?

    ☐☐ : ☐☐

16. Mark goes to the zoo on Saturday at 11:20.
    He leaves 30 minutes before the zoo closes.
    How long does he spend at the zoo?

    ☐ hours ☐☐ minutes

A plan of Adam's vegetable garden is shown on the right.
It is divided into smaller areas that are all the same size.

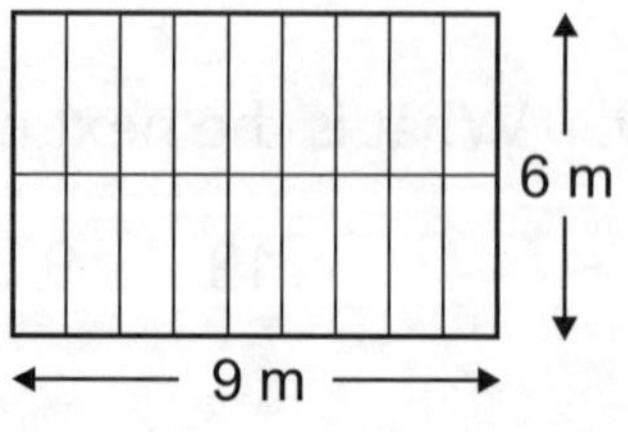

17. The vegetable garden is a rectangle.
    What is its total area?

    ☐☐ m²

    6 m
    9 m

18. Adam uses three of the smaller areas to grow tomatoes.
    What fraction of his vegetable garden is this?

    A 1/8 **B** 1/9 **C** 1/5 **D** 1/4 **E** 1/6

    / 18

    End of Test

Assessment Test 2

Assessment Test 3

Allow 8 minutes to do Section A and 15 minutes to do Section B.
Work as quickly and as carefully as you can.

You can print **multiple-choice answer sheets** for these questions from our website — go to cgpbooks.co.uk/11plus/answer-sheets. If you'd prefer to answer them in write-in format, either write your answers in the spaces provided or circle the **correct answer** from the options given.

Section A — Quick Maths
You have **8 minutes** to complete this section.
There are **20 questions** in this section.

1. Anthony has drawn the shape below. What type of shape is it?

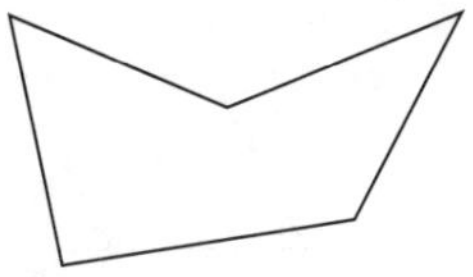

   A hexagon **C** octagon **E** triangle
   B pentagon **D** square

2. Three thousand and seventeen people took part in a singing contest. Write this number in figures.

3. Omar's class are split into teams of 5 children. There are 30 children in the class. How many teams are there?

   A 8 **B** 6 **C** 4 **D** 7 **E** 5

4. Jeremy's grandparents are 73 years old and 59 years old. What is the difference in their ages?

5. Class 4 made this pictogram to show the animals they saw on their country walk.

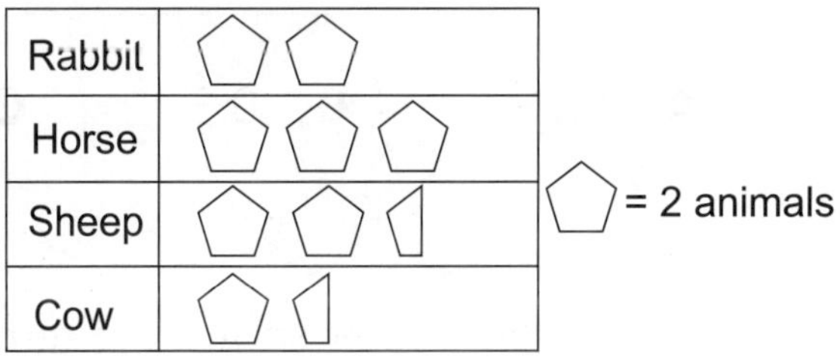

Rabbit	⬠⬠
Horse	⬠⬠⬠
Sheep	⬠⬠◁
Cow	⬠◁

   ⬠ = 2 animals

   How many sheep did they see?

6. This is a diagram of a school stage. What is its perimeter? ☐☐ m

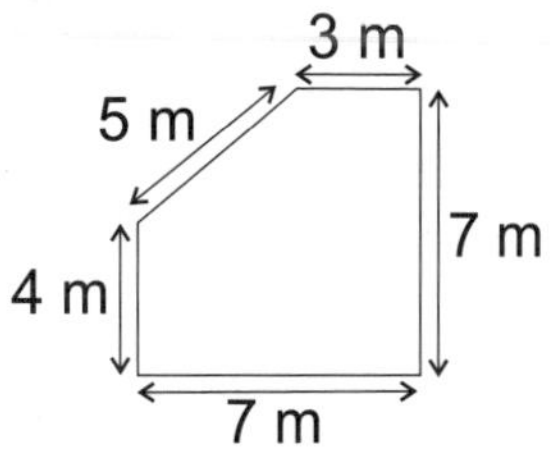

7. How many lines of symmetry does this equilateral triangle have?

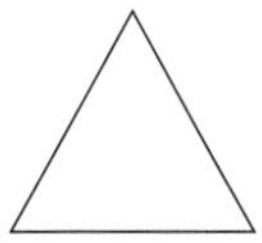

   A 3 **B** 4 **C** 2 **D** 6 **E** 1

Carry on to the next question → →

8. Edward draws this bar chart to show the favourite sports of children in his year group. Which sport did the fewest children choose?

   A Cricket   D Netball
   B Football   E Tennis
   C Rugby

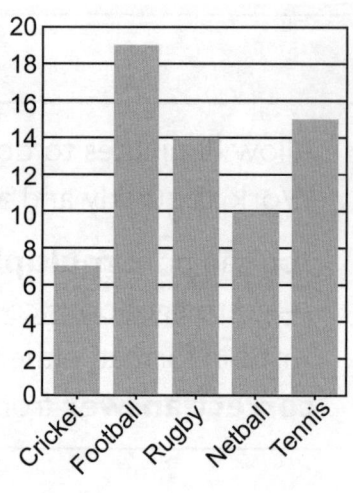

9. Lisa has 37 boxes of muffins. Each box contains 4 muffins. How many muffins does she have?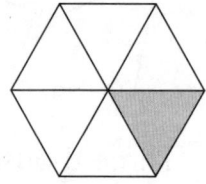

10. Katy thinks of a number. She multiplies it by 4 and gets 88. What number was Katy thinking of?

    A 44   B 92   C 84   D 22   E 352

11. What fraction of the hexagon is shaded?

    A ⅙   B ⅕   C ⅚   D ⅐   E ¼

12. Angle y is smaller than a right angle. Which of the following could be the size of angle y?

    A 120°   C 170°   E 180°
    B 40°   D 90°

    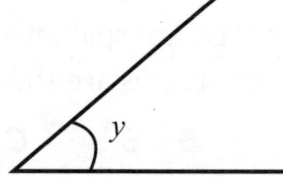

13. What number is the arrow pointing to on this number line?

    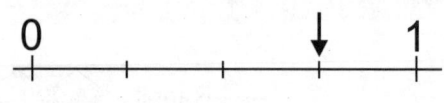

    A 0.25   B 0.5   C 7.5   D 0.75   E 0.33

14. The thermometer shows the temperature on a hilltop. The temperature is 3 °C warmer at the bottom of the hill.

    What is the temperature at the bottom of the hill?  °C

    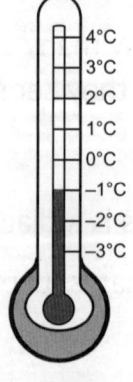

15. Which one of the following times is the same as twenty minutes to three?

    A 2:40   B 2:50   C 3:45   D 3:40   E 3:20

Assessment Test 3

16. Anton spent £2.35 on a sandwich. How much is this in pence? ☐☐☐ p

17. The diagram on the right shows part of a map of a zoo.
    Aki is visiting the giraffes (🦒).
    In which direction must he walk to reach the elephants (🐘)?

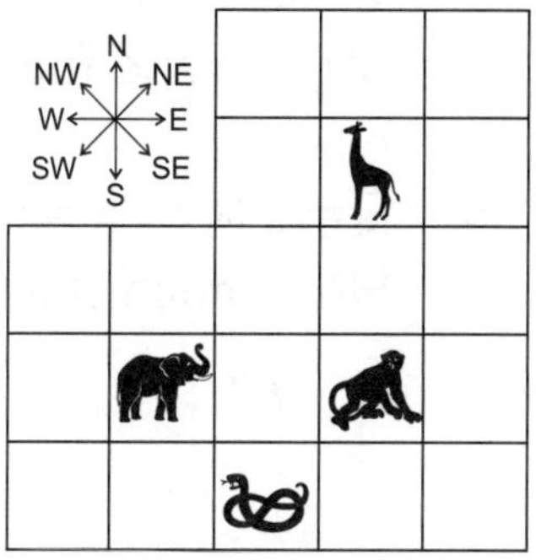

    A south-west   **C** east   **E** south-east
    B west   **D** south

18. Kelly makes a square-based pyramid.

    How many faces does it have? ☐

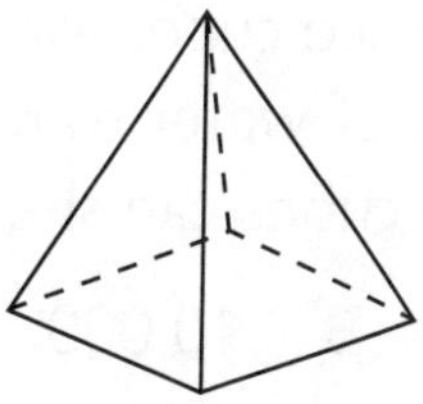

19. In a charity fun run Jo raised £36.90 in sponsorship money.
    During the fun run she collected a £1.50 more.
    How much did she raise in total?   £ ☐☐.☐☐

20. What are the coordinates
    of the point marked A?   (☐, ☐)

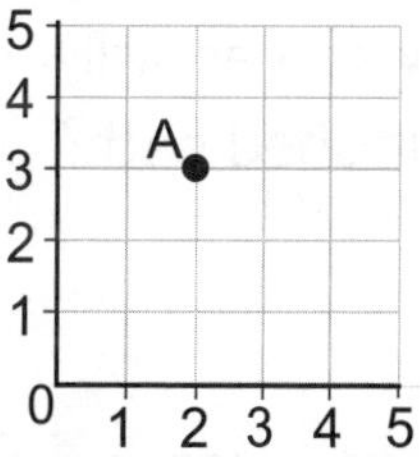

    / 20

Section B — Long Maths
You have **15 minutes** to complete this section.
There are **18 questions** in this section.

---

1. Which of the following pairs of numbers are both multiples of 9?

   A 90 and 72   **C** 14 and 36   **E** 56 and 18
   B 27 and 42   **D** 62 and 15

2. Which of these numbers does not equal 480 when it is rounded to the nearest 10?

   A 485   **B** 475   **C** 480.5   **D** 478   **E** 484.5

3. Saroo started with the number 3 and used the rule "add 4"
   to make a sequence. What is the 5th number in her sequence?

   A 7   **C** 17   **E** 20
   B 15   **D** 19

   Carry on to the next question → →

   Assessment Test 3

The pictures on the right show the prices of a glass of juice and a cookie.

4. What would be the price of a glass of juice and four cookies?

   £ ☐ . ☐ ☐

   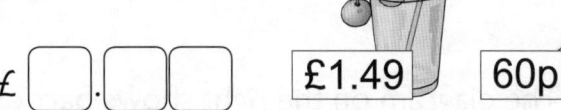

5. Freya buys a glass of juice and a cookie. How much change does she get from £5.00?

   A £3.19   **B** £3.91   **C** £2.91   **D** £2.10   **E** £2.19

6. Fiona is making ice cubes for a party. She uses 10 ml of water to make each ice cube. How many ice cubes can she make from one litre of water?

   A 1000   **B** 10 000   **C** 10   **D** 1   **E** 100

7. Mr Tran is making a path through his vegetable patch using hexagonal stones. Before lunch he lays a third of the stones. The diagram shows the path so far.

   How many stones will be in the finished path? ☐☐

   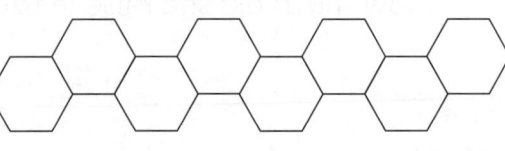

Look at the quadrilaterals on the right.

8. Which quadrilateral has the smallest area?

   A   **B**   **C**   **D**

9. Which quadrilateral has the biggest perimeter?

   A   **B**   **C**   **D**

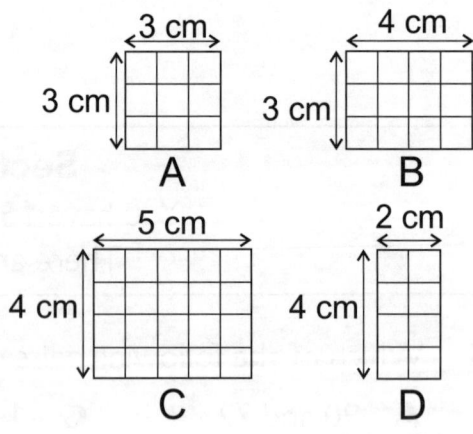

The ingredients for a salad are shown on the right.

10. Olive oil comes in 450 ml bottles. What fraction of the bottle should be used in the salad?

    A $\frac{1}{1000}$ **B** $\frac{1}{5}$ **C** $\frac{1}{10}$ **D** $\frac{1}{100}$ **E** $\frac{1}{3}$

    130 g lettuce
    6 tomatoes
    2 peppers
    45 ml olive oil
    juice of 1 lemon

11. Tomatoes come in packs of 8. What fraction of a pack is needed for the salad?

    A $\frac{2}{3}$ **B** $\frac{3}{4}$ **C** $\frac{1}{4}$ **D** $\frac{5}{6}$ **E** $\frac{1}{8}$

12. In the diagram on the right the shaded area represents the amount of each cake that has been eaten.

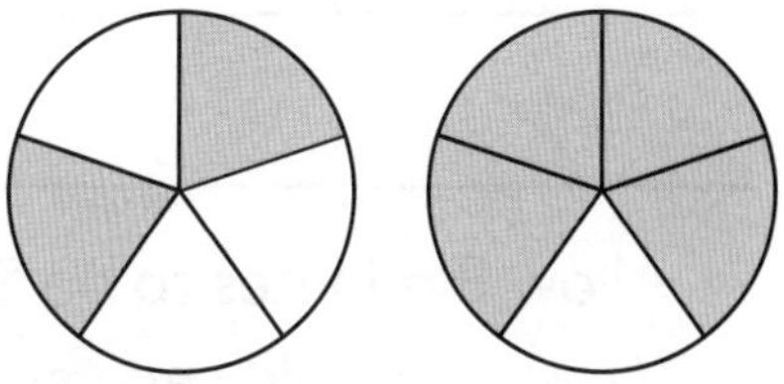

    How much more of cake B has been eaten than cake A?

    A ⅖ **B** ⅕ **C** ⅓ **D** ⅗ **E** ⅔

    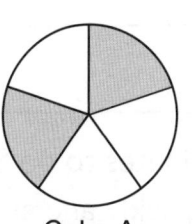
    Cake A   Cake B

13. Henry is measuring the width of the school tennis court using his stride. His stride measures 80 centimetres. The court is 9 strides wide. What is the width of the court to the nearest metre?

    A 7 m **B** 9 m **C** 72 m **D** 6 m **E** 8 m

14. The timetable on the right shows some bus times. Denise gets the 8:20 am bus from Markham to Shipford and then gets the 8:52 am bus from Shipford to Uptown.

Bus stop	Time	
Markham	8:20 am	—
Shipford	8:28 am	8:52 am
Uptown	—	9:10 am

    How long does Denise have to wait in Shipford? ☐☐ minutes

The bar chart shows the number of hours a group of lawyers spent at work last week.

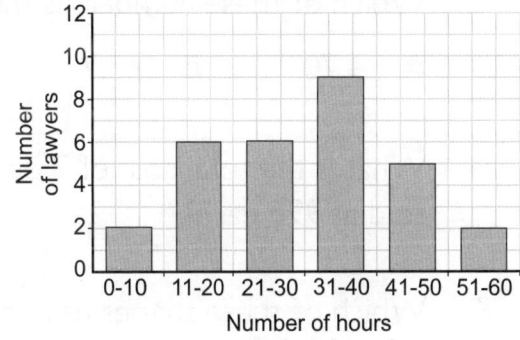

15. How many lawyers worked 31 or more hours? ☐☐

16. How many more lawyers worked 11-30 hours than 41-60 hours? ☐☐

17. Which of the following statements is true?

    A Most lawyers worked 21-30 hours.
    B The total number of lawyers shown in the bar chart is 28.
    C The same number of lawyers worked less than 11 hours as more than 50 hours.
    D More lawyers worked over 40 hours than under 40 hours.
    E 2 more lawyers worked 31-40 hours than 21-30 hours.

18. Laura has a cube and 2 square-based pyramids. She sticks them together to construct the shape shown on the right.

    How many faces does the new shape have? ☐☐

    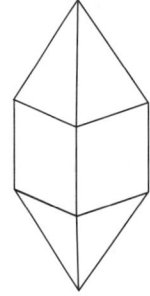

/ 18

End of Test

Assessment Test 3

Assessment Test 4

Allow 8 minutes to do Section A and 15 minutes to do Section B.
Work as quickly and as carefully as you can.

You can print **multiple-choice answer sheets** for these questions from our website — go to cgpbooks.co.uk/11plus/answer-sheets. If you'd prefer to answer them in write-in format, either write your answers in the spaces provided or circle the **correct answer** from the options given.

Section A — Quick Maths
You have **8 minutes** to complete this section.
There are **20 questions** in this section.

1. Which of these shapes is a hexagon?

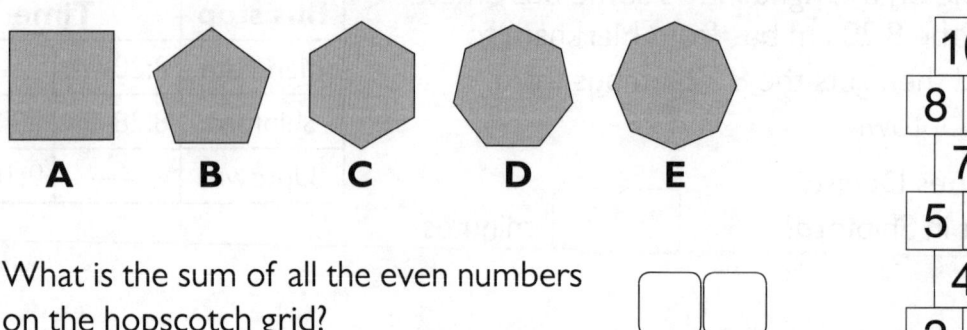

2. What is the sum of all the even numbers on the hopscotch grid?

3. Which of these numbers is the smallest?

   A   4.70   B   40.7   C   0.47   D   7.4   E   70.4

4. What is the total cost of 7 pens sold at 99p each?   £

5. Which of these shapes has only one line of symmetry?

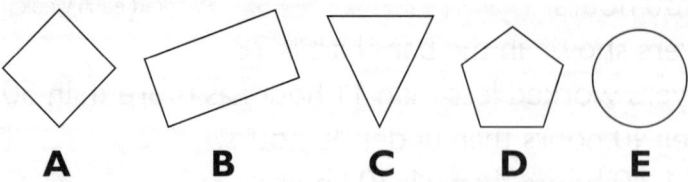

6. Which of the following is the most likely mass of an apple?

   A   0.3 kg   B   3 g   C   0.3 g   D   3 kg   E   30 kg

7. The temperature in Norway is −5 °C.
   The temperature in Dubai is 26 °C.
   What is the difference between these two temperatures?    °C

8. This pictogram shows the numbers of sweets sold by a sweet shop in one day. How many strawberry laces were sold?

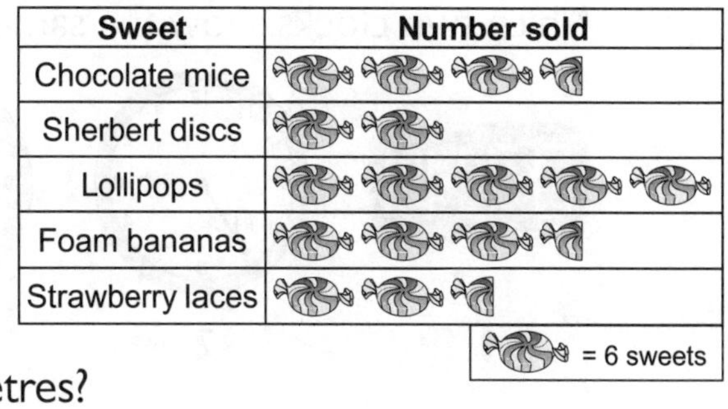

Sweet	Number sold
Chocolate mice	🍬🍬🍬🍬
Sherbert discs	🍬🍬
Lollipops	🍬🍬🍬🍬🍬
Foam bananas	🍬🍬🍬🍬
Strawberry laces	🍬🍬🍬

🍬 = 6 sweets

9. How many centimetres are there in 17.04 metres?

   A 170400 cm
   B 17040 cm
   C 1704 cm
   D 170.4 cm
   E 170.04 cm

10. May makes 32 fairy cakes. She sells ¼ of them at a cake sale. How many cakes did May sell?

11. There are 24 children in a class. Every child in the class needs one of each type of book shown in the bar chart. Which books are there not enough of?

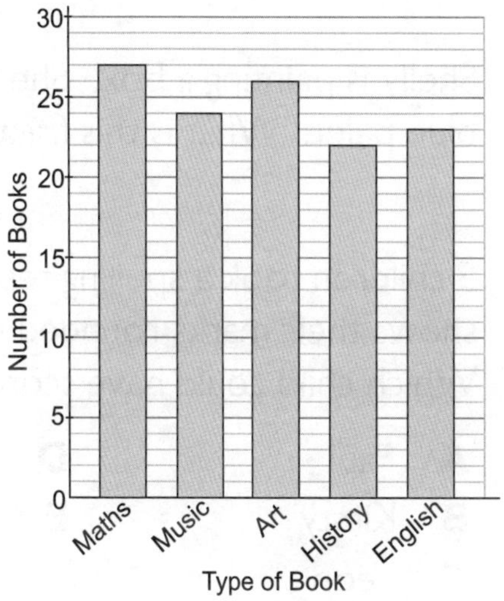

    A Maths and Art
    B Music only
    C History and Music
    D History and English
    E Music, History and English

12. A teacher wants to split 56 children into teams of 6. How many complete teams can he make?

13. Which of these is the best estimate for the size of angle *a* in this shape?

    A 90°
    B 80°
    C 120°
    D 45°
    E 180°

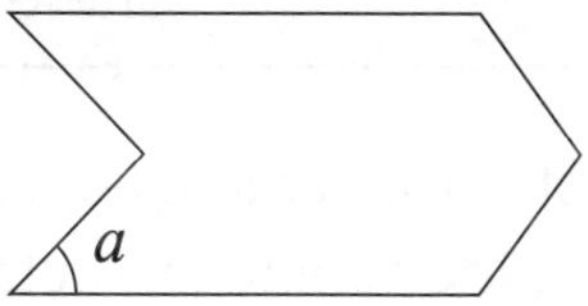

14. James and Oliver are running a race. Oliver finishes in 312 seconds. James finished 14 seconds earlier. How long did it take James to run the race? ☐☐☐ seconds

15. Which of these numbers is closest to 5000?

    A 4892   B 5029   C 4972   D 5100   E 4962

16. 64 passengers are divided equally between 8 minibuses. How many passengers are on each minibus?

Carry on to the next question → →

Assessment Test 4

17. Which two clocks show the same time?

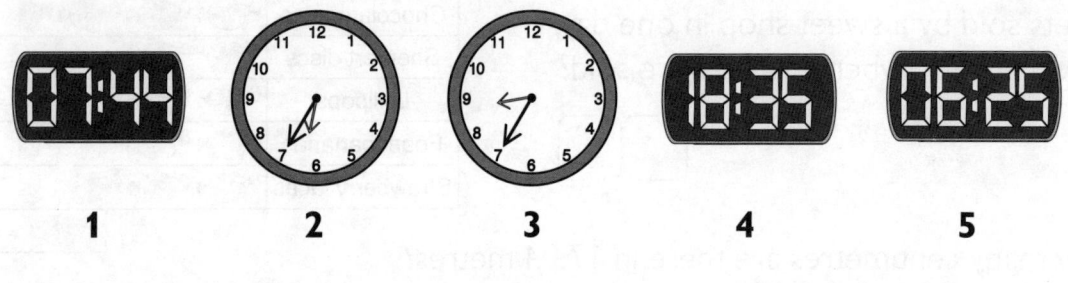

    1   2   3   4   5

A 1 and 2   **B** 3 and 5   **C** 1 and 3   **D** 2 and 4   **E** 2 and 5

18. What number is the arrow pointing to on this number line?

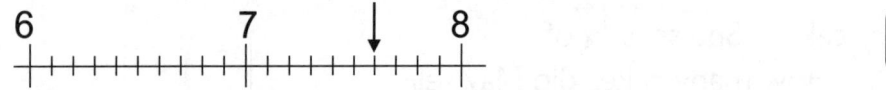

19. Shelly is painting a box. She paints ¼ of the box with blue paint. What is this fraction as a decimal?

20. 5 children took a spelling test. The table shows their marks rounded to the nearest 10. Which child could have scored 74 in the test?

    A Paul   **D** Hemish
    B Kirsty   **E** Fiona
    C Leon

Name	Rounded Mark
Paul	80
Kirsty	50
Leon	100
Hemish	70
Fiona	60

Section B — Long Maths
You have **15 minutes** to complete this section.
There are **18 questions** in this section.

This is a net for a 3D shape. It is made of two identical squares and four identical rectangles.

1. What is the total area of the net?

    ☐☐ cm²

2. What shape will the net make if it is folded together along the dashed lines?
    A A cuboid   **D** A polygon
    B A triangular prism **E** A quadrilateral
    C A square-based pyramid

Sally went rockpooling. She recorded the animals that she found in the table below.

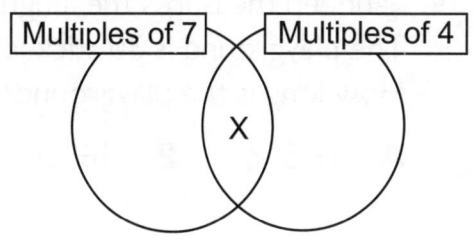

Animal	Number
Sea Snail	7
Pipefish	19
Shrimp	15
Crab	6
Starfish	4

3. What fraction of animals found were sea snails?

   A 7/50   **B** 1/7   **C** 7/51   **D** 7/52   **E** 7/53

4. 1/5 of the shrimp were orange and 3/5 were pink. The rest were grey. What fraction of the shrimp were either orange or pink?

   A 1/5   **B** 2/5   **C** 5/4   **D** 4/5   **E** 3/25

5. Lindsey writes a list of numbers. She starts with the number 13 and counts backwards in steps of 4. Which of these numbers will be on her list?

   A 8   **B** 4   **C** 0   **D** −3   **E** −8

6. Which of the numbers given below should go in the area labelled X on this Venn diagram?

   A 14   **D** 35
   B 21   **E** 43
   C 28   **F** 32

7. A rectangle is split in half into two triangles. What type of triangle must each of these triangles be?

   A Quadrilateral   **B** Right-angled   **C** Equilateral   **D** Isosceles

8. Ranji buys a loaf of bread and three cans of cola. He pays a total of £3.00. The shop charges 90p for a loaf of bread. How much does one can of cola cost?

    p

This table shows the amount of money collected by each stall at a fair.

Stall	Money Collected	
	Morning	Afternoon
Tombola	£18.00	£11.00
Coconut Shy	£15.00	£17.00
Penalty Shoot-out	£16.00	£22.00
Pony Ride	£21.00	£19.00
Bash the Rat	£13.00	£20.00

9. In the morning, how much more money did Pony Ride make than Bash the Rat?

   £

10. Which stall collected the most money over the whole day?

    A Tombola   **C** Penalty Shoot-out   **E** Bash the Rat
    B Coconut Shy   **D** Pony Ride

Carry on to the next question → →

Assessment Test 4

11. Esther buys a box of 100 ice pops for £36. She works out how much each ice pop cost her to buy and sells each ice pop for 14p more than this amount. How much money does Esther sell each ice pop for?  p

Sasha is playing a guessing game with a friend. She thinks of a number.

12. Sasha multiplies the number by 8, then adds 3. The number she ends up with is 51. What number did Sasha start with?

13. Sasha takes the same starting number, multiplies it by 5 and subtracts 12. What number does Sasha end up with?

14. Sandeep measures the length of the playground with a stick. The playground is 30 stick lengths long. The stick is 55 cm long. How long is the playground?

   A 16.5 m   **B** 165 m   **C** 65 m   **D** 160 cm   **E** 1650 m

15. Points A, B and C lie on the corners of a rectangle. Point D lies on the fourth corner of the rectangle. What are the coordinates of point D?

   A (7, 5)   **D** (2, 8)
   B (8, 4)   **E** (4, 8)
   C (5, 7)

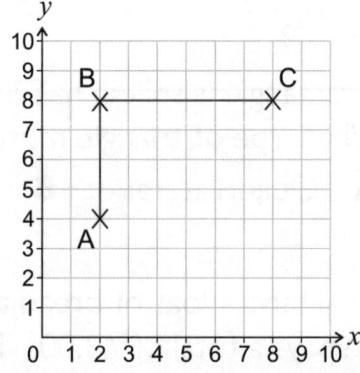

Elaine is decorating her sitting room with Christmas lights. Her sitting room is made up of one small rectangle joined to one larger rectangle.

16. What is the perimeter of her sitting room?

    m

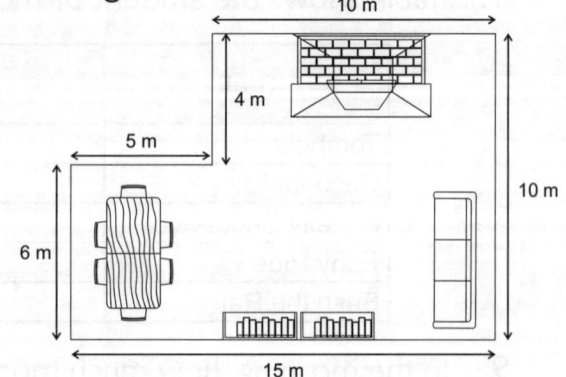

17. Christmas lights come in strands of 6 metres. How many strands of lights will Elaine need to go the whole way around the sitting room?

18. Christmas lights cost £7 for a 6 metre strand. How much will it cost Elaine to buy enough lights to go the whole way around her room? £

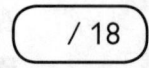 / 18

End of Test

Assessment Test 5

Allow 8 minutes to do Section A and 15 minutes to do Section B.
Work as quickly and as carefully as you can.

You can print **multiple-choice answer sheets** for these questions from our website — go to cgpbooks.co.uk/11plus/answer-sheets. If you'd prefer to answer them in write-in format, either write your answers in the spaces provided or circle the **correct answer** from the options given.

Section A — Quick Maths
You have **8 minutes** to complete this section.
There are **20 questions** in this section.

1. Which number is in the wrong section of this Venn diagram?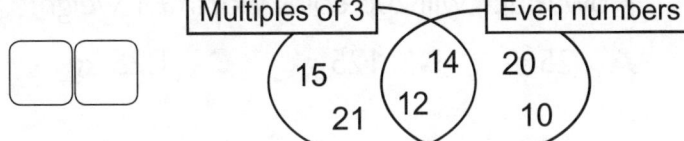

2. Mr Button is buying some tiles for his bathroom.
   He wants tiles which have 6 equal sides.
   What shape should his tiles be?

   A circle   **C** triangle   **E** square
   B regular hexagon   **D** regular pentagon

3. One minibus has space for 9 passengers.
   How many minibuses are needed for 72 passengers?

   A 8   **B** 6   **C** 12   **D** 7   **E** 15

4. Chris is making flapjacks. The scales show the weight of the sugar that he uses.

   How much sugar does Chris use?  g

   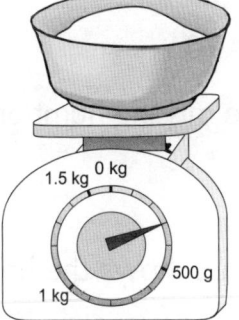

5. Which of the following is the most likely height of a house?

   A 0.85 km   **C** 8.5 m   **E** 80.5 m
   B 850 mm   **D** 85 cm

6. Aaron is laying concrete blocks to make a path Each block has a mass of 3 kg.
   How much would three blocks weigh in grams?

   A 90 g   **B** 9000 g   **C** 9.9 g   **D** 900 g   **E** 3000 g

   Carry on to the next question → →

7. Which pair of numbers can go in the shaded box of the table?

   A 8 and 12   C 3 and 6   E 9 and 10
   B 7 and 9   D 6 and 8

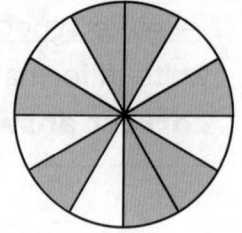

8. What fraction of this shape is shaded?

   A $\frac{3}{12}$ B $\frac{5}{12}$ C $\frac{7}{12}$ D $\frac{4}{12}$ E $\frac{8}{12}$

9. Round 17.48 m to the nearest 0.1 m. ☐☐.☐ m

10. One 20p coin weighs 5 g.
    How much will 20p coins worth £1 weigh?

    A 25 g   B 125 g   C 1.25 kg   D 250 g   E 2.5 kg

11. What is 1000 − 567?

    A 437   B 441   C 563   D 433   E 537

12. The table shows the temperature in Antarctica on five days.

    What was the difference in temperature between Wednesday and Thursday?

    A 6 °C   C 4 °C   E 5 °C
    B 7 °C   D 12 °C

Day	Temperature (°C)
Monday	−6
Tuesday	−4
Wednesday	−7
Thursday	−12
Friday	−8

13. ☐ ÷ 8 = 70

    What is the missing number in this calculation? ☐☐☐

14. The bar chart shows the heights of six buildings.

    What is the difference in height between building 3 and building 5? ☐☐ m

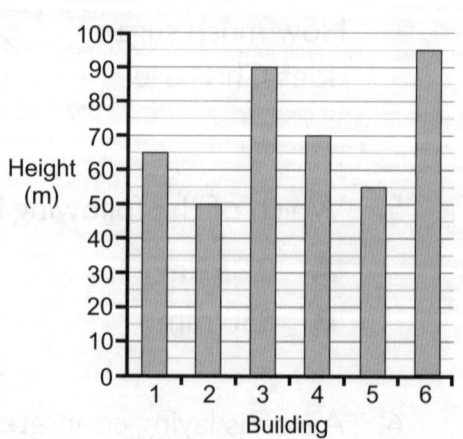

15. Here is part of a sequence: ...24, 48, 96, 192...

    The rule for the sequence is 'double the previous number'.
    Which number came before 24 in the sequence? ☐☐

Assessment Test 5

16. A train leaves Birmingham at 8:57 and arrives in Manchester at 10:45.
    How long did the journey take?

    A 2 hours and 48 minutes **D** 1 hour and 48 minutes
    B 1 hour and 45 minutes   **E** 1 hour and 42 minutes
    C 2 hours and 12 minutes

17. Which of these numbers is not a multiple of 3 and 5?

    A 15 **B** 30 **C** 35 **D** 60 **E** 45

18. Akmal folds up a net to make a cube.
    Which of the following nets could he have used?

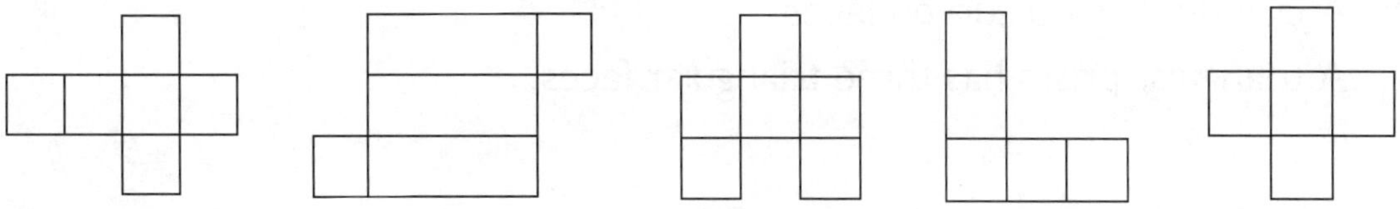

    A **B** **C** **D** **E**

19. Shape X is reflected in a vertical mirror line.
    Which of the following shapes is the reflection of shape X?

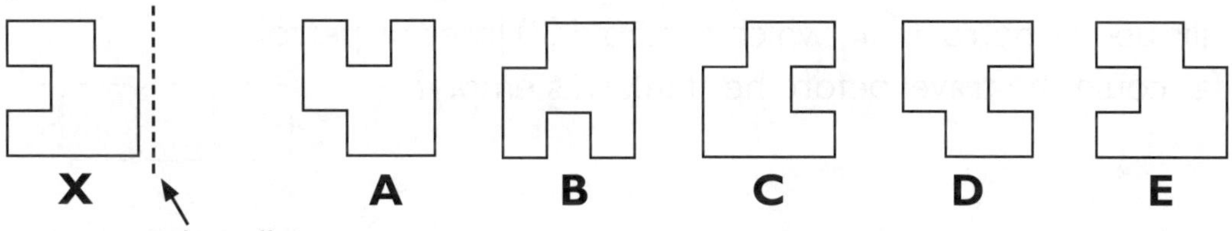

    X mirror line **A** **B** **C** **D** **E**

20. Alia's cat eats 80 g of tinned meat a day.
    How much tinned meat does her cat eat in a week?

    A 720 g **B** 560 g **C** 640 g **D** 480 g **E** 820 g

/ 20

Section B — Long Maths
You have **15 minutes** to complete this section.
There are **18 questions** in this section.

1. Each chapter in a book is eight pages long.
   Susi reads the first 8 chapters and 5 pages of chapter 9.

   How many pages has Susi read?

2. Kirsten's bookshelf is 1 m long.
   She has some books which are all 7 cm thick.
   How many books can she fit on her bookshelf?

   A 7 **B** 15 **C** 13 **D** 14 **E** 16

   Carry on to the next question → →

3. Point P on the grid is moved three squares down and two squares right.

   Which option below gives the correct coordinates of the new position of point P?

A	B	C	D	E
(6, 3)	(2, 3)	(7, 4)	(3, 6)	(4, 7)

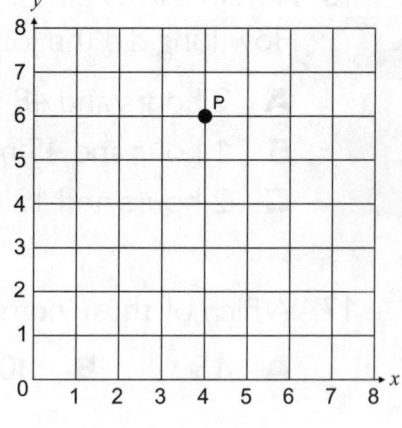

4. Which of these statements is true?
   - **A** A cube has four faces.
   - **B** A triangle-based pyramid has one rectangular face.
   - **C** A square-based pyramid has four triangular faces.
   - **D** A cylinder has no curved faces.
   - **E** A triangular prism has three triangular faces.

Paula has just bought a new car that uses 3 litres of petrol to travel 50 km.

5. The distance between Broggington and Frogsley is just under 200 km. How many litres of petrol would she need for this journey?

   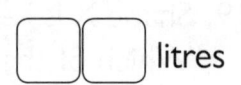 litres

6. Paula fills up her petrol tank, which can hold 30 litres of petrol. How far could she travel before her tank was empty?

   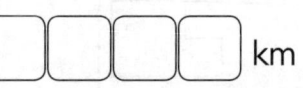 km

7. Harvey draws points A and B on this coordinate grid. He draws point C and then draws a line between points B and C to make a right angle.
   Which of the following could be the coordinates of point C?

   A (2, 4)   **B** (3, 2)   **C** (2, 1)   **D** (3, 3)   **E** (5, 4)

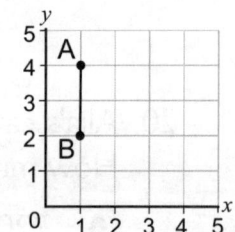

8. Liz makes this shape using six white cubes. She paints the outside of the shape blue and then breaks the shape apart into cubes again. How many cube faces are white?

   A 10   **B** 12   **C** 8   **D** 5   **E** 7

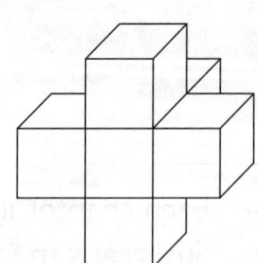

9. The battery of Darren's mobile phone lasts for 50 hours before he has to charge it again. The battery is fully charged at 9 am on Sunday morning. When will Darren have to charge the battery again?

   - **A** 1 pm Tuesday
   - **B** 11 pm Monday
   - **C** 11 am Wednesday
   - **D** 11 am Tuesday
   - **E** 5 am Wednesday

Assessment Test 5

The pictogram shows the scores of four teams in a quiz.

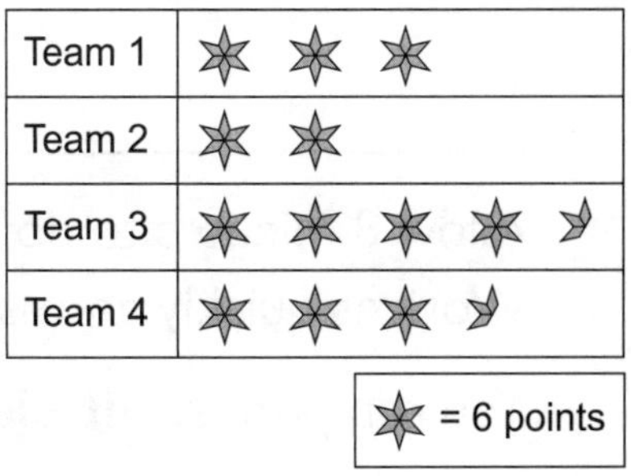

Team 1	★ ★ ★
Team 2	★ ★
Team 3	★ ★ ★ ★ ⟩
Team 4	★ ★ ★ ⟩

★ = 6 points

10. What is the difference between the scores of Team 2 and Team 4?

11. What was the total number of points scored by all the teams?

Jimmy and Gordon count the number of trees in their orchards.

12. Jimmy says, "Exactly $\frac{1}{7}$ of the trees in my orchard are apple trees".
    How many trees could Jimmy have in total?

    A 27   B 12   C 15   D 21   E 20

13. Gordon says, "$\frac{1}{8}$ of my trees are apple trees. $\frac{3}{8}$ of my trees are pear trees".
    What fraction of Gordon's trees are either apple or pear trees?
    Give your answer in its simplest terms.

    A $\frac{5}{8}$ B $\frac{4}{8}$ C $\frac{1}{2}$ D $\frac{2}{4}$ E $\frac{3}{4}$

The bar chart on the right shows the number of days it rained in Ulverthwaite in each of the last six months of the year.

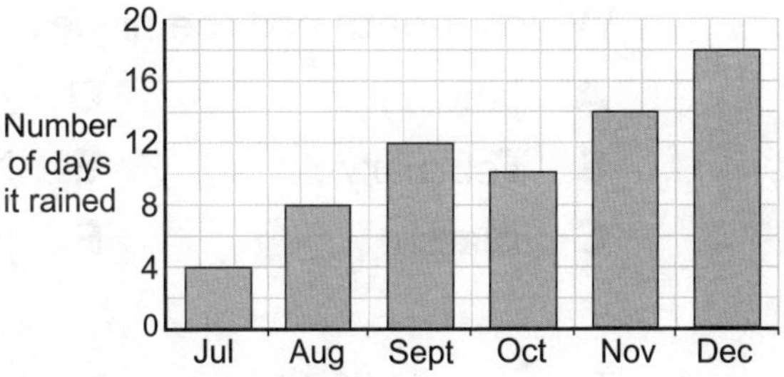

14. What was the total number of days it rained in the last three months of the year?

15. How many more days did it rain in December than in July and August combined?

16. A jug contains 3 litres of water.
    Maxine pours six 200 ml glasses of water from the jug.
    How much water is left in the jug?

    A 1200 ml   B 1800 ml   C 600 ml   D 2400 ml   E 1500 ml

17. Kaya buys 4 oranges at 49p each. She pays with a £10 note.
    How much change will she be given?

    A £1.96   B £8.04   C £7.62   D £7.96   E £4.90

18. Georgina drew the shape on the right and reflected it in the mirror line.

    What is the total perimeter of the shape and its reflection? ___ cm

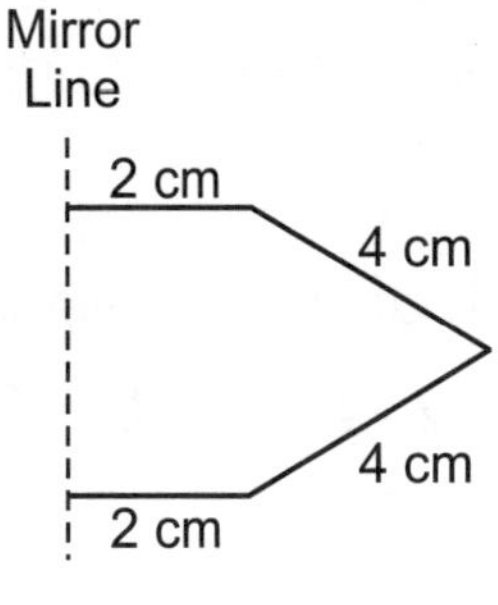

/ 18

End of Test

Assessment Test 5

Assessment Test 6

Allow 8 minutes to do Section A and 15 minutes to do Section B.
Work as quickly and as carefully as you can.

You can print **multiple-choice answer sheets** for these questions from our website — go to cgpbooks.co.uk/11plus/answer-sheets. If you'd prefer to answer them in write-in format, either write your answers in the spaces provided or circle the **correct answer** from the options given.

Section A — Quick Maths
You have **8 minutes** to complete this section.
There are **20 questions** in this section.

1. Which of these numbers is the largest?

   A 113   B 134   C 3.4   D 13   E 34

2. The bar chart shows the rainfall on an island during the first six months of a year. Which month had the highest rainfall?

   A January   D April
   B February   E May
   C March   F June

   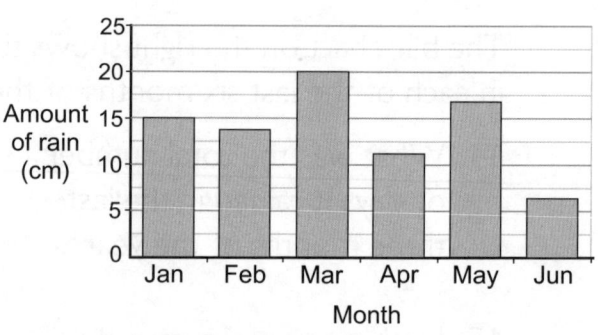

3. There are 1000 fans in a football stadium. 110 are away fans. The rest are home fans. How many home fans are in the stadium?

   A 880   B 910   C 990   D 890   E 900

4. Mick adds up the 7 digits on this barcode. What answer does he get?

   0 5 1 5 6 4 7

5. There are 606 chickens at Raven Farm. There are 149 fewer chickens at Shrove Farm. How many chickens are there at Shrove Farm?

   A 567   B 457   C 543   D 467   E 563

6. Which number is in the wrong section of this Venn diagram?

   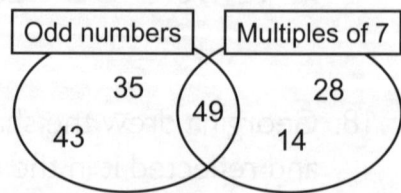

7. Which of these weights is closest to 3 kg?

   A 3.2 kg   B 2.8 kg   C 2.9 kg   D 2.5 kg   E 3.3 kg

8. The pictogram shows the number of hours of sunshine on five days. How many more hours of sunshine were there on Thursday than on Monday?

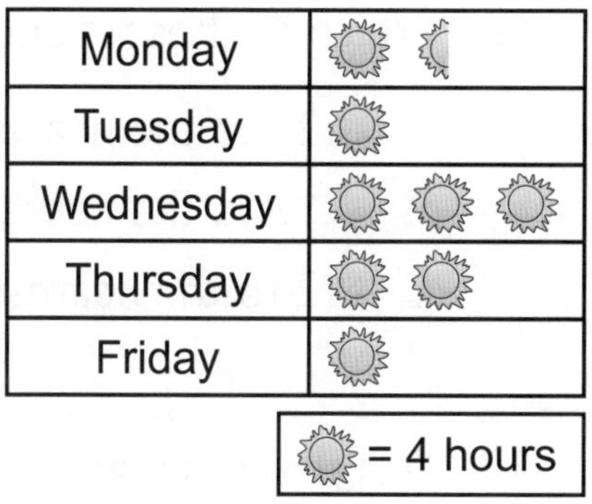

    ☐☐ hours

Monday	
Tuesday	
Wednesday	
Thursday	
Friday	

    ☀ = 4 hours

9. Taj starts at 17 and counts back in steps of 5. Which of these numbers will be in his sequence?

    A 1 **B** 2 **C** 3 **D** 4 **E** 5

10. Olivia draws this triangle on a coordinate grid. Which of these squares is not inside the triangle?

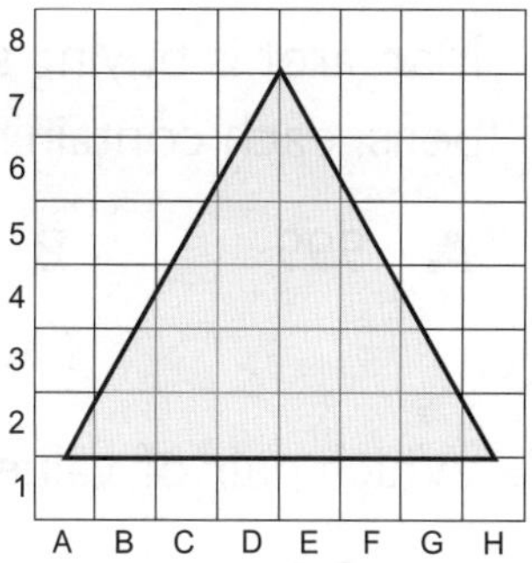

    A C3 **C** E5 **E** F7
    B D5 **D** D2

11. A TV programme starts at 5:45 pm and lasts for 57 minutes. What time does the programme finish?

    ☐☐:☐☐ pm

12. Anne-Marie can make 4 necklaces out of 320 beads. Each necklace has the same number of beads. How many beads are there in each necklace?

    A 90 **B** 160 **C** 80 **D** 100 **E** 140

13. Priya draws this shape on some squared paper. Each square on the paper has an area of 1 cm². What is the area of Priya's shape?

    ☐☐ cm²

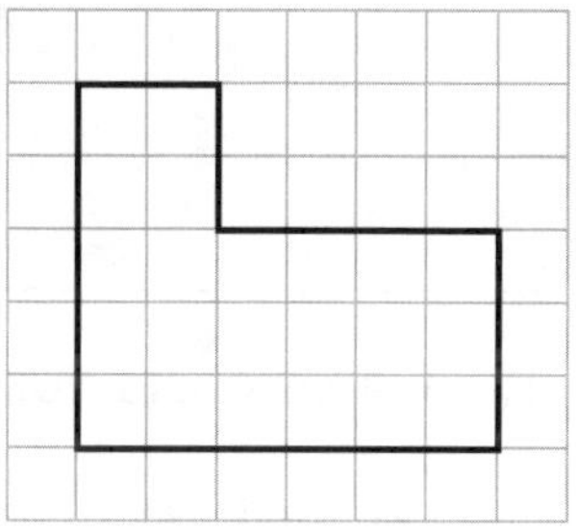

14. 37 people are on a bus. At a bus stop, 12 people get off and 6 people get on. How many people are on the bus after the stop?

    A 25 **B** 55 **C** 31 **D** 24 **E** 27

15. How many lines of symmetry does the shape on the right have?

    ☐

Carry on to the next question → →

Assessment Test 6

16. Which of these is equal to 120?

   A 121 to the nearest 100
   B 117 to the nearest 10
   C 12 to the nearest 100
   D 119.4 to the nearest whole number
   E 125 to the nearest 10

17. This shape is made from two identical rectangles. What is the perimeter of the shape? ☐☐ cm

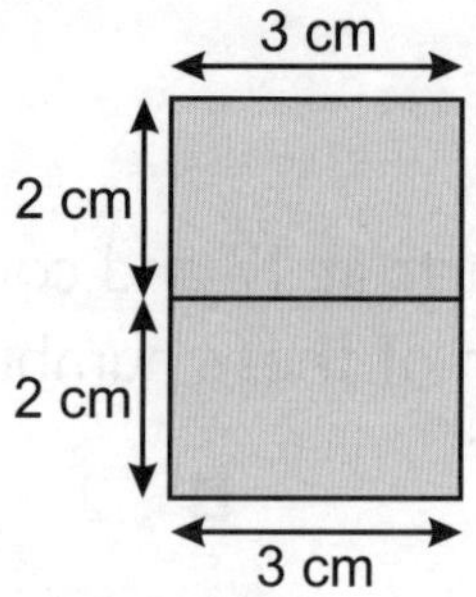

18. Margaret is buying stationery for a school. She buys 90 packets of pens, each containing 9 pens. How many pens did she buy in total?

   A 999   **B** 891   **C** 900   **D** 890   **E** 810

19. Which pair of values are equal?

   A 0.1 and ¼
   B ³⁄₁₀ and 0.4
   C ¾ and 0.25
   D ⁷⁄₁₀ and 0.5
   E ½ and 0.5

20. Chelsea reflected this rectangle in the mirror line. Which point shows the reflection of point Z?

   A   **B**   **C**   **D**   **E**

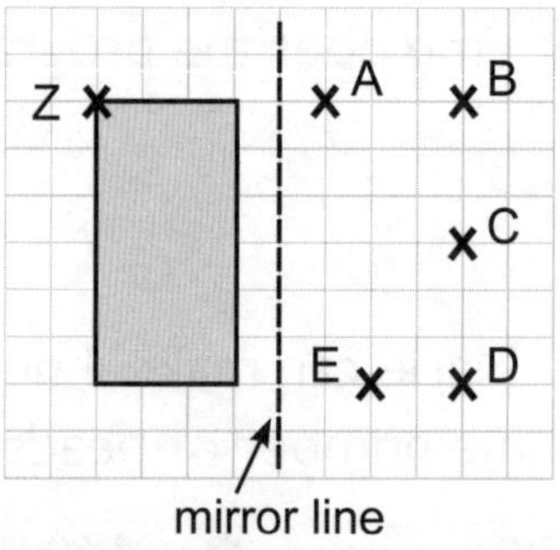

/ 20

Section B — Long Maths

You have **15 minutes** to complete this section.
There are **18 questions** in this section.

---

1. Cards costs 40p. Jo buys three cards. How much change does she receive from £5?

   A £1.20   **B** £3.80   **C** £4.60   **D** £4.00   **E** £4.20

Michelle is building a tower out of bricks following a sequence. The first 4 levels are shown in the picture.

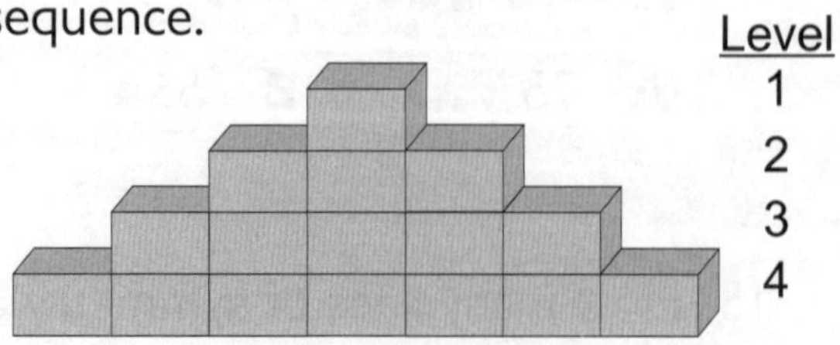

2. How many bricks will be in the 6th level? ☐☐

3. If the bottom level of the tower is made of 15 bricks, how many levels are in the tower? ☐☐

Assessment Test 6

7) B

To make a right angle, Harvey needs to draw a horizontal line from point B. This means that the point needs to have the same *y*-coordinate as point B (2). The only possible option is (3, 2).

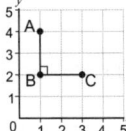

8) A

Each of the five cubes on the outside of the shape are attached to the middle cube on 1 face. The middle cube is attached to other cubes on 5 faces. So the total number of white faces will be: (1 × 5) + 5 = 5 + 5 = 10.

9) D

There are 24 hours in 1 day so there are 2 × 24 = 48 hours in 2 days.
So 50 hours is 2 days and 2 hours.
Count on 2 hours from 9 am on Sunday to get to 11 am. Then count on 2 days to get to 11 am on Tuesday. So the battery will need to be charged at 11 am on Tuesday.

10) 9

Each symbol on the pictogram shows 6 points. There are 2 symbols for Team 2, so they have 2 × 6 = 12 points.
There are 3½ symbols for Team 4.
½ of 6 is 3 and 3 × 6 = 18.
So Team 4 have 3 + 18 = 21 points.
So the difference between the two teams is 21 − 12 = 9 points.
(Or you could work out that Team 4 has 1½ symbols more than Team 2.
1½ symbol = 6 ÷ 2 = 3,
so the difference = 6 + 3 = 9 points.)

11) 78

Count up the number of symbols in the pictogram. There are 12 full symbols and 2 half symbols (which make another full symbol when combined) so 13 symbols in total. Each symbol represents 6 points.
Split up 13 × 6 into 10 × 6 = 60 and 3 × 6 = 18. 60 + 18 = 78 points.
(Or you could find the points each team scored and add them together.
Team 1: 18, Team 2: 12, Team 3: 27, Team 4: 21. 18 + 12 + 27 + 21 = 78 points)

12) D

The total number of trees must divide exactly by 7. 21 ÷ 7 = 3.

13) C

Add the fraction of trees that are apple trees to the fraction that are pear trees — the denominators are the same, so just add the numerators together. ⅛ + ⅜ = 4⁄8.
4 is half of 8, so the fraction is ½ in its simplest terms.

14) 42

Find the height of the bars for October (10), November (14) and December (18) and add them together. 10 + 14 = 24, 18 can be split up into 10 + 8 and added in parts to 24: 24 + 10 = 34, 34 + 8 = 42.

15) 6

It rained for 18 days in December. It rained for 4 days in July and 8 days in August, which is 12 days in total. 18 − 12 = 6 days.

16) B

There are 1000 ml in 1 litre so there is 3 × 1000 = 3000 ml of water in the jug. The amount of water Maxine pours into glasses is 6 × 200 ml = 1200 ml.
This means that there is 3000 − 1200 = 1800 ml left in the jug.

17) B

Round 49p up to 50p.
4 × 50p = £2.00. You added an extra 1p to each price, so in total you added 4 × 1p = 4p. Subtract 4p from your rounded answer to find the actual cost of 4 oranges: £2.00 − 4p = £1.96.
Subtract £1.96 from £10 to work out the change that Kaya is given:
£10 − £1.96 = £8.04.

18) 24 cm

The diagram shows the shape after it has been reflected. Add up the length of every side to find the perimeter of the shape:
2 + 4 + 4 + 2 + 2 + 4 + 4 + 2 = 24 cm.

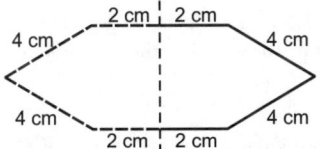

Assessment Test 6
Section A — Pages 66-68

1) B

Look at the place value of the first digit in each of the numbers given.
Both 113 and 134 have 1 hundred.
Then look at the place value of the second digit in the next column on the right.
113 has 1 ten, and 134 has 3 tens.
So 134 is the biggest number.

2) C

The month with the highest amount of rain will have the tallest bar — March.

3) D

Break up 110 into 100 + 10 and subtract each part from 1000.
1000 − 10 = 990,
990 − 100 = 890 fans.

4) 28

To add up the 7 digits try and group the digits up into numbers that add to 10.
5 + 5 = 10, 6 + 4 = 10 and 1 + 7 = 8.
10 + 10 + 8 = 28.

5) B

Subtract 149 from 606 to find the number of chickens at Shrove Farm.
You could do this by counting back from 606 to 149, then adding up the numbers you counted back. 606 − 6 = 600, 600 − 400 = 200, 200 − 50 = 150, 150 − 1 = 149,
6 + 400 + 50 + 1 = 457 chickens.
Alternatively you could partition 149 and subtract each number from 606.
149 splits into 100 + 40 + 9.
606 − 9 = 597, 597 − 40 = 557,
557 − 100 = 457 chickens.

6) 35

35 is an odd number and a multiple of 7 (7 × 5 = 35). It should be in the middle section of the Venn diagram.

7) C

Look for the biggest number under 3 kg and the smallest number above 3 kg.
Then look at the difference between 3 kg and these two numbers.
The difference between 2.9 kg and 3 kg is 3 − 2.9 = 0.1 kg. The difference between 3.2 kg and 3 kg is 3.2 − 3 = 0.2 kg.
So 2.9 kg is closest to 3 kg.

8) 2 hours

There are 2 symbols on Thursday and only 1½ symbols on Monday.
This is a difference of ½ a symbol.
1 symbol represents 4 hours, so
½ a symbol represents 4 ÷ 2 = 2 hours.

9) B

Count back in 5s from 17 until you reach one of the options: 17, 12, 7, 2...
2 is the only option that's in the sequence.

10) E

To work out the position of each square you count across the horizontal axis until you find the letter. Then you count up the vertical axis until you find the number.
F7 is not inside the triangle.

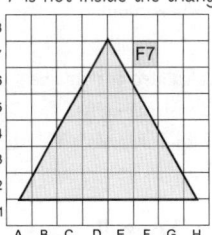

11) 6:42 pm

57 minutes is only 3 minutes less than 1 hour. So add an hour and then subtract 3 minutes to find the finish time.
1 hour on from 5:45 pm is 6:45 pm, and 3 minutes back from 6:45 pm is 6:42 pm.

12) C

You know from your times tables that 8 × 4 = 32, so 32 ÷ 4 = 8. 320 is ten times larger than 32, so the answer will be ten times larger: 320 ÷ 4 = 80 beads.

13) 22 cm²

Count the number of squares inside the shape to find its area. The area of each square is 1 cm² and there are 22 squares inside the shape, so the area of the shape is 22 cm².

14) A
Multiply the number of stick lengths by the length of the stick to find the length of the playground in centimetres: 30 × 55 cm. You could partition 55 into 50 + 5 to make the multiplication easier.
30 × 50 = 1500 cm. 30 × 5 = 150 cm.
1500 + 150 = 1650 cm.
1 m = 100 cm, so divide by 100 to find the length in metres: 1650 ÷ 100 = 16.5 m.

15) B
The shape is a rectangle so it has two pairs of equal sides. This means that the x-coordinate of corner D is the same as corner C (8). The y-coordinate of corner D is the same as corner A (4).
So the coordinates of corner D are (8, 4).

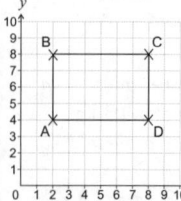

16) 50 m
You need to add up all the individual lengths of the walls.
10 + 10 + 15 + 6 + 5 + 4.
15 splits into 10 + 5.
Add the tens first:
10 + 10 + 10 = 30
Then add the units:
5 + 5 + 6 + 4 = 20
Then add them both together
30 + 20 = 50 m

17) 9
Elaine needs enough Christmas lights to go around 50 m of wall. If lights come in strands of 6 m, you need to find the first multiple of 6 that is bigger than 50.
You need to use your 6 times table:
8 × 6 = 48 is too small. 9 × 6 = 54.
This is greater than 50 so will mean there is enough to cover the whole room.

18) £63
In question 17 you calculated that Elaine needs 9 strands of Christmas lights.
Each strand costs £7 so 9 strands will cost 9 × 7 = £63.

Assessment Test 5
Section A — Pages 61-63

1) 14
The numbers in the middle section of the diagram should be multiples of 3 that are also even numbers.
14 is even, but it's not a multiple of 3, so it doesn't belong in the middle section.

2) B
A shape with 6 equal sides is a regular pentagon.

3) A
There are 72 passengers in total and each minibus can hold 9 passengers.
So the number of minibuses needed is 72 ÷ 9 = 8.

4) 300 g
There are 5 spaces on the scale between 0 kg and 500 g, so each space on the scale is worth 100 g. The arrow is pointing 3 spaces from 0 kg, so the weight of the sugar is: 3 × 100 g = 300 g.

5) C
850 mm and 85 cm are the same and both less than 1 m. An adult is usually between 1.5 m and 1.8 m tall, so these measurements are too small to be the height of a house.
80.5 m is roughly the height of a tower block, and 0.85 km is the same as 850 m, so both of these heights are far taller than a house — 8.5 m is the only realistic answer.

6) B
There are three 3 kg blocks so that would be 3 × 3 = 9 kg in total. 1 kg = 1000 g.
So 9 kg is 9 × 1000 = 9000 g.

7) D
< means 'is less than', so the numbers in the shaded box must be even numbers that are less than 10. 6 and 8 are both even and less than 10, so D is the correct answer.

8) C
The circle is split into 12 parts and 7 parts are shaded. As a fraction this is 7/12.

9) 17.5 m
17.45 is halfway between 17.4 and 17.5.
17.48 is more than 17.45, so 17.48 rounds up to 17.5 m.

10) A
100p ÷ 20p = 5, so there are five 20p coins in £1. The weight of the coins will be:
5 × 5 g = 25 g.

11) D
You can work this out by partitioning 567 into 500 + 60 + 7 and then subtracting each number from 1000 one at a time.
1000 − 500 = 500, 500 − 60 = 440,
440 − 7 = 433.

12) E
Count back from −7 °C. 3 °C takes you to −10 °C and 2 °C takes you to −12 °C.

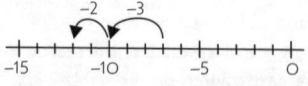

3 °C + 2 °C = 5 °C.

13) 560
The missing number is divided by 8 to give 70. So 70 × 8 must equal the missing number (because multiplying is the opposite of dividing). You know that 7 × 8 = 56.
70 is ten times larger than 7, so the answer will be ten times larger: 56 × 10 = 560.
So 560 ÷ 8 = 70.

14) 35 m
Building 3 is 90 metres tall and building 5 is 55 metres tall. So building 3 is:
90 − 55 = 35 metres taller than building 5.

15) 12
The previous number has been doubled to give 24. So find half of 24 to find the previous number: 24 ÷ 2 = 12.

16) D
Count on from 8:57 to 10:45.
8:57 to 9:00 is 3 minutes.
9:00 to 10:00 is 1 hour.
10:00 to 10:45 is 45 minutes.
1 hour + 45 minutes + 3 minutes
= 1 hour and 48 minutes.

17) C
35 is a multiple of 5 (5 × 7 = 35) but it's not a multiple of 3.

18) A
Imagine folding each of the nets and work out which edges will join together.
Net A is the only net that will fold up to make a cube.

19) C
The diagram shows shape X being reflected. Option C is the reflected shape.

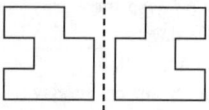

20) B
There are 7 days in a week, so the cat eats 7 × 80 g of tinned meat each week.
80 × 7 = 560 g (8 × 7 = 56 and 80 is ten times bigger than 8).

Section B — Pages 63-65

1) 69
Each chapter is 8 pages long, so the first 8 chapters will be 8 × 8 = 64 pages long. She has also read 5 pages of chapter 9, so in total she has read 64 + 5 = 69 pages.

2) D
There are 100 cm in 1 m, so you need to work out 100 ÷ 7. You can solve this by partitioning 100 into 70 + 30 and dividing each number by 7. Then you add together the results. 70 ÷ 7 = 10,
30 ÷ 7 = 4 r 2. 10 + 4 r 2 = 14 r 2.
So that means you can fit 14 books on the bookshelf, and there will be 2 cm of space left over.

3) A
3 squares down takes you to (4, 3).
2 squares right takes you to (6, 3).

4) C
A square-based pyramid has one square face and four triangular faces.

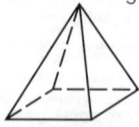

5) 12 litres
3 litres of petrol will take Paula 50 km.
To go 200 km she will need:
200 ÷ 50 = 4 times as much petrol.
So she will need 3 × 4 = 12 litres.

6) 500 km
3 litres of petrol will take Paula 50 km.
If she has 30 litres she will be able to go 30 ÷ 3 = 10 times further. So she will be able to go 10 × 50 = 500 km.

9) C

There are 100 cm in 1 m, so to convert 17.04 m into centimetres you multiply by 100: 17.04 × 100 = 1704 cm.

10) 8

$\frac{1}{4}$ of 32 is the same as 32 ÷ 4 = 8. So $\frac{1}{4}$ of 32 is 8 cakes.

11) D

For each child to be able to have one of each type of book, there needs to be 24 of each book. Look at which bars reach 24 books on the vertical axis.

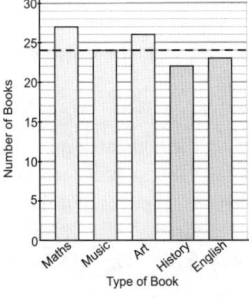

Both the History and English bars on the chart are below 24, so there aren't enough of these types of books.

12) 9

54 ÷ 6 = 9, so 54 children could be split to make 9 teams of 6. That would leave two children left over (56 − 54 = 2), which isn't enough to make another complete team.

13) D

A right angle is 90°. Angle a is smaller than a right angle so it's less than 90°. 80° is only slightly smaller than a right angle. 45° is half the size of a right angle, which most closely matches the picture.

14) 298 seconds

James was 14 seconds faster than Oliver. You need to work out 312 − 14. You can do this by counting back:

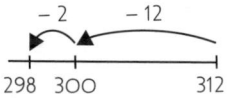

15) C

Find the highest number below 5000, and the lowest number above 5000 — one of these will be the closest number to 5000. Then just work out the difference between 5000 and these two numbers.
Highest number below 5000 = 4972
Lowest number above 5000 = 5029
5000 − 4972 = 28
5029 − 5000 = 29 so 4972 is closer to 5000.

16) 8

You need to divide 64 by 8 to find how many passengers are on each minibus.
64 ÷ 8 = 8.

17) D

First look at the number of minutes shown by each clock — only clocks 2, 3 and 4 match (they each show 35 minutes). The hour hand on clock 2 is between 6 and 7 so it shows 6:35. The time shown on clock 4 is in the 24-hour clock — subtract 12 from the number of hours to find the time in the 12-hour clock: 18 − 12 = 6. So the time on clock 4 is 6:35, which is the same as on clock 2.

18) 7.6

The space between 7 and 8 is split into 10 gaps — each gap is worth one tenth (0.1). The arrow is pointing at a line 6 gaps further along than 7, which must have a value of 6 tenths greater than 7.
7 + 0.6 = 7.6

19) 0.25

$\frac{1}{4}$ is the same as 0.25 (1 ÷ 4 = 0.25).

20) D

74 is being rounded to the nearest 10. 75 is halfway between 70 and 80. 74 is less than 75, so 74 rounds down to 70. Hemish is the only child who has a rounded score of 70, so Hemish could have scored 74 on the test.

Section B — Pages 58-60

1) 80 cm²

The area can be found by multiplying the length of each quadrilateral by its width or by counting the squares.
The area of each square is 2 × 2 = 4 cm².
So the area of the 2 squares together is 4 × 2 = 8 cm².
The rest of the net is made of 4 identical rectangles each with a length of 9 cm and a width of 2 cm.
The area of each rectangle is 9 × 2 = 18 cm².
The total area of the four rectangles is 4 × 18 cm².
Split 18 into 10 + 8:
4 × 10 = 40, 4 × 8 = 32,
so 4 × 18 = 40 + 32 = 72 cm²
So the total area of the net is
72 + 8 = 80 cm²

2) A

Imagine folding the net along the dotted lines and work out which edges of the net will join together. This net will fold up to be a cuboid.

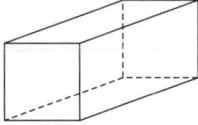

3) C

First work out the total number of animals found. This can be done by partitioning. 19 splits into 10 + 9 and 15 splits into 10 + 5.
Add the tens first: 10 + 10 = 20.
Add the units: 7 + 9 + 5 + 6 + 4 = 31.
Then add them together: 31 + 20 = 51.
The number of sea snails found was 7.
This gives a fraction of $\frac{7}{51}$.

4) D

Add the fraction of shrimps that are orange to the fraction that are pink — the denominators are the same, so just add the numerators together. $\frac{1}{5} + \frac{3}{5} = \frac{4}{5}$

5) D

Count back from 13 in steps of 4 until you reach one of the options.

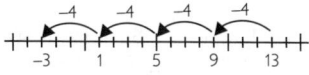

6) C

The number that goes into section X has to be a multiple of 7 and 4. Only 28 is a multiple of both 4 and 7 (4 × 7 = 28, 7 × 4 = 28).

7) B

A rectangle can only be split into two triangles by cutting it like this: This means each triangle will have a right angle — so option B is correct.

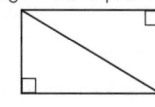

8) 70p

Subtract the cost of a loaf of bread from the total cost to find the cost of the three cans of cola:
£3.00 − 90p = 300p − 90p = 210p.
Divide 210p by 3 to find the price of each can of cola. 21 ÷ 3 = 7. 210 is ten times bigger than 21, so 210 ÷ 3 will be 10 times bigger than 7. That means the price of a can of cola is 7 × 10 = 70p

9) £8

In the morning, the Pony Ride made £21.00 and Bash the Rat made £13.00.
£21.00 − £13.00 = £8.00

10) D

Add up the number of pounds raised by each stall during the day to find the total amount collected by each stall.
Tombola: 18 + 11 = £29
Coconut Shy: 15 + 17 = £32
Penalty Shoot-out: 16 + 22 = £38
Pony Ride: 21 + 19 = £40
Bash the Rat: 13 + 20 = £33
So Pony Ride collected the most money.

11) 50p

Esther paid £36 for 100 ice pops.
So the amount she paid for each ice pop = £36 ÷ 100, which is the same as 3600p ÷ 100 = 36p.
Add 14p to find the price she charges for each ice pop. 36p + 14p = 50p

12) 6

Work backwards through Sasha's calculation to find the number she started with.
She adds 3 to a number to get 51, so subtract 3 from 51:
51 − 3 = 48. 48 is the start number multiplied by 8. So divide by 8 to find Sasha's start number: 48 ÷ 8 = 6.

13) 18

Her starting number from question 12 is 6.
6 × 5 = 30. 30 − 12 can be done using partitioning. 12 splits into 10 + 2.
30 − 10 = 20. 20 − 2 = 18.

15) A
Twenty minutes to three means that it is twenty minutes before three o'clock. There are 60 minutes in an hour, so 'twenty minutes to' is the same as 60 − 20 = 40 minutes past the previous hour. So twenty minutes to three is the same as 2:40.

16) 235p
In £1 there are 100 pence. So in £2 there are 100 × 2 = 200 pence. So in £2.35 there will be 200 + 35 = 235 pence.

17) A
Draw an arrow to the elephants from the giraffes. It will be pointing in the same direction as the SW arrow on the compass. So the elephants are south-west of the giraffes.

18) 5
There is 1 square face for the base, and 4 triangular faces. This is 5 faces in total.

19) £38.40
£1.50 more than £36.90 is:
£36.90 + £1.50. Partition £1.50 into £1 + 50p and add each bit separately:
£36.90 + £1 = £37.90.
£37.90 + 50p = £38.40

20) (2, 3)
Read down from point A to the horizontal axis for the first coordinate (2). Then read across from point A to the vertical axis for the second coordinate (3). So A is at (2, 3).

Section B — Pages 53-55

1) A
90 and 72 are both in the 9 times table, so they are both multiples of 9.
(90 = 10 × 9, 72 = 8 × 9)

2) A
485 is exactly halfway between 480 and 490, so 485 rounds up to 490. All the other options round up or down to 480.

3) D
Count on in 4s from 3: 3, 7, 11, 15, 19.

4) £3.89
Four cookies will cost:
4 × 60p = 240p = £2.40
(4 × 6 = 24, so 4 × 60 = 240).
Now add on the price of a glass of juice:
£2.40 + £1.49, split £1.49 into
£1 + £0.40 + £0.09 and add each part in turn:
£2.40 + £1 = £3.40,
£3.40 + £0.40 = £3.80
£3.80 + £0.09 = £3.89.

5) C
The juice is £1.49 and the cookie is 60p, so £1.49 + 60p = £2.09.
To find the change from £5 you need to work out: £5 − £2.09. £2.09 can be partitioned into £2 + 9p.
£5 − £2 = £3.
£3 − 9p = £2.91

6) E
1 litre = 1000 ml. Each ice cube is 10 ml. So the number of ice cubes she can make is 1000 ÷ 10 = 100.

7) 24
$\frac{1}{3}$ of the path is made of 8 stones, so there will be three times as many stones in the whole path. 8 × 3 = 24 stones.

8) D
Find the area of each quadrilateral by either counting the small squares or multiplying length by width:
Quadrilateral A: 3 × 3 = 9 cm².
Quadrilateral B: 4 × 3 = 12 cm².
Quadrilateral C: 5 × 4 = 20 cm².
Quadrilateral D: 2 × 4 = 8 cm².
Quadrilateral D has the smallest area.

9) C
Find the perimeter of each rectangle:
Quadrilateral A: 3 + 3 + 3 + 3 = 12 cm.
Quadrilateral B: 4 + 3 + 4 + 3 = 14 cm.
Quadrilateral C: 5 + 4 + 5 + 4 = 18 cm.
Quadrilateral D: 4 + 2 + 4 + 2 = 12 cm.
Quadrilateral C has the biggest perimeter.

10) C
450 ÷ 45 = 10. So $\frac{1}{10}$ of the bottle is used in the salad.

11) B
$\frac{6}{8}$ of a pack is needed. Divide the numerator and the denominator by 2 to get an equivalent fraction. 6 ÷ 2 = 3 and 8 ÷ 2 = 4, so $\frac{6}{8} = \frac{3}{4}$.

12) A
In cake A, 2 out of 5 slices have been eaten which is $\frac{2}{5}$ as a fraction.
In cake B, 4 out of 5 slices have been eaten which is $\frac{4}{5}$ as a fraction.
So the difference in the amount of each cake eaten is $\frac{4}{5} - \frac{2}{5} = \frac{2}{5}$.

13) A
The court is nine 80 cm strides wide.
So the width is 9 × 80 = 720 cm.
1 m = 100 cm, so 720 cm is 7.2 m.
So the court is 7 m wide to the nearest metre.

14) 24 minutes
The 8:20 am bus from Markham gets to Shipford at 8:28 am. Denise then has to wait till 8:52 am for the bus to Uptown. So she waits from 8:28 am until 8:52 am. The hours are the same so find the difference in the minutes: 52 − 28 = 24 minutes.

15) 16
The lawyers who work 31 or more hours make up the last 3 bars of the bar chart. Add together the heights of these bars:
9 + 5 + 2 = 16 lawyers.

16) 5
Lawyers who work 11-30 hours make up the second and third bars which have heights of 6 + 6 = 12 lawyers. Lawyers who work 41-60 hours make up the last two bars which have heights of 5 + 2 = 7 lawyers. The difference is 12 − 7 = 5 lawyers.

17) C
The number of lawyers who work less than 11 hours is just the first bar which shows 2 lawyers. The number of lawyers who work more than 50 hours is the last bar which shows 2 lawyers.
So the same number of lawyers work less than 11 hours as more than 50 hours.

18) 12
The original cube has 6 faces but two faces are covered by sticking the square based pyramids to them, so 4 faces are showing. The two square based pyramids have 5 faces each but one face of each is stuck to the cube so they both have 4 faces showing. All 3 shapes have 4 faces showing which is 3 × 4 = 12 faces in total.

Assessment Test 4
Section A — Pages 56-58

1) C
Hexagons have 6 sides, so shape C is the only possible answer.

2) 30
The even numbers on the hopscotch grid are 2, 4, 6, 8 and 10. This addition can be done using partitioning. The tens and the units can be added separately.
2 + 4 + 6 + 8 = 20. 20 + 10 = 30.

3) C
Look at the place value of the first number in each of the values given. 0.47 has no units and is the only number to have no values greater than tenths.
So 0.47 is the smallest number.

4) £6.93
Round up 99p to £1 and multiply by 7:
7 × £1 = £7. You added an extra 1p to each price, so in total you added 7 × 1p = 7p extra. Subtract this from your rounded answer to find the correct price:
£7.00 − 7p = £6.93

5) C
C is the only shape that has only one line of symmetry.

6) A
An apple is easy to pick up and feels quite light, so 3 kg and 30 kg are too heavy. A feather weighs around 1 g, so 0.3 g and 3 g are much too light to be the weight of an apple. 0.3 kg is the correct answer.

7) 31 °C
Count up from −5 to 26 to find the difference between them.

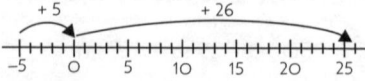

Add 5 to get from −5 to 0.
Add 26 to get from 0 to 26.
5 + 26 = 31 °C

8) 15
Each sweet symbol on the pictogram shows 6 sweets. There are 2 and a half symbols shown for strawberry laces.
Half a symbol = 6 ÷ 2 = 3 sweets.
So the number of strawberry laces sold was 6 + 6 + 3 = 15.

6) 280 cm
A whole cube would need 12 matchsticks. A cube that shares a face would need 12 − 4 = 8 matchsticks, so the total number of matchsticks used is 12 + 8 + 8 = 28. Each matchstick is 10 cm in length. To work out the total length you need to calculate 10 × 28. When multiplying by 10 you need to move the digits one place to the left. 10 × 28 = 280 cm.

7) C
Work out how long the party is:
From 4 pm to 6 pm is 2 hours.
From 6 pm to 6:30 pm is 30 minutes.
So the party lasts for 2 hours 30 minutes.
They have the cake halfway through the party and half of 2 hours 30 minutes is 1 hour 15 minutes.
Count on 1 hour 15 minutes from the start time of 4:00 pm:
4:00 pm + 1 hour = 5:00 pm
5:00 pm + 15 minutes = 5:15 pm.

8) 8
One guest leaves every two minutes with the first one leaving at 6:30. At 6:32 two guests have left, at 6:34 three guests have left, etc. By 6:44, 8 guests will have left — after that is longer than 15 minutes, so 8 is the answer.

9) −7
Find the difference between the numbers in the sequence to work out the rule. The difference between 13 and 9 is 13 − 9 = 4. The difference between 9 and 5 is 9 − 5 = 4, etc.
So the rule of the sequence is subtract 4.

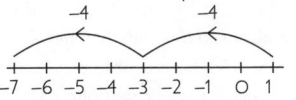

The next number in the sequence is −7.

10) 5
If Azra starts with 20 slices, $\frac{1}{4}$ of the cake is 20 ÷ 4 = 5 slices.
$\frac{1}{2}$ of the cake is 20 ÷ 2 = 10 slices.
In total, Azra has given away 10 + 5 = 15 slices.
He has 20 − 15 = 5 slices left.

11) £25.50
The children's tickets cost £3.50 × 3. You can work this out by partitioning: £3.50 splits into £3 + 50p.
£3 × 3 = £9, 50p × 3 = £1.50.
£9 + £1.50 = £10.50.
The adults' tickets cost £7.50 × 2. You can work this out by partitioning: £7.50 splits into £7 + 50p.
£7 × 2 = £14, 50p × 2 = £1.
£14 + £1 = £15.
So the total cost for the whole family is:
£10.50 + £15 = £25.50.

12) C
Find the price of 3 hotdogs:
£1.25 can be split up into £1 and 25p.
£1 × 3 = £3, 25p × 3 can be split up into 20p × 3 = 60p and 5p × 3 = 15p
£3 + 60p + 15p = £3 + 75p = £3.75
Now subtract £3.75 from £10.00. You can do this by counting up from £3.75 to £10.00:
£3.75 + £0.25 = £4.00.
£4.00 + £6.00 = £10.00
£0.25 + £6.00 = £6.25 change.

13) 8 days
1 litre = 1000 ml, so
2 litres = 2 × 1000 ml = 2000 ml.
The horse has 250 ml a day, so after 2 days it has had: 250 + 250 = 500 ml.
After 3 days: 500 + 250 = 750 ml
After 4 days: 750 + 250 = 1000 ml.
If 1000 ml lasts for 4 days, 2000 ml will last twice as long. So 2000 ml will last 2 × 4 days = 8 days.

14) E
Monday: open for 8 hours
Tuesday: open for $8\frac{1}{2}$ hours
Wednesday: open for 7 hours
Thursday: open for 8 hours
Friday: open for 9 hours
Saturday: open for $7\frac{1}{2}$ hours
Sunday: open for 7 hours.
Friday has the longest opening hours.

15) 8:55
The zoo opens at 7:30 on a Tuesday. You need to work out what time is 1 hour and 25 minutes after this.
1 hour later than 7:30 is 8:30.
25 minutes after 8:30 is 8:55.

16) 5 hours 40 minutes
If Mark leaves 30 minutes before the zoo closes, he leaves at:
17:30 − 30 minutes = 17:00.
Count on between 11:20 and 17:00 to find the difference:
From 11:20 to 12:00 is 40 minutes.
From 12:00 to 17:00 is 5 hours.
40 minutes + 5 hours
= 5 hours 40 minutes

17) 54 m²
To find the area of the vegetable garden, multiply the width by the length:
9 m × 6 m = 54 m².

18) E
18 ÷ 3 = 6, so 3 out of 18 strips is equivalent to $\frac{1}{6}$.

Assessment Test 3
Section A — Pages 51-53

1) B
The shape has 5 sides so it's a pentagon.

2) 3017
There are 3 thousands, so put 3 in the thousands column. There are no hundreds, so put zero in the hundreds column.
17 is one ten and 7 units:

Thousands	Hundreds	Tens	Units
3	0	1	7

3) B
30 children are split into teams of 5. So the number of teams is 30 ÷ 5 = 6.

4) 14
To find the difference, you could count back from 73 to 59.
73 − 3 = 70
70 − 10 = 60
60 − 1 = 59
3 + 10 + 1 = 14

5) 5
Each symbol shows 2 animals, so half a symbol shows 1 animal. There are $2\frac{1}{2}$ symbols for sheep, which shows 2 + 2 + 1 = 5 sheep.

6) 26 m
The perimeter is the total distance around the edge of the shape, so add up the lengths of each side:
5 m + 3 m + 7 m + 7 m + 4 m = 26 m

7) A
There are 3 lines of symmetry:

8) A
The sport that was chosen by the fewest children has the shortest bar.
7 children chose cricket, which is fewer than any other sport.

9) 148
37 × 4 can be worked out by partitioning 37 into 30 + 7 and multiplying each part by 4 separately: 30 × 4 = 120, 7 × 4 = 28. Now add the products together to get the answer: 120 + 28 = 148.

10) D
Katy's number multiplied by 4 is 88. So Katy's number will be 88 ÷ 4, because division is the opposite of multiplication. To do this calculation, partition 88 into 40 + 40 + 8, then divide each part by 4:
40 ÷ 4 = 10, 8 ÷ 4 = 2
So 88 ÷ 4 = 10 + 10 + 2 = 22.

11) A
The hexagon is split into 6 equal sections. 1 section is shaded, which is $\frac{1}{6}$ of the hexagon.

12) B
A right angle is 90° and angle y is smaller than a right angle. The only answer option that is smaller than 90° is 40°.

13) D
The arrow is pointing to the mark $\frac{3}{4}$ of the way from 0 to 1. $\frac{3}{4}$ is equivalent to 0.75. Alternatively, you can work it out by looking at the possible options. The point in the middle, halfway between 0 and 1, is $\frac{1}{2}$ or 0.5. So the arrow is pointing to a number between 0.5 and 1. The only option which has a value between 0.5 and 1 is D, 0.75.

14) 2 °C
To find the temperature that is 3 °C warmer than the temperature shown on the thermometer (which is −1 °C), count up 3 °C. This brings you to 2 °C.

15) 4:30 pm
It takes Siti 45 minutes to cycle into town and 45 minutes to cycle back.
45 + 45 = 90 minutes. This is the same as an hour and a half. You then need to add this to the hour and a half that Siti spent in town. 1½ hours + 1½ hours = 3 hours.
If she set off at 1:30 pm then she arrived back at home 3 hours later. Count on from 1:30 pm by 3 hours to get to 4:30 pm.

16) C
There are 11 sheep in the pen in total.
6 of them are white.
This gives a fraction of 6/11.

17) 12
The fraction of white sheep from question 16 is 6/11. 1/11 of 22 = 22 ÷ 11 = 2.
6/11 of 22 = 2 × 6 = 12.

18) E
Add the fraction of wool dyed red and the fraction dyed blue together.
The denominators are the same, so just add the numerators:
2/9 + 5/9 = 7/9

Assessment Test 2
Section A — Pages 46-48

1) D
The 7 is in the thousands column, so it is worth seven thousand.

Thousands	Hundreds	Tens	Units
7	0	5	2

2) A
There are 4 edges around the top of the cube, 4 edges down the sides of the cube and 4 edges around the bottom of the cube.
4 + 4 + 4 = 12 edges.

3) C
To have an equal number of pens in 8 pencil cases with none left over, the number of pens must be in the 8 times table. 72 is the only option in the 8 times table, so this must be the correct answer.

4) C
C is the only shape with a line of symmetry.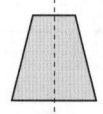

5) B
0.35, 0.98 and 0.65 are the smallest three numbers, because they have 0 units.
0.35 has three tenths, 0.98 has nine tenths and 0.65 has six tenths, so from smallest to largest the order is 0.35, 0.65, 0.98.
1.03 and 1.30 both have 1 unit, but 1.03 is smaller than 1.30 because it has 0 tenths whereas 1.30 has 3 tenths. So the order is 0.35, 0.65, 0.98, 1.03, 1.30.

6) £29
£87 is divided equally between 3 people.
So each person gets £87 ÷ 3.
You can work this out by partitioning 87 into 60 + 27. Then divide each part by 3.
60 ÷ 3 = 20, 27 ÷ 3 = 9.
So 87 ÷ 3 = 20 + 9 = 29.
Each person gets £29.

7) C
Triangle C is a right-angled triangle. Right-angled triangles can be scalene or isosceles, but they're never equilateral.

8) B
In 5 packs there will be 5 × 6 = 30 apples, which isn't enough for 32 children.
In 6 packs there will be 6 × 6 = 36 apples, which is enough for 32 children.

9) 11
The highest bar shows the most popular type of dog — it is 'Beagle'. Read off the value on the vertical axis to find out how many children chose 'Beagle' — 11 children.

10) D
5250 is halfway between 5200 and 5300. 5240 is less than 5250, so 5240 rounds down to 5200.

11) A
The first coordinate (1) is the distance across the horizontal axis.
The second coordinate (4) is the distance up the vertical axis.
Going 1 unit across and 4 units up takes you to point A.

12) E
A week has 7 days, so if she visits her grandma on 12th February, she'll visit again on 12 + 7 = 19th February.

13) 1 °C
Find the bar for Wednesday and read across to the vertical axis, the temperature was 2 °C. Find the bar for Saturday and read across to the vertical axis, the temperature was 3 °C. To find the difference in temperature subtract the lower temperature from the higher temperature:
3 °C − 2 °C = 1 °C.

14) 323
You're told that 60 − 37 = 23, so you just need to subtract the hundreds in 560 − 237 and add 23.
500 − 200 = 300. 300 + 23 = 323

15) D
To divide a number by 100 you move the digits two places to the right.
4500 ÷ 100 = 45 parcels in each lorry.

16) 5
Each wheel symbol shows 4 vehicles.
So each quarter of a wheel shows
4 ÷ 4 = 1 vehicle.
Motorbikes: 2 quarters of a wheel = 2.
Buses: 3 quarters of a wheel = 3.
The total of motorbikes and buses is:
2 + 3 = 5.

17) C
1 kg = 1000 g so
2 kg = 1000 g × 2 = 2000 g
½ kg = half of 1000 g
     = 1000 g ÷ 2 = 500 g
2½ kg = 2000 g + 500 g = 2500 g.

18) 2
Turning from north to south means going through 2 right angles.

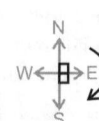

19) E
Turning a shape anti-clockwise through 90° is the same as turning it by a right angle. The diagram below shows the direction of movement.

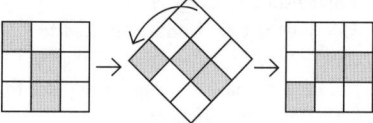

20) B
< means 'is less than'. So the number that goes in the gap must be less than 4652. 4599 is less than 4652 because although they both have the same number of thousands, 4599 has a smaller number of hundreds.

Section B — Pages 48-50

1) E
Vikram's dog weighs 16 kg, which means it comes under the 'up to 30 kg' category.
So the dog should have 4 biscuits a day. There are 7 days in a week, so Vikram's dog should have 4 × 7 = 28 biscuits per week.

2) 25
The squares gain an extra row and an extra column each time. The next square will have 4 + 1 = 5 rows and 4 + 1 = 5 columns of counters. To calculate the number of counters in the next square multiply 5 by 5 (5 rows of 5 counters).
5 × 5 = 25 counters.

3) 55
In question 2, you worked out that Tom needs 25 counters for the 5th square in the pattern. For all 5 squares together, he will need: 1 + 4 + 9 + 16 + 25 counters.
You can work this out using partitioning and adding the tens and units separately.
16 splits into 10 + 6.
25 splits into 20 + 5.
1 + 4 + 9 + 6 + 5 = 25
10 + 20 = 30
25 + 30 = 55 counters.

4) B
6 packets of raisins weigh 6 × 65 g.
You can work this out by partitioning:
65 g splits into 60 g + 5 g.
6 × 60 g = 360 g, 6 × 5 g = 30 g.
360 g + 30 g = 390 g.
Round 390 g to the nearest 100 g:
350 is halfway between 300 and 400. 390 is more than 350, so 390 g rounds up to 400 g.

5) 8
Alex wants to make the following model:

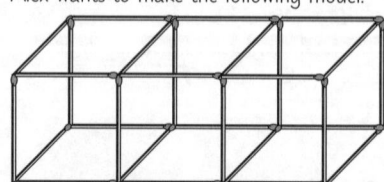

A whole cube has 12 edges, so it would need 12 matchsticks. Alex's new cube shares a face with his model though, so he would need 4 fewer than 12 matchsticks.
He will need 12 − 4 = 8 matchsticks.

5) D

A line of symmetry passes through each of the 5 corners:

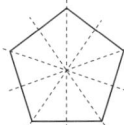

6) B

A 90° angle is a right angle. The only angle bigger than a right angle is B.

7) 6

Divide the total number of treats by the number of treats in each bag to get the number of bags. 48 ÷ 8 = 6 bags.

8) D

XXX is 30, V is 5 and II is 2. Added together it makes 30 + 5 + 2 = 37.

9) D

80 is ten times bigger than 8. So the answer will be 10 times bigger than 56. 56 × 10 = 560.

10) B

You can find the difference between £998 and £1029 by counting up:

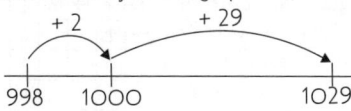

Add £2 to get to £1000, and then add £29 to get to £1029. £2 + £29 = £31

11) B

A regular shape has sides that are all the same length. Only the square has all sides the same length.

12) 328

You can multiply 41 by 8 using partitioning. 41 splits into 40 + 1. Now multiply both parts by 8: 4 × 8 = 32. 40 is 10 times bigger than 4, so the answer will be 10 times bigger. 32 × 10 = 320. 1 × 8 = 8. Add them together: 320 + 8 = 328

13) C

There are 10 gaps between 68 and 69. So each gap represents 1 tenth or 0.1. The arrow points to 5 gaps after 68, which is 68 + 0.5 = 68.5.

14) 36p

10 stamps cost £3.60, so 1 stamp will cost £3.60 ÷ 10. Divide by 10 by moving the digits one place to the right. So £3.60 ÷ 10 = £0.36 = 36p.

15) C

Think of a shape divided into 8 equal parts. 1/8 of this shape is 1 of these parts:

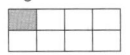

3/8 of this shape is 3 of the 8 parts, so 3/8 is bigger than 1/8.
1/4 of this shape is 2 of the 8 parts, so 1/4 is bigger than 1/8.
3/4 is bigger than 1/4, so 3/4 is bigger than 1/8.
1/2 of this shape is 4 of the 8 parts, so 1/2 is bigger than 1/8.
So 1/8 is the smallest fraction.

16) 100 m

The playground is a rectangle, so it has two sides of 20 m and two sides of 30 m. Adding the lengths of all the sides together gives you the perimeter:
20 m + 20 m + 30 m + 30 m = 100 m

17) 3

He gets £2.40 a week, so after 2 weeks he will have £2.40 + £2.40. Partition one lot of £2.40 into £2 + 40p and then add the parts one at a time: £2.40 + £2 = £4.40, £4.40 + 40p = £4.80.
After 3 weeks he will have:
£4.80 + £2.40. £4.80 + £2 = £6.80, £6.80 + 40p = £7.20, so after 3 weeks he will have saved £7.20.

18) B

Shape B has 5 faces: two triangular faces at the ends, and three rectangular faces in the middle. It also has 9 edges.

19) B

7 + 7 + 7 + 7 = 28. So 28 = ☐ × 2.
28 ÷ 2 = 14

20) 75

Read across from the brown hair and black hair rows on the table to find the number of children with each hair colour. There are 140 children with brown hair and 65 children with black hair. Subtract 65 from 140 by partitioning 65 into 60 + 5.
140 − 60 = 80, 80 − 5 = 75

Section B — Pages 43-45

1) E

Convert the measurements into the same units: 1 m = 100 cm, so 2 m = 2 × 100 cm = 200 cm.
Total length of ribbon cut from the roll = 75 cm × 2 = 150 cm.
Length of ribbon left = 200 − 150 = 50 cm.
There are 100 cm in 1 m, so 50 cm = 50 ÷ 100 = 0.5 m.

2) 150 cm²

In question 1, you calculated that there was 0.5 m of ribbon left on the roll.
1 m = 100 cm, so 0.5 m = 0.5 × 100 = 50 cm.
Area = width × length, so the area of ribbon left on the roll = 50 × 3 = 150 cm².

3) 2

Read the numbers of children off the vertical scale. 9 children go to choir and 7 children go to dance club. 9 − 7 = 2.

4) D

Work backwards from 50. The last thing she does is add 1 to a number to get 50. So subtract 1 from 50 to find this number: 50 − 1 = 49. She multiplied her start number by 7 to get 49. So divide 49 by 7 to find her start number: 49 ÷ 7 = 7. So she started with 7.

5) B

36 is in both the 6 times table and the 9 times table (6 × 6 = 36 and 4 × 9 = 36). So 6 and 9 are both factors of 36.

6) 19

The sequence Jessica follows is to increase the number of sweets by 3 in each layer. Continue the sequence: 1, 4, 7, 10, 13, 16, 19...

7) 10

Continue the sequence, increasing the number of sweets added by 3 each time:
1, 4, 7, 10, 13, 16, 19, 22, 25, 28...
28 is the 10th number.

8) 15

The number of tubes needed is the first multiple of 20 which is greater than 287.
2 × 10 = 20, so 20 × 10 = 200. Ten tubes of sweets will give her 200 sweets. Another 5 tubes of sweets will give her 5 × 20 = 100 more sweets.
10 + 5 = 15 tubes would give her 200 + 100 = 300 sweets. One tube fewer would give her 300 − 20 = 280 sweets which would not be enough, so she needs 15 tubes.

9) D

First work out how much carbohydrate and protein there is in 100 g of bread by reading off the table. There is 12 g of protein and 48 g of carbohydrate which gives 12 + 48 = 60 g in total. To get from 100 g of bread to 150 g you multiply by 1.5, so you need to multiply 60 g by 1.5 to get the answer — this is the same as adding a half. Half of 60 is 60 ÷ 2 = 30, so there is 60 + 30 = 90 g of carbohydrate and protein in 150 g of bread.

10) D

Claire gives half of 80 stickers to Luke — so Luke gets 80 ÷ 2 = 40 stickers. Luke gives one quarter of his 40 stickers to Jenny — so Jenny gets 40 ÷ 4 = 10 stickers.

11) 44 m²

To work out the area of the lawn, first work out the area of the entire garden.
Area of the entire garden = 6 × 10 = 60 m².
Then work out the area of the patio:
4 × 4 = 16 m². The area of the lawn is the area of the entire garden minus the area of the patio: 60 − 16 = 44 m².

12) C

Work out how much the temperature changed by between the different days to find the greatest change in temperature.
Monday to Tuesday: 6 − 3 = 3 °C
Tuesday to Wednesday: 3 − 2 = 1 °C
Wednesday to Thursday: the difference between 2 °C and 0 °C is 2 °C. The difference between 0 °C and −2 °C is 2 °C. Add these together to find the total difference. 2 °C + 2 °C = 4 °C
Thursday to Friday: the difference between −2 °C and 0 °C is 2 °C. The difference between 0 °C and 1 °C is 1 °C. Add these together to find the total difference.
2 °C + 1 °C = 3 °C
The greatest difference is between Wednesday and Thursday.

13) B

Go through each option and see if it is the correct label: 4 is not a multiple of 3.
They are both even numbers.
Neither of them are odd.
Neither of them are multiples of 7.
6 is not a factor of 8.
So the correct label must be "Even numbers".

14) E

The numbers in the central part of the Venn diagram have to be both even and multiples of 5.

11

11) 7:50 am
The time on the clock face is ten past eight, which is 8:10. You need to subtract 20 minutes from 8:10.
20 minutes before 8:10 am can be split up. 10 minutes before 8:10 is 8:00 and 10 minutes before 8:00 is 7:50.

12) 3:05 pm
The time on the clock face is quarter to three, which is 2:45.
You need to add on 20 minutes to 2:45. 20 minutes after 2:45 am can be split up. 15 minutes after 2:45 am is 3:00 and 5 minutes after 3:00 is 3:05.

13) 25 minutes
You can look at any of the bus times to get this answer. E.g. the first bus leaves Whitdale at 10:15 and gets to the hospital at 10:40. The difference between these two times is 40 − 15 = 25 minutes.

14) B
Read across the 'hospital' row for the arrival times at the hospital. The latest bus that Sarah can get arrives at 10:55.
You're asked for the time that this bus leaves Whitdale, which is 10:30.

15) 9:55
It takes Peter 30 minutes to get to Thornby and the bus leaves at 10:25, so you need to find 30 minutes before 10:25. 25 minutes before 10:25 is 10:00 and 5 minutes before 10:00 is 9:55.

16) 3 weeks
There are 31 days in May, and she's on holiday from the 24th day — this means there are 23 days in May that she's not on holiday for. So she is on holiday for 31 − 23 = 8 days in May. She is also on holiday for 13 days in June, so altogether she is away for 8 + 13 = 21 days. There are 7 days in a week, so the number of weeks she's on holiday for is 21 ÷ 7 = 3 weeks.

17) 7:55 pm
1 hour = 60 minutes. So:
70 minutes = 1 hour + 10 minutes.
1 hour later than 6:45 pm is 7:45 pm.
10 minutes later than 7:45 pm is 7:55 pm.

18) 19:55
To convert a pm time into the 24-hour clock you need to add 12 to the hours.
7 + 12 = 19 so 7:55 pm is the same as 19:55.

19) 2:35 pm
It takes Mrs Brown 35 minutes to drive and 5 minutes to park, so you need to subtract these times from 3:15 pm. Subtract 5 minutes from 3:15 pm to get to 3:10 pm. Subtract 35 minutes from 3:10 by first subtracting 10 minutes to get 3:00 and then subtract 25 minutes to get to 2:35 pm.

20) 2 hours and 50 minutes
The concert starts at 3:15 pm and finishes at 6:05 pm. Start with 3:15 pm and add on 45 minutes which takes you to 4:00 pm. Then add on 2 hours which takes you to 6:00 pm. Then add on 5 minutes to take you to 6:05 pm.
45 minutes + 2 hours + 5 minutes is equal to 2 hours and 50 minutes.

21) D
To add on 11 hours, add on 12 hours then subtract 1 hour. 12 hours later than 10:15 am is 10:15 pm (remember, am is morning and pm is evening).
Subtracting 1 hour gives 9:15 pm.

Section Seven — Mixed Problems
Pages 39-40

1) D
Shape D has two pairs of sides which are equal in length and four right angles, so it could be placed in the shaded area of the Venn diagram.

2) £45.00
The total number of hours that Anna worked is $4\frac{1}{2} + 5\frac{1}{2}$ = 10 hours. She was paid £4.50 for each hour of work, so the amount of money she earns in total is:
10 × £4.50 = £45.00.

3) £2.40
There are 1000 ml in 1 litre.
2 × 500 ml = 1000 ml, or 1 litre.
One 500 ml bottle of water costs 40p, so 1 litre of water would cost 2 × 40p = 80p.
So 3 litres of water costs:
80p × 3 = 240p, or £2.40.

4) C
Three out of the five shapes have one line of symmetry. This is written as $\frac{3}{5}$.

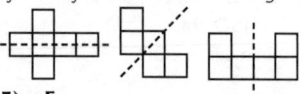

5) E
The amount of time it takes Hilda to wash all eight cars is 8 × 10 = 80 minutes, or 1 hour and 20 minutes. Count 1 hour and 20 minutes on from 4:45 pm. 1 hour on takes you to 5:45 pm and a further 20 minutes on takes you to 6:05 pm.

6) 2000 metres
There are 60 minutes in an hour, so 15 minutes is $\frac{1}{4}$ of an hour (60 ÷ 4 = 15). So the distance Lucy runs in 15 minutes is 8 ÷ 4 = 2 km. There are 1000 m in 1 kilometre so to convert this into metres, multiply by 1000: 2 × 1000 = 2000 m.

7) A
The diagram shows the shape after it has been reflected. Add up the length of every side to find the perimeter of the shape:
4 + 4 + 3 + 5 + 5 + 3 = 24 cm.

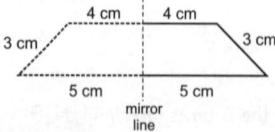

8) 15
2.5 kg = 2500 g. It takes 500 g of flour to make 3 bases, so Jenny would be able to make 2500 ÷ 500 = 5 times the number of pizza bases (5 × 5 = 25,
so 500 × 5 = 2500).
5 × 3 = 15 pizza bases.

9) C
Work out the value of each option:
A: 20 (the number of tenths is 5 or more so you need to round the number up).
B: 40 ÷ 2 = 20.
C: 70 − 40 = 30
    30 − 6 = 24
D: 200 ÷ 10 = 20.
E: The sequence is adding 4 each time, so the next number will be 19 + 4 = 23.
So the biggest number is given by option C.

10) £0.20
Pierre is buying 3 packs for each of his 4 friends, so he is buying 3 × 4 = 12 packs in total. Each pack costs 40p, 12 × 40 can be split up. 10 × 40 = 400p,
2 × 40 = 80p, so
400 + 80 = 480p = £4.80.
He pays with £5.00 so he will get
£5.00 − £4.80 = £0.20 change.

11) $\frac{11}{20}$
The grid shows the path that Paddy has walked on:
4 north, 3 east and
3 south. He walked on
11 of the 20 squares
which is $\frac{11}{20}$ as a fraction.

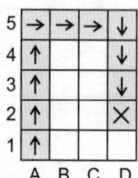

12) 12
First you need to add up her four weekly scores. Add up the units first:
3 + 5 + 9 + 1 = 18
Then add up the tens:
10 + 10 + 10 = 30
18 + 30 = 48
Now divide 48 by 4. 48 ÷ 4 = 12.

13) 12 cm
The number of sides increases by 1 each time. The 3rd shape has 5 sides so the 4th shape will have 6 sides. Each one of the 6 sides will have a length of 2 cm, so the perimeter of the shape will be
6 × 2 = 12 cm.

Assessment Test 1
Section A — Pages 41-43

1) C
You could add up the pounds and then add up the pence: £2 + £1 = £3.
5p + 2p + 2p = 9p.
Then add them together: £3 + 9p = £3.09

2) C
This is the route taken:

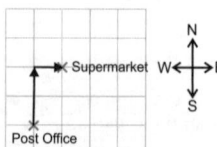

3) E
295 kg is half way between 300 kg and 290 kg, so it rounds up to 300 kg when rounded to the nearest 10.

4) B
The key tells you that each symbol represents 2 plants, so half a symbol represents 1 plant. There are 2½ symbols on the pictogram for beans.
2 + 2 + 1 = 5 bean plants.

6) **2**

A rectangle has two lines of symmetry.

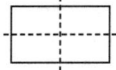

7) **N**

The letter 'N' has no lines of symmetry.

8) **D**

The diagram shows the reflection of the shape. This shape is option D.

9) **C**

Point X is 3 squares above the mirror line. So the reflection of X will be 3 squares below the mirror line. This is shown by C.

Page 33

The thick and dotted lines show the shape's edges — this helps you to see the number of faces the shape has.

1) B
2) A
3) E
4) C
5) D
6) C

The net is made up of 6 square faces so it could only make a cube.

7) E

Shape E has 2 pentagonal faces and 5 rectangular faces.
It is the only option that has 7 faces.

8) D

The net is made up of 4 triangles.
It will fold up to make a triangle-based pyramid — option D is correct.

9) C

The shape in the middle section of the Venn diagram should have 1 or more curved faces and 1 or more triangular faces. A cuboid has neither curved faces nor triangular faces, so it should not be in the Venn diagram.

Page 34

For questions 1-5, you need to count the number of cubes in each shape.

1) A
2) C
3) B
4) E
5) D
6) C

When one of the tiles is flipped, the two tiles in option C can fit together to make shape X.

7) D

Option D shows the shape after it has been reflected.

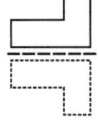

8) B

Shape W has been rotated 180° to give option B.

Page 35

To find the coordinates of each object, read down from the object to find the letter. Then read across from the object to find the number.

1) B3
2) A2
3) E6
4) D1
5) F4
6) E

Read up from the letter B and across from the number 3 to find the square B3.
Carlos has drawn a triangle in this square.

7) E5

The star is in square D4, if you go directly north east of this you get to the square that contains the hexagon.
The coordinates of this square are E5.

8) A

Read down from point B to find the x-coordinate (3) and then across from point B to find the y-coordinate (7).
The coordinates of point B are (3, 7).

9) C

To go from A to B, you need to move A left and up. Count how many squares A needs to move — it moves three left and one up.

Section Six — Units and Measures

Page 36

1) C

The only volumes are 0.3 litres and 5 ml. 5 ml is far too little liquid for a full mug of tea.

2) E

The only lengths are 100 m and 7 cm. 100 m is far too long for a finger.

3) B

This is the only mass measurement.

4) D

The only volumes are 0.3 litres and 5 ml. 0.3 litres is far too much liquid for a teaspoon.

5) A

The only lengths are 100 m and 7 cm. 7 cm is far too short for the length of a football pitch.

6) **275 ml**

There are 4 spaces between the 200 ml mark and the 300 ml mark. So 4 spaces are equal to 300 ml − 200 ml = 100 ml.
1 space = 100 ml ÷ 4 = 25 ml.
The liquid is 1 mark below the 300 ml line. So there is 25 ml less than 300 ml in the bottle: 300 ml − 25 ml = 275 ml.

7) **180 cm**

Mrs Patel bought 30 cm + 1.5 m of chain. Make 1.5 m the same unit as 30 cm:
1 m = 100 cm,
so 1.5 m = 1.5 × 100 = 150 cm
She bought 30 cm + 150 cm = 180 cm of chain in total.

8) **4**

1 litre = 1000 ml,
2 litres = 2 × 1000 ml = 2000 ml
Each bottle is 500 ml, 4 × 500 = 2000, so 4 bottles are needed to fill the jug.

9) A

Total weight of all the bags:
10 × 350 g = 3500 g. 1000 g = 1 kg,
so: 3500 g = 3500 ÷ 1000 = 3.5 kg.

10) C

There is 10 km − $9\frac{3}{4}$ km = $\frac{1}{4}$ km left.
1 km = 1000 m, so:
$\frac{1}{4}$ km = $\frac{1}{4}$ of 1000 m
= 1000 m ÷ 4 = 250 m

Pages 37-38

1) A

There are 60 minutes in an hour, so ten minutes to five o'clock is the same as 4:50.

2) D

Half past seven means half an hour past seven o'clock. Half an hour is 30 minutes, so the digital time is 7:30.

3) B

Quarter to six means 15 minutes before six o'clock. This is the same as 5:45.

4) E

Quarter to seven is the same as 6:45. 6:15 is half an hour (30 minutes) before 6:45.

5) C

Ten minutes to five is the same as 4:50.
Add twenty minutes on:
10 minutes takes you to 5 o'clock.
Another 10 minutes takes you to 5:10.

6) **15 minutes**

There are 60 minutes in 1 hour,
so in a quarter of an hour there are
60 ÷ 4 = 15 minutes.

7) **21 days**

There are 7 days in 1 week.
In 3 weeks there are 7 × 3 = 21 days.

8) **6 months**

There are 12 months in 1 year,
so in half a year there are
12 ÷ 2 = 6 months.

9) **6:00 am**

The time on the clock face is quarter to seven, which is 6:45.
You need to subtract 45 minutes from 6:45.
45 minutes before 6:45 am is 6:00.

10) **2:30 pm**

The time on the clock face is twenty past two, which is 2:20. You need to add on 10 minutes to 2:20. 10 minutes after 2:20 am is 2:30.

11) 36
Each symbol on the pictogram shows 8 matches. There are 3 symbols for 2 goals, so 2 goals were scored in 3 × 8 = 24 matches. There are 1½ symbols for 3 goals. ½ of 8 is 4 and 1 × 8 = 8. So 3 goals were scored in 4 + 8 = 12 matches. To find the total number of matches in which they scored 2 or more goals you add them together: 24 + 12 = 36 matches.

12) D
The graph shows that 4 children play 251-300 minutes of sport each week, so option D is true.

13) 2
7 people voted for salt and vinegar and 5 people voted for ready salted. So 7 − 5 = 2 more people voted for salt and vinegar than ready salted.

14) 6
5 people voted for ready salted, 8 people voted for cheese and onion and 7 people voted for salt and vinegar. The total who voted for these 3 flavours is 5 + 8 + 7 = 20 people. There were 26 people asked in total, so the number who voted for prawn cocktail is 26 − 20 = 6 people.

Section Five — Shape and Space

Page 29
Make sure you know what a 90° angle looks like. 90° is also called a right angle. A 180° angle is twice the size of a 90° angle (so it's the same as two right angles).

1) C

2) D
Angle D is smaller than 90°.

3) B

4) A
Angle A is larger than 90° but not as large as 180°.

5) C
There are 2 right angles in the shape.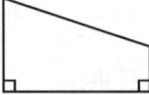

6) 3
The numbers 12 and 3 on a clock are at 90° to each other.

7) 6
The numbers 12 and 9 on a clock are at 90° to each other. The numbers 9 and 6 are also at 90° to each other. Two right angles are the same as 180°, so the hand will be pointing at 6.

8) D
D is the only obtuse angle — it's between 90° and 180°. You can see it's bigger than a right angle (90°) but smaller than the angle on a straight line (180°).

9) 2
Josie turns through 1 right angle as she turns from south to west, and one right angle as she turns from west to north. So she turns through 2 right angles in total.

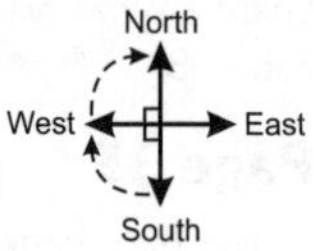

10) 45°
Angle a is smaller than a right angle. 45° is the only option that is smaller than 90°, so this is the size of a.

Page 30

1) B
A pentagon has 5 sides and 5 corners — so it's shape B.

2) D
A circle has no corners — so it's shape D.

3) E
An equilateral triangle has 3 equal sides and 3 equal angles — so it's shape E.

4) A
An isosceles triangle has only 2 equal sides — so it's shape A.

5) C
A square has 4 equal sides and 4 right angles — so it's shape C.

6) B
All the sides of a scalene triangle are different lengths, so that's triangle B. A is an equilateral triangle (all three sides the same length) and C, D and E are isosceles (two sides the same length).

7) B
A quadrilateral has 4 sides. Shape B has 5 sides so it is not a quadrilateral.

8) E
To go in the shaded box, the shape must have at least one right angle and sides that are the same length. A square has 4 right angles and all of its sides are equal in length. So it can be placed in the shaded box.

9) C
A shape is irregular if some of the angles are different. In a regular (equilateral) triangle each angle is 60°. Shape C is a right-angled triangle so contains a 90° angle — shape C is irregular.

Page 31

1) 12 cm
3 + 3 + 3 + 3 = 12 cm

2) B
3 + 2 + 3 + 2 = 10 cm

3) 12 cm²
There are twelve 1 cm² squares inside shape D.

4) 9 cm²
There are nine 1 cm² squares inside shape C.

5) 14 cm
4 + 3 + 4 + 3 = 14 cm

6) 24 cm
Add up the length of the six sides to find the perimeter of the hexagon.
4 + 4 + 4 + 4 + 4 + 4 (or 6 × 4) = 24 cm.

7) 18 cm²
Count the number of squares within the triangle to find its area. There are 15 full squares and 6 half squares. 2 half squares added together make 1 whole square, so the 6 half squares make up 3 full squares in total. So the area of the triangle is 15 + 3 = 18 cm².

8) 32 cm
Add up the length of every side of the shape to find its perimeter.
3 + 5 + 6 + 2 + 9 + 7 = 32 cm.

9) E
Find the area of both rectangles, then add them together. The area of any rectangle is its length times its width.
Rectangle A: 5 × 3 = 15 cm²
Rectangle B: 9 × 2 = 18 cm²
15 cm² + 18 cm² = 33 cm²

10) E
The perimeter of the vegetable patch is found by adding up the four sides. The two longest sides are both 10 m, so the total length of the two shortest sides is 28 − 10 − 10 = 8 m. The two short sides add up to 8 m, so the length of each side is 8 ÷ 2 = 4 m. So the width of the vegetable patch is 4 m.

11) 40 m²
The length is 10 m and the width (from question 10) is 4 m.
So the area is 4 × 10 = 40 m².

Page 32
A line of symmetry is a straight line that divides a shape into two parts that are reflections of each other.

1) B
Shape B has four lines of symmetry.

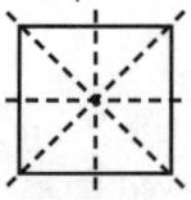

2) D
Shape D has one line of symmetry.

3) E
Shape E has three lines of symmetry.
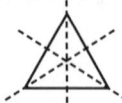

4) A
Shape A has two lines of symmetry.

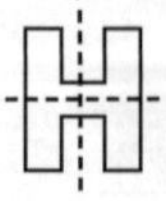

5) C
Shape C has five lines of symmetry.
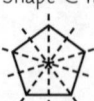

8) B

The number of matches Nicola's dad has seen is a multiple of 6. The only option that's a multiple of 6 is B — 6 × 6 = 36.

9) £9.00

Mr Bracken paid £15 for 10 litres of fuel so the cost of 1 litre is £15 ÷ 10 = £1.50.
He used 6 litres to get to his aunt's house, so the cost of the journey is £1.50 × 6 = £9.

10) A

You could test each of the options until you find one that gives the same answer as Robin's calculation.
Robin's calculation starting with 3:
3 × 8 = 24. 24 ÷ 6 = 4.
Option A: 3 × 4 = 12. 12 ÷ 3 = 4.

11) 500 g

To make pasta carbonara for 4 people you use 400 g of pasta, so the amount of pasta for each person is 400 g ÷ 4 = 100 g.
So, to make pasta carbonara for 5 people you need 5 × 100 g = 500 g.

12) 15 m

9 rabbit costumes is three times as many as 3 rabbit costumes, and 6 squirrel costumes is three times as many as 2 squirrel costumes. So, if Mrs Price can make 3 rabbit costumes and 2 squirrel costumes with 5 m of fabric, she needs
5 m × 3 = 15 m of fabric to make 9 rabbit costumes and 6 squirrel costumes.

13) D

Divide the height of the stack by the height of each pack of butter to find the number of packs of butter in the stack:
12 ÷ 4 = 3 packs of butter. Each pack of butter has a mass of 200 g, so 3 packs would have a mass of 3 × 200 g = 600 g.

14) 6

The cost of 6 hair clips is £1.50 × 6 = £9. This means that Martha has
£10 − £9 = £1 left over, which is not enough to buy another hair clip.

15) 8

2 hair clips would cost 2 × £1.50 − £0.50 = £3.00 − £0.50 = £2.50.
Count up in lots of £2.50 until you reach £10: £2.50, £5, £7.50, £10.
You can buy 4 × 2 = 8 hair clips.

Section Four — Data Handling

Pages 25-26

For questions 1-5 you need to carefully read the data from the table.

1) 3

Look in the 'Number Ordered' column and read across from the 'Shirt' row. 3 shirts have been ordered.

2) £12.99

Look in the 'Price' column and read across from the 'Jumper' row.
The cost of a jumper is £12.99.

3) D

Look in the 'Number Ordered' column. The shorts have a 2 in this column, which means they have been ordered twice.

4) E

Look in the 'Price' column. The blazer is the most expensive item at £19.99.

5) £5

Trousers cost £10.99 and shorts cost £5.99. The difference in price is
£10.99 − £5.99 = £5.

6) 18

Add up the number of children who own 2 or more pets. So that's the number of children for columns 2, 3, 4 and 5.
8 + 3 + 4 + 3 = 18 people.

7) E

The number of shops in Herdnell and Nolanbeck is 112 and the number of parks is 4.

8) 24

Dellville has 136 shops. Nolanbeck has 112 shops. To work out how many more shops Dellville has than Nolanbeck, you need to work out 136 − 112. This can be done through partitioning.
112 splits into 100 + 10 + 2.
136 − 2 = 134
134 − 10 = 124
124 − 100 = 24
The difference in the number of shops between Dellville and Nolanbeck is 24.

9) 31

Add together the number of boys and girls in Year 5 to find the total number of children: 17 + 14 = 31.

10) B

Look at the difference between each pair of values in the table. The temperature fell from 39 °C at 12:30 to 34 °C at 13:00.
39 °C − 34 °C = 5 °C.

11) B

There are 40 children in total and 8 travel to school by car. So the number who did not travel by car is 40 − 8 = 32.

12) 7

Onions cost 20p each and Mrs Chung spent £1.40 on onions in total.
£1.40 ÷ 7 = 20p. So Mrs Chung bought 7 onions.

13) 70p

The total cost of the baked beans was £2.80. This is the same as 280p. She bought 4 tins of baked beans, so you need to calculate 280 ÷ 4. 28 ÷ 4 = 7. 280 is ten times larger than 28, so the answer will be ten times larger:
280p ÷ 4 = 70p.

14) 11

There were 18 cookies sold in total and 7 were sold in the morning. So 18 − 7 = 11 cookies were sold in the afternoon.

15) 7

There were 26 doughnuts sold in total and 10 were sold in the afternoon, so
26 − 10 = 16 doughnuts were sold in the morning. To find the number of brownies sold in the morning, subtract the number of doughnuts and cookies sold in the morning from the total number of items sold in the morning: 30 − 16 − 7 = 7.

16) C

The total number of doughnuts and cookies sold over the day can be read from the table. 26 doughnuts and 18 cookies were sold. In question 15 you worked out 7 brownies were sold in the morning. The total number of brownies sold is 7 + 24 = 31.
So, the number of brownies sold is more than cookies or doughnuts.

Pages 27-28

1) D

The day when the most tomatoes were picked will have the tallest bar — Thursday.

2) E

Find 10 on the vertical axis and read across until you find a bar which is exactly at 10. Mr Potter picked 10 tomatoes on Friday.

3) 11

Look at the top of the bar for Monday and read across to the vertical axis.
Mr Potter picked 11 tomatoes on Monday.

4) 32

Mr Potter picked 22 tomatoes on Thursday and 10 tomatoes on Friday.
22 + 10 = 32 tomatoes.

5) E

Each symbol on the pictogram shows 4 buttons. There are 2½ symbols for red buttons. ½ of 4 is 2, 2 × 4 = 8.
2 + 8 = 10 red buttons in total.

6) C

Each square up the vertical axis is worth 100 ice creams, so if you count up 3 squares on the vertical axis you'll reach 300. Read across from 300 to find the month which is exactly at 300 — March.

7) 9

Each symbol on the pictogram shows 6 birds. There are 3 symbols for ducks, so she saw 3 × 6 = 18 ducks. There are 1½ symbols for turkeys. ½ of 6 is 3,
1 × 6 = 6. So she saw 3 + 6 = 9 turkeys in total. Find the difference by subtracting the number of turkeys from the number of ducks: 18 − 9 = 9. (Or you could work out that there are 1½ more symbols for ducks than turkeys. 1 symbol = 6, ½ a symbol = 6 ÷ 2 = 3. So, she saw 6 + 3 = 9 more ducks than turkeys.)

For questions 8-10 you will need to use the tally chart. One strike is equivalent to one person. A diagonal strike helps to quickly identify units of five.

8) 16

There are three diagonal strikes plus one strike. This shows 3 × 5 + 1 = 15 + 1 = 16 people who said tennis was their favourite sport.

9) 12

3 people said running and 9 people said netball. 9 + 3 = 12.

10) 12

17 people said football was their favourite sport. 5 people said swimming was their favourite sport. 17 − 5 = 12.

9) $4/9$
The denominators of the fractions are the same, so just subtract the numerators:
$8/9 - 4/9 = 4/9$

10) $5/8$
Add the fractions to find the total fraction used. The denominators of the fractions are the same, so just add the numerators:
$1/8 + 4/8 = 5/8$

11) $7/15$
Add the fractions to find the total fraction eaten. The denominators are the same, so just add the numerators:
$1/15 + 4/15 + 2/15 = 7/15$

12) $2/7$
Add the fractions to find the fraction that are red or silver. The denominators are the same, so just add the numerators:
$3/7 + 2/7 = 5/7$
The fraction that are white = $7/7 - 5/7 = 2/7$

Page 20
Make sure you know common fractions as decimals: $1/4 = 0.25$, $1/2 = 0.5$, $3/4 = 0.75$. If the fraction is out of 10, then you need to put the numerator in the tenths column to make the decimal.
For example, $2/10$ is 0.2.
1) 0.5   4. 0.75
2) 0.25 5. 0.8
3) 0.1   6. 1

For questions 7-9, convert the fractions to decimals and find the largest value in each row.

7) A
$1/2 = 0.5$ and $1/4 = 0.25$. The values are 0.8, 0.5, 0.2, 0.75 and 0.25, so 0.8 is largest.

8) B
$6/10 = 0.6$, $3/4 = 0.75$ and $1/2 = 0.5$. The values are 0.6, 0.75, 0.5, 0.4 and 0.5, so 0.75 ($3/4$) is the largest.

9) A
$1/4 = 0.25$, $1/10 = 0.1$ and $2/10 = 0.2$. The values are 0.25, 0.2, 0.1, 0.1 and 0.2, so 0.25 ($1/4$) is the largest.

10) 0.7
$7/10$ means 7 tenths.
Put 7 in the tenths column to make 0.7.

11) $1/2$
Elizabeth got £0.50, which is $1/2$ of £1.00, £0.50 × 2 = £1.00.

12) E
The total amount of pizza eaten by Micah and Rose is $2/4 + 1/4 = 3/4$. This means that there is $1/4$ of the pizza left over. $1/4$ is 0.25 as a decimal.

13) C
$3/10$ means 3 tenths. Put 3 in the tenths column to make 0.3.
Susan ate this amount of the cake.

14) 3
$1/4 = 0.25$. $3/4 = 0.75$.
$1/4 + 1/4 + 1/4 = 3/4$
so there are three quarters in 0.75.

Section Three — Number Problems
Pages 21-22
To find the rule in a sequence, try to find how to get from one number to another. It can help to look at the difference between the numbers, or try to spot a pattern, e.g. the numbers double each time.

1) 19
The rule of the sequence is add 3.

2) 30
The rule of the sequence is add 6.

3) 20
The rule of the sequence is subtract 2.

4) 10.5
The rule of the sequence is add 0.5.

5) 16
The rule of the sequence is double the last number.

6) 8
The sequence is 2, 5, 8...

7) 20
The sequence is 8, 14, 20...

8) 1
The sequence is 0, 0.5, 1...

9) 8
The sequence is 20, 14, 8...

10) 26
The sequence is 36, 31, 26...

11) 20
The rule of the sequence is add 5.
The term before the missing number is 15.
15 + 5 = 20

12) 25
The rule of the sequence is add 4.
The term before the missing number is 21.
21 + 4 = 25

13) 54
The rule of the sequence is add 2.
The term before the missing number is 52.
52 + 2 = 54

14) 39
The rule of the sequence is subtract 3.
The term before the missing number is 42.
42 − 3 = 39

15) 49
The rule of the sequence is subtract 7.
So, add 7 to 42 to find the missing number,
42 + 7 = 49.

16) C
Count on in 6s from 18 until you reach one of the given numbers: 18, 24, 30, 36...

17) 15
In each row there is one more tile than in the previous row, so in the 4th row there will be 4 tiles. In the 5th row there will be 5 tiles. So the total number of tiles on the roof will be 1 + 2 + 3 + 4 + 5 = 15.

18) B
Count back in steps of 3 from 16:
16, 13, 10, 7, 4, 1...

19) C
Count on in steps of 2.5 from 10:
10, 12.5, 15, 17.5...

20) E
Count back in 5s from 7: 7, 2, −3, −8...

21) 21
The 6th number in Jesper's sequence is 5 + 8 = 13, so the 7th number will be 8 + 13 = 21.

22) A
Count on in steps of 5 from 2:
2, 7, 12, 17, 22, 27...

23) 13
Gina plants 3 more seeds in each pot than she planted in the pot before. She plants 7 seeds in the 3rd pot, so she'll plant 7 + 3 = 10 seeds in the 4th pot and 10 + 3 = 13 seeds in the 5th pot.

24) 7
Gina plants 3 more seeds in each pot than she planted in the pot before. From question 23, she planted 13 seeds in the 5th pot. This means she'll plant 13 + 3 = 16 seeds in the 6th pot and 16 + 3 = 19 seeds in the 7th pot.

25) 16 minutes
Count back in 8s from 40 for each of the 4 coats of paint. The second coat will take 40 − 8 = 32 minutes, the third coat will take 32 − 8 = 24 minutes and the fourth coat will take 24 − 8 = 16 minutes.

Pages 23-24
1) £1.00
Subtract the cost of the banana milkshake from the total cost to find the cost of the 2 mugs of hot chocolate:
£2.50 − 50p = £2. The cost of each mug of hot chocolate is £2 ÷ 2 = £1.

2) 1280
Multiply the number of boxes by the number of sweets in each box to find the total number of sweets:
10 × 128 = 1280 fizzy sweets.

3) 44p
The cost of 4 chews is 4 × 8p = 32p.
The cost of 1 chocolate mouse is 12p.
So the total cost is 32p + 12p = 44p.

4) £3.00
Waleed was given £2 change, so the total cost of the 6 tickets is £20 − £2 = £18. Divide the total cost by the number of tickets to find the cost of each ticket:
£18 ÷ 6 = £3.

5) A
Jodie has £20 and she needs to save another £20 (£40 − £20 = £20) to buy the jacket. She saves £4 each week, so the number of weeks that it will take her to save £20 is 20 ÷ 4 = 5 weeks.

6) A
To find the number Callum started with you need to work backwards from 6. He divided his number by 4, so do the opposite and multiply his answer by 4 to find the starting number: 6 × 4 = 24.

7) C
The cost of 2 scarves is 2 × £1.50 = £3.
The cost of 1 bottle of perfume is £7.
So the total cost is £3 + £7 = £10.

10) 2

Work out the first part of the function machine. 7 × 4 = 28. Then think what you need to divide 28 by to give 14. 28 ÷ 2 = 14.

11) C

A: (3 + 5) − (4 × 1) = 8 − 4 = 4
B: (3 × 5) − (4 + 1) = 15 − 5 = 10
C: (3 + 5) + (4 × 1) = 8 + 4 = 12
C is the largest.

12) B

Lizzy puts 3 + 12 individual items in each bag. This is 3 + 12 = 15 items in total. She makes 8 separate party bags. So she uses 15 × 8 items in total.
15 can be split into 10 + 5.
8 × 5 = 40. 8 × 10 = 80.
80 + 40 = 120.

13) A

The calculation you're given shows you how to work out the cost of the pounds column for all the tickets:
2 adult tickets (2 × £5)
1 student ticket (1 × £4)
3 child tickets (3 × £3)
2 senior tickets (2 × £4).
Now for the pence. You need to add on 10 pence for each ticket bought:
2 + 1 + 3 + 2 = 8. 8 × 10p = 80p.

Section Two — Number Knowledge

Page 16

1) C

Start by finding the option with the lowest number of units. Both 0.2 and 0.7 have no units. Compare the digit in the tenths column. 2 is less than 7 so 0.2 is the lower number.

2) C

Start by looking to see if there are any negative numbers in the row. There's only one, −1, so it must be the smallest number.

3) B

The biggest negative number will have the lowest value. It will be the furthest number to the left on a number line.
So −6 is a lower number than −2.

> means 'is greater than' and < means 'is less than'. The correct symbol should be added to show whether the number on the left is greater than or smaller than the number on the right.

4) >   **5)** <

6) B

60 is written as 50 + 10 in Roman numerals, so it's LX. 4 is 5 − 1, which is written as IV in Roman numerals.
So together 64 is LXIV.

7) 5 °C

The lowest temperature is −3 °C on Monday and the highest temperature is 2 °C on Wednesday. The difference between −3 °C and 0 °C is 3 °C, and the difference between 0 °C and 2 °C is 2 °C. So, the total difference is 3 °C + 2 °C = 5 °C.

8) E

19 − 9 = 10, which is an even number.

9) −48

2 less than −26 is −28, and 20 less than −28 is −48.

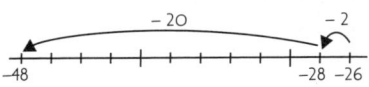

10) 4

4 should not be in the right-hand circle of the Venn diagram. This circle is for numbers that are greater than 5.

11) D

2 is the only even number in the list that is greater than −3. 1, 7 and 5 are all odd numbers, and −6 is less than −3.

12) 25

The odd numbers that are between 0 and 10 are 1, 3, 5, 7 and 9. The sum of these numbers is 1 + 3 + 5 + 7 + 9 = 25.

Page 17

1) 9, 12

The multiples of 3 are just the 3 times table. The third and fourth multiples are missing: 3 × 3 = 9 and 4 × 3 = 12.

2) 21, 28

The multiples of 7 are just the 7 times table. The third and fourth multiples are missing: 3 × 7 = 21 and 4 × 7 = 28.

3) 24

The first three multiples of 4 are 4, 8 and 12. So Rabin's age is 4 + 8 + 12 = 24.

4) E

8 × 6 = 48 and 4 × 12 = 48.
48 is not divisible by 9, so 9 is not a factor.

5) C

3 × 6 = 18 and 2 × 9 = 18.
So 18 is a multiple of both 6 and 9.

6) E

The number of children in each team needs to be a factor of 36 to have equal teams. 8 is not a factor of 36, so you can't have equal teams of 8.

7) E

Some multiples of three are even (e.g. 6, 12, 18, 24 etc.) so Cathy is incorrect. All of the multiples of 4 are even numbers (e.g. 4, 8, 12, 16 etc.) so Dolly is correct. Not all multiples of 2 are also multiples of 4 (e.g. 2, 6, 10, 14 etc. are multiples of 2 but not 4), so Ellie is incorrect.

8) D

3, 5 and 6 are all factors of 30.
(10 × 3 = 30 and 5 × 6 = 30).
7, 4 and 8 are not factors of 30.

9) C

16 is a multiple of 2: 8 × 2 = 16.
20 is a multiple of 2 and 5: 10 × 2 = 20 and 4 × 5 = 20. 25 is a multiple of 5: 5 × 5 = 25.

Page 18

To find what fraction of each shape is shaded, count up the total number of sections — this will be the denominator (bottom number) of the fraction.
Then count the number of shaded sections — this will be the numerator (top number) of the fraction.

1) E   **4)** F
2) C   **5)** A
3) B   **6)** D

7) 4

Lakshmi eats $\frac{1}{4}$ of 16 sweets.
$\frac{1}{4}$ of 16 is the same as 16 ÷ 4 = 4.

8) B

There are 12 squares in total and 5 of the squares are shaded.
As a fraction this is $\frac{5}{12}$.

9) D

The number line has been split into quarters with points at $\frac{1}{4}$, $\frac{2}{4}$ and $\frac{3}{4}$.
Arrow D is pointing at $\frac{3}{4}$.

10) 20p

You need to find $\frac{1}{3}$ of 60p. $\frac{1}{3}$ of 60p is the same as 60 ÷ 3 = 20p.

11) B

The fraction of the circle that is shaded is $\frac{1}{4}$.
The fraction of circle B that is shaded is $\frac{2}{8}$.
These two fractions are equal (see diagrams).

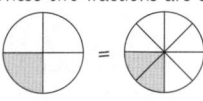

Page 19

1) E

$\frac{2}{6}$ of the circle is shaded. Divide the numerator and denominator by 2.
2 ÷ 2 = 1, 6 ÷ 2 = 3. So $\frac{2}{6} = \frac{1}{3}$.

2) A

$\frac{3}{6}$ of the star is shaded. Divide the numerator and denominator by 3.
3 ÷ 3 = 1, 6 ÷ 3 = 2. So $\frac{3}{6} = \frac{1}{2}$.

3) D

$\frac{6}{8}$ of the rectangle is shaded. Divide the numerator and denominator by 2.
6 ÷ 2 = 3, 8 ÷ 2 = 4. So $\frac{6}{8} = \frac{3}{4}$.

4) C

$\frac{2}{10}$ of the pentagon is shaded. Divide the numerator and denominator by 2.
2 ÷ 2 = 1, 10 ÷ 2 = 5. So $\frac{2}{10} = \frac{1}{5}$.

5) B

20 ÷ 4 = 5, so $\frac{4}{20}$ is equivalent to $\frac{1}{5}$.

6) B

9 ÷ 3 = 3, so $\frac{3}{9}$ is equivalent to $\frac{1}{3}$.

7) C

Divide the numerator and denominator of $\frac{2}{12}$ by 2: 2 ÷ 2 = 1, 12 ÷ 2 = 6.
So $\frac{2}{12} = \frac{1}{6}$. This means $\frac{2}{12}$ can't be equivalent to $\frac{1}{3}$.

8) $\frac{4}{5}$

The denominators of the fractions are the same, so just add the numerators:
$\frac{3}{5} + \frac{1}{5} = \frac{4}{5}$

16) 4
Use the nine times table to work out the missing number. 4 × 9 = 36.
Or you can use division find the answer, 36 ÷ 9 = 4.
17) 168
You need to work out 24 × 7.
24 splits into 20 + 4. 7 × 20 = 140.
7 × 4 = 28. 140 + 28 = 168 stickers.
18) 48
If Carol removes 2 stickers from each page, then she has removed 2 × 24 stickers in total. 24 splits into 20 + 4.
2 × 20 = 40. 2 × 4 = 8. 40 + 8 = 48.
19) 35 m
You can find the length of the roll of ribbon by multiplying the length of each part by the number of parts. 5 m × 7 = 35 m.
20) 270
3 × 9 = 27. 30 is ten times larger than 3, so the answer will be 10 times larger.
27 × 10 = 270.
21) A
6 × 7 = 42 so option A is correct.
22) C
Round up 99p to £1. 3 × £1 = £3.
You added an extra 1p to the cost of each DVD, so in total you added 3 × 1p = 3p extra. So the total cost of the DVDs is £3 − 3p = £2.97.
23) A
3 × 7 = 21. 30 is ten times larger than 3, so the answer will be ten times larger:
21 × 10 = 210.
24) B
33 splits into 30 + 3. 30 × 4 = 120,
3 × 4 = 12. 120 + 12 = 132 people.
25) 48
You need to work out 6 × 8 = 48.
26) 200
The number of Lemon Drops is 40 × 5.
To multiply by 40, first multiply by 4 and then by 10. 5 × 4 = 20.
20 × 10 = 200 Lemon Drops.
27) 340
The number of Chocolate Mice is 5 × 28.
28 can be split into 20 + 8.
20 × 5 = 100. 8 × 5 = 40.
100 + 40 = 140 Chocolate Mice.
From question 26, you know Hannah ordered 200 Lemon Drops.
In total, this is 200 + 140 = 340 sweets.

Pages 13-14
1) 8
8 × 2 = 16, so 16 ÷ 2 = 8.
2) 9
9 × 3 = 27, so 27 ÷ 3 = 9.
3) 7
7 × 6 = 42, so 42 ÷ 6 = 7.
4) 6
6 × 6 = 36, so 36 ÷ 6 = 6.
5) 9
9 × 9 = 81, so 81 ÷ 9 = 9.

You could use partitioning to find the answer to more difficult division problems.
Break up the number you're dividing into more easily divisible parts and divide each of the parts separately.
6) 1
18 ÷ 2 = 9.
19 is 18 + 1, so 19 ÷ 2 = 9 r 1.
7) 4
42 ÷ 6 = 7.
46 = 42 + 4, so 46 ÷ 6 = 7 r 4.
8) 6
63 ÷ 9 = 7.
69 = 63 + 6, so 69 ÷ 7 = 7 r 6.
9) 3
You can split 68 into 50 + 18.
50 ÷ 5 = 10, 18 ÷ 5 = 3 r 3.
10 + 3 r 3 = 13 r 3.
10) 4
You can split 88 into 70 + 18.
70 ÷ 7 = 10, 18 ÷ 7 = 2 r 4.
10 + 2 r 4 = 12 r 4.
11) 23
You can split 69 into 30 + 30 + 9.
30 ÷ 3 = 10, 30 ÷ 3 = 10, 9 ÷ 3 = 3.
10 + 10 + 3 = 23 books.
12) B
You can split 96 into 80 + 16.
80 ÷ 8 = 10, 16 ÷ 8 = 2.
10 + 2 = 12 chocolates.
13) C
8 × 7 = 56 so 56 ÷ 7 = 8.
58 ÷ 7 = 8 r 2 so option C is incorrect.
14) 14
You can split 86 into 60 + 26.
60 ÷ 6 = 10, 26 ÷ 6 = 4 r 2.
10 + 4 r 2 = 14 r 2. There are 14 full boxes.
15) £4
4 × 4 = 16 so £16 ÷ 4 = £4.
16) £15
You can split £75 into £50 + £25.
£50 ÷ 5 = £10, £25 ÷ 5 = £5.
£10 + £5 = £15.
17) £16
You can split £96 into £60 + £36.
£60 ÷ 6 = £10, £36 ÷ 6 = £6.
£10 + £6 = £16.
18) £32
You can split £128 into £100 + £28.
£100 ÷ 4 = £25, £28 ÷ 4 = £7.
£25 + £7 = £32.
19) £19
You can split £57 into £30 + £27.
£30 ÷ 3 = £10, £27 ÷ 3 = £9.
£10 + £9 = £19.
20) D
You can split 60 into 40 + 20.
40 ÷ 4 = 10, 20 ÷ 4 = 5.
10 + 5 = 15. So, 60 ÷ 4 = 15.
21) 7
Find the number in the 9 times table that's nearest to 68, and is also less than 68.
9 × 7 = 63, so 63 ÷ 9 = 7.
68 is 5 more than 63, so 68 ÷ 9 = 7 r 5.
So 7 is the missing number.

22) 12
Find the number in the 7 times table that's nearest to 79, and is also less than 79.
7 × 11 = 77, so 77 ÷ 7 = 11. 79 is 2 more than 77, so 79 ÷ 7 = 11 r 2. Phoebe has enough coins to fill 11 complete pages with 2 coins left over. So she will need 1 more page. 11 + 1 = 12 pages in total.
23) C
June divides 39 brownies into boxes of 9, so you need to work out 39 ÷ 9. Find the number in the 9 times table that's nearest to 39, and is also less than 39. 4 × 9 = 36, so 36 ÷ 4 = 9. 39 is 3 more than 36, so 39 ÷ 4 = 9 r 3. There is a remainder of 3, so June has 3 brownies left over.
24) 20
You need to find 180 ÷ 9.
You can split 180 up into 90 + 90.
9 × 10 = 90, so 90 ÷ 9 = 10.
10 + 10 = 20.
25) 12
Grace makes 9 necklaces. So there are 108 ÷ 9 red beads per necklace.
You can split 108 up into 90 + 18.
9 × 10 = 90, so 90 ÷ 9 = 10 red beads.
9 × 2 = 18, so 18 ÷ 9 = 2 red beads.
So Grace uses 10 + 2 = 12 red beads on each necklace.
26) £6
Grace sells 9 necklaces and makes £54.
So each necklace sold for £54 ÷ 9 = £6.

Page 15
For the questions 1-5 make sure you work out the calculation in the brackets first. Then use this to work out the answer.
1) 22
11 + 17. 11 can be split into 10 + 1.
17 + 1 = 18. 18 + 10 = 28. 28 − 6 = 22
2) 14
44 ÷ 4 = 11
11 + 3 = 14
3) 30
7 × 6 = 42
42 − 12. 12 can be split into 10 + 2.
42 − 2 = 40. 40 − 10 = 30
4) 14
12 ÷ 2 = 6
8 + 6 = 14
5) 9
12 ÷ 4 = 3
3 × 3 = 9
6) 23
9 + 17 = 26
26 − 3 = 23
7) 66
4 + 7 = 11
11 × 6 = 66
8) 13
81 ÷ 9 = 9
9 + 4 = 13
9) 7
Work out the first part of the function machine. 42 ÷ 2 = 21. Then think what you need to subtract from 21 to give 14.
21 − 7 = 14

4

10) 22p
Count back from £1 to 78p to find the difference between them.
£1 − 20p = 80p, 80p − 2p = 78p.
20p + 2p = 22p.
Alternatively, you could count up from 78p to £1 and find the amount you've added on.
78p + 2p = 80p. 80p + 20p = £1.
20p + 2p = 22p.

11) £1.50
Count back from £5 to £3.50 to find the difference between them. £5 − £1 = £4,
£4 − 50p = £3.50. £1 + 50p = £1.50.

12) £2.40
Count back from £5 to £2.60 to find the difference between them. £5 − £2 = £3,
£3 − 40p = £2.60. £2 + 40p = £2.40.

13) £5.70
Count back from £10 to £4.30 to find the difference between them.
£10 − £5 = £5, £5 − 70p = £4.30.
£5 + 70p = £5.70.

14) £2.15
Count back from £10 to £7.85 to find the difference between them.
£10 − £2 = £8, £8 − 10p = £7.90,
£7.90 − 5p = £7.85.
£2 + 10p + 5p = £2.15.

15) 122 litres
You need to work out 167 − 45.
45 splits into 40 + 5.
167 − 5 = 162, 162 − 40 = 122.

16) 116
16 splits into 10 + 6. 132 − 6 = 126,
126 − 10 = 116.

17) 251
136 splits into 100 + 30 + 6.
387 − 6 = 381, 381 − 30 = 351,
351 − 100 = 251.

18) 197 seconds
You need to work out 215 − 18.
18 splits into 10 + 8.
215 − 8 = 207. 207 − 10 = 197 seconds.

19) 16 seconds
To work out how many seconds Peter's time has improved by since his first week of training you need to work out 197 − 181. When the numbers are so close together it is easiest to count up: 181 + 9 = 190,
190 + 7 = 197. 9 + 7 = 16 seconds.

20) D
48 splits into 40 + 8. 71 − 8 = 63,
63 − 40 = 23.

21) C
The tallest sunflower is 213 cm and the shortest sunflower is 163 cm, so you need to work out 213 − 163. One way to do this would be to count back from 213 to 163.

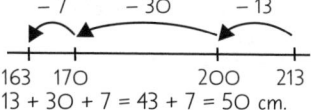

13 + 30 + 7 = 43 + 7 = 50 cm.

22) D
Count back from £10 to £6.65 to find the difference between them.
£10 − £3 = £7, £7 − 30p = £6.70,
£6.70 − 5p = £6.65.
£3 + 30p + 5p = £3.35.

23) 279
38 splits into 30 + 8. 317 − 8 = 309,
309 − 30 = 279.

24) 203
Martin starts with 250 milk bottles.
He delivers 47 at Barrowford so you need to work out 250 − 47. 47 splits into 40 + 7.
250 − 7 = 243. 243 − 40 = 203 bottles.

25) 117
From question 24, after he's been to Barrowford he will have 203 bottles.
After he's been to Canton he will have 203 − 70 = 133 bottles. After he's been to Morristone he will have 133 − 16 bottles.
16 splits into 10 + 6.
133 − 10 = 123, 123 − 6 = 117 bottles.

26) 20
From question 25, he has 117 bottles left after Morristone. You need to work out
117 − 64 − 33. 64 splits into 60 + 4.
117 − 4 = 113. 113 − 60 = 53.
33 splits into 30 + 3. 53 − 3 = 50.
50 − 30 = 20 bottles remaining.

Page 10
When you multiply by 10, move the digits one place to the left. When you multiply by 100, move the digits two places to the left. (Use zeros to fill any places to the left of the decimal point which are left empty.)
When you're dividing by 10 or 100, you move the digits the same number of places, but to the right.

1) 700
Move 70 one place to the left.

2) 620
Move 62 one place to the left.

3) 2800
Move 28 two places to the left.

4) 51
Move 510 one place to the right.

5) 60
Move 6000 two places to the right.

6) 150
The chickens lay 15 eggs in one day, so after 10 days they will have laid 15 × 10 eggs.
Move 15 one place to the left to give 150.

7) 720p
A packet of crisps costs 72p, so the box costs 10 × 72p. Move 72 one place to the left to give 720p.

8) B
Divide the total amount by the cost of each ticket to find out how many tickets were sold, 6210 ÷ 10. Move 6210 one place to the right to give 621.

9) D
The length of each piece is 500 ÷ 10.
Move 500 one place to the right to give 50 cm.

10) D
The missing number has been divided by 10 to give 44, so do the opposite and multiply 44 by 10 to find the missing number. 44 × 10 = 440.

11) 6700
George has 670 chickens so David has 10 × 670 chickens. Move 670 one place to the left to give 6700 chickens.

12) 67
David has 6700 chickens (from question 11). Shaun has 6700 ÷ 100 chickens.
Move 6700 two places to the right to give 67 chickens.

Pages 11-12
Use your 4, 5, 6 and 7 times tables to help you answer questions 1-4.

1) £25
5 × £5 = £25

2) £28
4 × £7 = £28

3) £36
6 × £6 = £36

4) £32
8 × £4 = £32

5) 120
3 × 4 = 12. 30 is ten times larger than 3, so the answer will be ten times larger:
12 × 10 = 120.

6) 450
9 × 5 = 45. 90 is ten times larger than 9, so the answer will be ten times larger:
45 × 10 = 450.

7) 420
6 × 7 = 42. 70 is ten times larger than 7, so the answer will be ten times larger:
42 × 10 = 420.

8) 180
6 × 3 = 18. 60 is ten times larger than 6, so the answer will be ten times larger:
60 × 3 = 180.

9) 400
8 × 5 = 40. 80 is ten times larger than 8, so the answer will be ten times larger:
40 × 10 = 400.

You could use partitioning to find the answer to questions 10-14. Break up one number into units, tens, hundreds, etc. and multiply each of the parts with the other number, one at a time — then add them together.
Or you could use a written method.

10) 90
15 splits into 10 + 5. 10 × 6 = 60,
5 × 6 = 30. 60 + 30 = 90.

11) 81
27 splits into 20 + 7. 20 × 3 = 60,
7 × 3 = 21. 60 + 21 = 81.

12) 215
43 splits into 40 + 3. 40 × 5 = 200,
3 × 5 = 15. 200 + 15 = 215.

13) 144
36 splits into 30 + 6. 30 × 4 = 120,
6 × 4 = 24. 120 + 24 = 144.

14) 225
45 splits into 40 + 5. 40 × 5 = 200,
5 × 5 = 25. 200 + 25 = 225.

15) 48
The number of pencils Ross buys is the number of pencils in each pack multiplied by the number of packs. 6 × 8 = 48.

20) 3300
3250 is halfway between 3200 and 3300. 3264 is more than 3250, so 3264 rounds up to 3300.

21) 78.5 kg
78.45 is halfway between 78.4 and 78.5. 78.49 is more than 78.45, so 78.49 kg rounds up to 78.5 kg.

22) B
5500 is halfway between 5000 and 6000. 5495 is less than 5500, so 5495 rounds down to 5000. The population of Thelston is 6000, so 5495 can't be the answer.

23) E
645 is halfway between 640 and 650. 646.1 is more than 645, so 646.1 rounds up to 650.

24) B
145 is halfway between 140 and 150. 147.5 is more than 145, so Josie's height rounds up to 150 cm. 145.3 is more than 145, so Martina's height also rounds up to 150 cm. This means that Martina and Josie have the same rounded height.

25) 148 cm
147.5 is halfway between 148 and 147. Josie's height of 147.5 is equal to 147.5, so 147.5 cm rounds up to 148 cm.

Pages 6-7

You can add numbers using partitioning — breaking up one number into units, tens, hundreds, etc. and adding each of the parts to the other number, one at a time. It's usually easier to partition the smaller of the two numbers you're adding. You can also use a different written method such as the column method.

1) 42
33 + 9 = 42.

2) 70
23 splits into 20 + 3. 47 + 3 = 50, 50 + 20 = 70.

3) 101
16 splits into 10 + 6. 85 + 6 = 91, 91 + 10 = 101.

4) 113
48 splits into 40 + 8. 65 + 8 = 73, 73 + 40 = 113.

5) 265
54 splits into 50 + 4. 211 + 4 = 215, 215 + 50 = 265.

6) 378
38 splits into 30 + 8. 340 + 8 = 348, 348 + 30 = 378.

7) 704
19 splits into 10 + 9. 685 + 9 = 694, 694 + 10 = 704.

8) 689
182 splits into 100 + 80 + 2. 507 + 2 = 509, 509 + 80 = 589, 589 + 100 = 689.

9) £24.70
A jacket costs £22.50 and a hat costs £2.20, so find £22.50 + £2.20. £2.20 splits into £2.00 + £0.20.
£22.50 + £0.20 = £22.70, £22.70 + £2.00 = £24.70.

10) £22.90
A scarf costs £7.40 and a jumper costs £15.50, so find £7.40 + £15.50. £7.40 splits into £7.00 + £0.40. £15.50 + £0.40 = £15.90, £15.90 + £7.00 = £22.90.

11) £29.90
A scarf costs £7.40 and a jacket costs £22.50, so find £7.40 + £22.50. £7.40 splits into £7.00 + £0.40. £22.50 + £0.40 = £22.90, £22.90 + £7.00 = £29.90.

12) £19.70
A shirt costs £12.30 and a scarf costs £7.40, so find £12.30 + £7.40. £7.40 splits into £7.00 + £0.40. £12.30 + £0.40 = £12.70, £12.70 + £7.00 = £19.70.

13) £27.80
A jumper costs £15.50 and a shirt costs £12.30, so find £15.50 + £12.30. £12.30 splits into £10.00 + £2.00 + £0.30. £15.50 + £0.30 = £15.80, £15.80 + £2.00 = £17.80, £17.80 + £10.00 = £27.80.

14) 407
191 splits into 100 + 90 + 1. 216 + 1 = 217, 217 + 90 = 307, 307 + 100 = 407.

15) 766 g
320 splits into 300 + 20. 446 + 20 = 466, 466 + 300 = 766 g.

16) 665 g
315 splits into 300 + 10 + 5. 350 + 5 = 355, 355 + 10 = 365, 365 + 300 = 665 g.

17) 460 cm
133 splits into 100 + 30 + 3. 327 + 3 = 330, 330 + 30 = 360, 360 + 100 = 460 cm.

18) 377 ml
Round 199 up to 200 by adding 1. Then do the calculation 200 + 178 = 378. To get the answer, you then just have to subtract the 1 you added to 199 at the beginning. 378 − 1 = 377.

19) 39
The total of all of the numbers is: 4 + 5 + 6 + 7 + 8 + 9 = 39.

20) B
336 splits into 300 + 30 + 6. 582 + 6 = 588, 588 + 30 = 618, 618 + 300 = 918.

21) 299 seconds
147 splits into 100 + 40 + 7. 152 + 7 = 159, 159 + 40 = 199, 199 + 100 = 299 seconds.

22) C
33 splits into 30 + 3. 57 + 3 = 60, 60 + 30 = 90.

23) 91
45 splits into 40 + 5. 46 + 5 = 51, 51 + 40 = 91.

24) 135
To work out the number of new tulips: 15 splits into 10 + 5. 29 + 5 = 34 34 + 10 = 44 tulips.
Then add them to the number of tulips worked out in question 23:
44 splits into 40 + 4. 91 + 4 = 95 95 + 40 = 135.

25) £3.71
Fish costs £2.46 and chips cost £1.25, so find £2.46 + £1.25. £1.25 splits into £1.00 + £0.20 + £0.05. £2.46 + £0.05 = £2.51, £2.51 + £0.20 = £2.71, £2.71 + £1.00 = £3.71.

26) 222
25 splits into 20 + 5, 85 splits into 80 + 5, 54 splits into 50 + 4 and 58 splits into 50 + 8.
Add the tens and the units separately: 20 + 80 + 50 + 50 = 200. 5 + 5 + 4 + 8 = 22.
Add the totals to find the answer. 200 + 22 = 222.

Pages 8-9

You could use partitioning to find the answers to these subtractions. Break up the smaller number into units, tens, hundreds, etc. and subtract each of the parts from the other number, one at a time. You can also use a different written method such as the column method.

1) 61
12 splits into 10 + 2. 73 − 2 = 71, 71 − 10 = 61.

2) 35
34 splits into 30 + 4. 69 − 4 = 65, 65 − 30 = 35.

3) 53
47 splits into 40 + 7. 100 − 7 = 93, 93 − 40 = 53.

4) 48
77 splits into 70 + 7. 125 − 7 = 118, 118 − 70 = 48.

5) 126
72 splits into 70 + 2. 198 − 2 = 196, 196 − 70 = 126.

6) 24
225 splits into 200 + 20 + 5. 249 − 5 = 244, 244 − 20 = 224, 224 − 200 = 24.

7) 87
36 splits into 30 + 6. 123 − 6 = 117, 117 − 30 = 87.

8) 121
Count back from 166 to 45 to find the number that's been subtracted.
166 − 66 = 100, 100 − 50 = 50 and 50 − 5 = 45.
66 + 50 + 5 = 116 + 5 = 121.

9) 49
Count back from 71 to 22 to find the number that's been subtracted.
71 − 1 = 70, 70 − 40 = 30 and 30 − 8 = 22. 1 + 40 + 8 = 41 + 8 = 49.

4. Brian made this bar chart to record how much his plant grew each week. How much did the plant grow in total during weeks 4, 5 and 6?

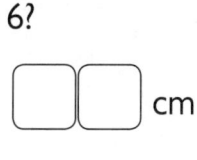 cm

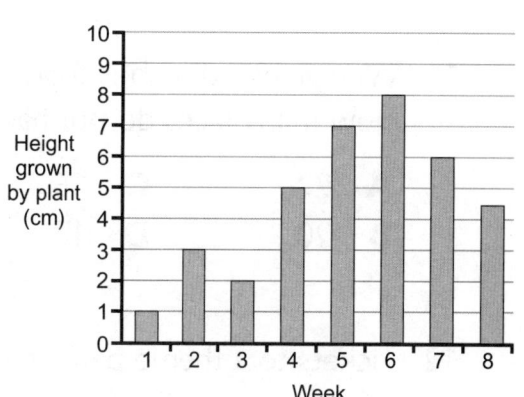

David has two jugs of orange juice, shown on the right.

5. How much orange juice does David have in total?

   A 2.5 litres   C 4.05 litres   E 1.75 litres
   B 3.5 litres   D 4 litres

6. David has some glasses with a capacity of 300 ml each. He pours out 6 full glasses from his jugs of orange juice. How many millilitres of orange juice does he have left in the jugs?

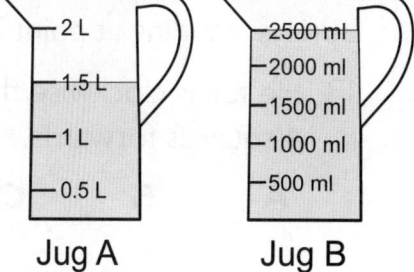 ml

7. A shop keeps ice cream in a freezer at −16 °C. The freezer breaks down at 4 am and the temperature in the freezer rises by 1 °C every hour. At what time will the temperature in the freezer reach −9 °C?

   A 10 am   B 7 am   C 1 pm   D 11 am   E 9 am

8. Hilary and Bill are selling cards at a fete. Hilary sells 13 more cards than Bill. Which pair of numbers could be the number of cards Hilary and Bill sold?

   A 61 and 55   C 44 and 56   E 34 and 48
   B 77 and 91   D 58 and 71

Ken is driving to visit his mother who lives 24 miles away.

9. He stops for a break after driving 8 miles. What fraction of the journey has he done?

   A ½   B ⅕   C ⅓   D ⅔   E ¼

10. Ken listens to the radio for the first ⅛ of the journey and then a CD for the next ⁶⁄₈ of the journey. He does not listen to anything for the rest of the journey. What fraction of the journey was he listening to something for?

    A ⅝   B ⅞   C ¾   D ⁶⁄₈   E ²⁄₄

Carry on to the next question → →

Assessment Test 6

11. Wen glues five cubes together to make this shape.
    How many faces do not have glue on them?

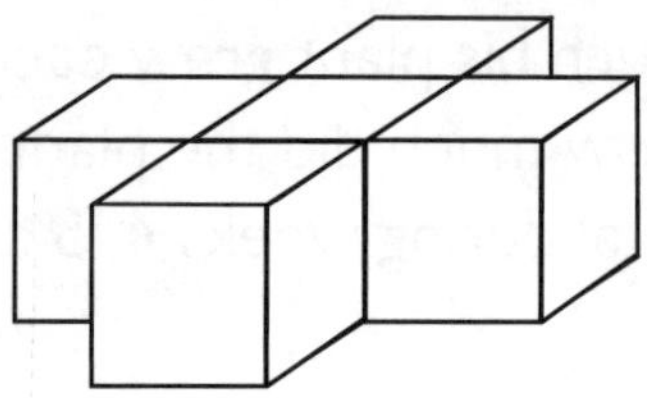

    A 22   **C** 16   **E** 24
    B 20   **D** 17

12. Tickets to a theme park cost £9.50.
    8 friends go to the theme park.
    How much do they spend on their tickets in total?   £ ☐☐.☐☐

Boris is standing at point X facing north.

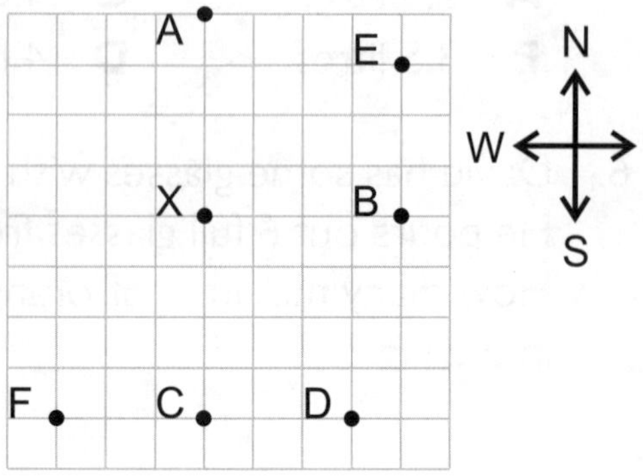

13. He turns clockwise through 180° and walks
    4 squares forwards. At what point is he standing?

    A   **B**   **C**   **D**   **E**   **F**

14. From this point Boris turns 90° anti-clockwise
    and walks 3 squares forwards.
    At what point is he standing?

    A   **B**   **C**   **D**   **E**   **F**

15. Mara bought a block of cheese and two packs of butter. The three
    items weighed 920 g in total. The block of cheese weighed 470 g.
    What is the weight of one pack of butter?   ☐☐☐ g

16. Mr Green started filling in this table to record
    the number of children from Years 4 and 5
    who were going on a school trip.
    How many Year 4 girls went on the trip?   ☐☐

	Year 4	Year 5	Total
Boys	22	9	31
Girls	?		28
Total		26	59

Tony works in a shop. He worked 5 hours on Monday and 7 hours on Tuesday.

17. In total on Monday and Tuesday he earned £60.
    How much was he paid per hour?   £ ☐☐.☐☐

18. At the weekend, he earns £7.50 per hour.
    On Saturday he worked for 6.5 hours and
    on Sunday he worked for 3.5 hours.
    How much did he earn in total over the weekend?   £ ☐☐.☐☐

End of Test

Assessment Test 6

Breckland Portraits

Recollections of a Norfolk Par[ish]

REV. CHARLES HUGH RICHARDSON HARPER

"HUGH the HARP"

Rector of West Harling
1899-1915

Rector of Riddlesworth
with Gasthorpe and Knettishall
1915-1924

Edited by
DAVID O'NEALE

ISBN 1 901470 03 2

First published in 1997 by
TAVERNER PUBLICATIONS
Taverner House, Harling Road, East Harling, Norfolk

Printed by
POSTPRINT
Taverner House, Harling Road, East Harling, Norfolk

About this Edition

The earlier and companion book, 'A Breckland Time Piece' mainly featured the Breckland poems of "Hugh the Harp" coupled with his own accounts which related to the verses.

'Breckland Portraits' dwells almost entirely on the remaining Breckland episodes contained within his unpublished autobiography, 'Birds'-Eye Castle'. A few further poems have been revealed as having Breckland connections and are included here.

Harper's "Portraits" cover a wide range: his own domestic routine; various characters and social groupings (landed gentry, clergy, gamekeepers, labourers, servants, shopkeepers and royalty); the coming of the motor car and cycle to Breckland; the natural environment and distinctive buildings concluding with the effects of the Great War in the Harling area.

Throughout all this, not only is one aware of Harper's gentle good humour, but also his love of humanity. He found inspiration of his own life in many Breckland characters, writing with equal fondness of the Nugent family at West Harling and Charles and Mary Bennett who ended their days in the workhouse. He had a particular affection for Charles and Thirza Brundle; indeed, his complete autobiography opens with words of wisdom from Charles, who died in 1920 aged 95.

"Breckland Portraits" testifies to the memorial inscription of Charles Hugh Richardson Harper and his sister-wives in far away Jerusalem:

"We believe in the eternal goodness".

Acknowledgements

I would like to thank Christine Doughty for her exquisite illustrations and all those at Postprint who have helped compile this book: Peter and Carole Lee, Jeremy Warren, Stephen Ellis, Pam Banks, Roberta Rees and Diane Green.

In addition, I received considerable assistance from many people as they supplied photographs and/or information.

Jimmy Alderton (Rev. Blunt's driver), Eileen Barker, Peter and Miriam Barry, Howard and Joan Bell (once of Stonehouse Farm), Oliver Bone (Ancient House Museum Thetford), Stan Brown, Maggie Burman and Vanessa Shipp (Wilson family of Stonehouse), Peggy Bunkall, Trevor Burlingham, Ivy Burlingham, Tony Cardy, Michael Carnell (Thetford Library), Margaret Cole, Christopher Dalton and The Churches' Conservation Trust (West Harling Church photographs), David Dean (Riddlesworth Hall School), Horace Denniss, Richard and Sue Evans (present owners of Stonehouse Farm), Lord Fisher, Ruth and Les Forder, Laura Fowler (Coote family), Enid Garnham, Maj. Edward Garnier M.C., William Gething, Christine Hewson, Cynthia Hustler, Molly King (Brundle family), Ceri Lamb, Charles Leeder, Harold Lock, Ian Lonsdale, John Martin (Roudham Hall), Sir Fergus Matheson of Matheson, Bt., Emily Mayer, David Napier, Malcolm Nebbett, Pru Nebbett (Davis family), Ena Nicholson (Riches family), Norfolk Record Office, Sir Robin Nugent, Bt., David Osborne, Ann and John Rich, Steve Snelling (E.D.P.), Laurence 'Boko' Steel, Marjorie Steel, Joan Terry, John Watson (Rev. Blunt photographs) Alan Wiggett, and the family of the author's nephew, the Rev. Paul Harper. Thank you all!

David O'Neale

*Outside the Dower House, previously Harper's West Harling Rectory, c. 1930.
L to R. Evelyn Nugent, Robin Nugent, Nannie Maunder, Stella Wright (granddaughter of
George and Margaretta Wilson of Stonehouse Farm), Dinah Nugent, Violet Nugent.*

Foreword

The value of a book such as this is immeasurable in terms of providing continuity of local history. In the course of preparation and research, people's memories are inevitably stirred; memories of names and events long forgotten but jogged by the sight of an unknown photograph extracted from some unexpected box. Allowing for obvious material inequalities, Hugh Harper's Breckland Portraits provide a clear structure of living in a small community from his introduction to the Nugent family, via a delightfully varied mixture of people, places and customs, to the moving account of the life and character of his friend Charles Brundle. Reading these Portraits one cannot help feeling that people then, of all walks of country life, enjoyed a depth of happiness and contentment sadly missing now.

My own jogged memory of West Harling is very limited, as I was only five years old when the Hall was demolished, but I do distinctly remember visiting my great-grandfather in bed shortly before he died, even though I can only have been three. I can still picture him as Harper describes him – a 'formidable' but kindly old gentleman. Of course we used to see Sir Edmund's two daughters, Evelyn and Violet, periodically until after the second world war and I was always amazed at how tirelessly they continued their work for the good of the community. They were known affectionately in the family as the 'Grenadier' Aunts because of their stature, and individually as Aunt M and Am Vo due to some child's inability to pronounce their names. But one indelible memory that I retain of them is their wonderfully liberal and very modern outlook to life around them – all this in spite of a strict and narrow Victorian upbringing.

I feel sure that, round about 1930 when my sister and I stayed at the Dower House for a fortnight or so, we were taken round the estate to meet some of the old families. Names that we can recall between us are Mabel and May Wiggett who looked after the church all by themselves and Reeve the butler and his wife. Reeve had the unenviable task of looking after the Hall in its desolate state prior to its sale and subsequent demolition.

They would all have been delighted to know that someone had taken the trouble to commit to paper this picture of their beloved Breckland during a very eventful period in history.

Sir Robin Nugent, Bt.

ABOUT THE AUTHOR

Charles Hugh Richardson Harper was born on 12 January 1869 at Redlands, Clifton, Bristol; the first of five children, four boys, (three of whom were to become clerics), and one girl. He was educated at Bristol Grammar School (1881-6) and was admitted to St. John's College, Cambridge in 1888. He was awarded his B.A. in 1890 and his M.A. in 1894.

He was, for a time in the 1890s, at Oxford University and curate of Holy Trinity 1892-5. He was ordained in 1893. Following the curateship of Portman Chapel 1895-6, he became association secretary of the Church Pastoral Aid Society from 1897 to 1899.

At the same time as undertaking these duties he was involved in frequent foreign travel, apparently linked to a medical condition. (He was advised by doctors to accept the West Harling position because of its climate, so his health difficulties may have been lung related). He was also advised, much against his nature, not to marry… was an early death prophesied? To make up for the 'quiet life' he travelled extensively: France, Italy, Egypt, South Africa, Ceylon and the Middle East!

In between, or perhaps before and after these journeys, he was rector of West Harling 1899-1915 and Riddlesworth (with Gasthorpe and Knettishall) 1915-1924. During these years he was on the staff of the London Daily Telegraph (re: bee-keeping) and a regular correspondent of two London magazines, one a weekly, the other a quarterly. At this time he also published a small book on a theological subject and wrote various articles on travel and motoring, followed later by 'The Motorist's Ceylon'!

He then resigned from clerical life, not because of his impending marriage but due to his dissatisfaction with the unbending dogmas of the Church: "The Christian Church has made bad mistakes in dogmatizing about the physical world. Should it not also review its dogmas in regard to spiritual matters? Hard-and-fast dogmas are not partners in the humility that is an essential ingredient of true wisdom." How he would have revelled in the debates of **our** time! In many ways he was ahead of his time as his writings clearly show.

In 1924 he 'retired' to the West Country and married Agnes Mary Wood, who died tragically and was buried in Jerusalem in 1928. In 1929 he married her sister, Grace Burton Wood. After further travelling they returned to the West Country before settling in Australia at the start of the second world war. Grace died following a fall in 1944, and Harper in 1947. Their ashes were interred in the grave of Agnes at Mount Zion.

He wrote over a hundred poems on various topics (childhood, Breckland, Australia, WWII, America and Love) as well as an autobiography entitled 'Bird's Eye Castle'.

In his will, in memory of his sister-wives, he endowed the annual Harper-Wood scholarship in English poetry and literature at St. John's College, Cambridge.

A MESSAGE FROM THE AUTHOR

In the second world war when we were far away from England, and my eyesight had failed, my wife felt it would lessen the tedium if I dictated to her an account of my life, unimportant as it was,

In these pages I have tried to call back hundreds of names and incidents, almost all being of no import or interest other than to myself. When we wrote them we were in Australia, without means of checking many matters of fact, which in the mists of time have become obscured for me. The war still rages and I am never likely to be able to correct my errors herein.

But one thing I hope, namely, that I have not spoken unkindly nor unjustly of any one of those it has been my lot to meet along the roads of life. It is my happiness, in the shadows of old age, to recall again so many faces and to hear in memory the voices of my friends, gentle and simple as all alike were to me, generous and patient beyond my power to thank them.

I should like to think that you may care to read some of these pages, for in that way we could become acquainted. My good wishes now reach forward to each one of you.

Charles Hugh Richardson Harper, Australia, 1944

WEST HARLING 1899 – 1915

Harling Road Station.

The Great Eastern rail journey from London to Harling Road station on the main line for Norwich was ninety-eight and a half miles, and took three hours. I was the only parson among the half-dozen passengers getting off the train, and was met on the platform by a tall, florid, heavily-built man in light-coloured tweeds, who introduced himself. Outside was a four-wheeled dog-cart, a light vehicle, my own cart, Sir Edmund explained, and particularly useful to him for "goin' shootin'," as it would carry himself, loader, groom and a friend and their paraphernalia. It was drawn by an old and beautiful silver-grey animal, still powerful and finely shaped. The squire gathered the reins, the man got up behind, and we started along a flat sandy road, with marshy looking meadows on either hand. Plainly there was water near, and soon we crossed a flat bridge, with a ford beside it. This was the river Thet, I learned. On the left a water-mill had once worked, and the old house and garden still remained. Above them on a little height, stood a beautiful flint church, with a spire that was visible far away. "East Harling church," said my mentor. We did not go into the village-town, our road turning to the right passed two comfortable seemly houses standing in ample grounds – "my agent's" Sir Edmund pointed his whip, and again – "East Harling rectory". [Ed. His agent was Caleb Barker, his house now known as 'The Beeches']. A few cottages were passed on the left, and the road descended

East Harling Water Mill.

again to the river-level whose course was marked by alders. Crossing a yard-wide stream, hidden by the road-culvert, the squire brightened, saying impressively, "we are now in West Harling."

The road was a lane, darkened by oak, ash, elm and sycamore, too close grown for size, and showing the poverty of the water-soaked, black-sand soil. In a little, on the right, appeared an old double cottage, and on the left four more, all standing in pretty gardens and facing a green. This, with an old farm house at the further end of the green, was Middle Harling, part of West Harling. We had now driven about two miles. The narrow road turned sharp to the left, still a tunnel of trees; but we pulled up for a moment before a high white gate, that was swiftly opened by a woman in a starched dress who ran from a lodge and curtsied deeply. Before us a gravelled road ran straight and flat through open park lands; as we approached its end a man came running from the stables on the left to open another white gate, and ran at the double across a curve to open a further gate and salute. At once we were before a flight of wide stone steps leading up to the door of a tall red brick Georgian house. On this northern side was a lawn, a dark sheet of water, and, beyond, a vista cut through alders to show, more than two miles away, the spire of East Harling church. A very tall, thin, cadaverous butler with pale face, black hair and melancholy eyes, with a young footman opened the double door, and ushered us into a small rectangular hall. To the left was a room used for family

The Church of St Peter & St Paul, East Harling.

prayers. On the right was the staircase, not very wide and rather steep. The walls were light-coloured painted wood almost hidden by oil paintings of no special interest. Two or three had watch-faces let into church towers and musical boxes at the back. Straight in front was the door into the saloon, a good specimen of the comfort and seemliness of a moderate sized Georgian country house. The permanent feature of this chief room was a number of copies of full-length well-known portraits by Velasquez that, with a good plain period mantelpiece, gave an air of ineffaceable dignity among a crowd of less harmonious subjects, such as oil lamps on brass standards, whatnotty furniture, an American organ, a grand piano with many framed photographs upon it, and feminine gimcracks of Victorian days round about. There was an air of lived-in comfort about this chamber, plenty of flowers and no smell of tobacco. Sir Edmund was a great smoker of pipes and cigars, but only in his own den downstairs, and out of doors. On the mantelpiece, among other objects, were one or two nice little bronzes … a Romulus and Remus under the she-wolf I always coveted. Two pennies, not antiques, lay near it. When, years after, I asked their significance, Violet Nugent laughed – "That's what happens here, things get left about, and no one moves them."

West Harling Hall.

THE NUGENT FAMILY

[as known to Harper]

Sir Edmund Charles Nugent 3rd Bt. = Lady Evelyn Henrietta Gascoigne
12 March 1839 – 4 Dec 1928   6 Nov 1839 – 12 Jan 1922

m. 30 April 1863

Children:

Brig. Gen. George Colborne Nugent M.V.O.
22 Feb 1864
31 May 1915

m. 8 Dec. 1891

Isabel May Gascoigne Bulwer
13 Sept 1867
13 Oct 1941

Rev. Edmund Frederick Nugent
4 Feb 1866
13 May 1950

Lt. Charles Henry Nugent
4 Feb 1866
30 April 1887

Claud Nugent
10 May 1867
2 April 1901

Evelyn Lilla Nugent
13 Oct 1869
2 Nov 1949

Violet Nugent
30 Mar 1871
2 July 1943

Children of George and Isabel:

Sir George Guy Bulwer Nugent 4th Bt.
5 Nov 1892 – 17 Aug 1970

Terence Edmund Gascoigne Nugent GCVO
1st Baron of West Harling (1960)
11 Aug 1895 – 27 April 1973

THE NUGENT FAMILY

*The Nugent family, 1900. Freddie, Violet, Claud, Evelyn.
Lady Evelyn, George, Sir Edmund.*

My host, his wife and two daughters were gathered to inspect the parson who might become their new rector. They were all urbanity, but the squire and his lady were evidently somewhat *formidable* in the French sense. Sir Edmund lost no time by taking me into the adjoining dining room, not for refreshment as I might have supposed, but to gaze upon the portrait by Gainsborough of the first and I think last Lord Nugent. This was a ruddy, portly gentleman with a fine leg, seated, bewigged, and handsomely attired. He was an Irishman who as plain Mr. Nugent had married and buried, three heiresses. A man-about-town, witty and wealthy, he frequented the circles of the Prince Regent, and was given an earldom in the Irish peerage. His son, also painted by Gainsborough, was here shown standing, in the brilliant uniform of the Grenadier Guards. He had sons, Sir Edmund explained by a beautiful lady who was not his wife, and the earldom became extinct. One son was an Admiral of the Fleet and the other received a field-marshal's baton and a baronetcy, hence the present squire. We returned to the saloon and Lady Nugent, a fine portly figure, told me she was a Gascoigne – the precise spelling of which, was impressed on me, unfortunately I have forgotten whether an 'i' or a 'g' or something else was the important difference. The daughters were very tall and thin – the elder, Evelyn, fair and aquiline, and Violet, darker and less so. They were the most devoted daughters possible, and friendly to everyone. These preliminaries being satisfactorily effected, I asked whether I might be shown the church and rectory.

Through glass doors we went into a glazed porch containing canaries and doves in cages. A few panels of old painted glass were here. The squire said they had been taken from the church windows by a former owner of the estate, whose life-size bust was in the chancel. When catechising, I once asked a small boy, Johnny Cross, what graven image we must not worship. "Him, Sir," he answered pointing to the bust. I agreed, since he had stolen our painted glass. Outside this porch a flight of stone steps descended into the garden, similar to those on the north side of the house. A geometrical pattern of flower beds formed this part of the garden. There was a summer house and a tulip tree. Beyond the fence was grassland with trees, ending with a ha-ha. A long vista similar to that on the north was cut through coverts, the ground slightly raising to open distance a mile or two away.

A gravelled path, led to a bridle-way through a wood on the right. Before reaching this, the church was passed on the left surrounded by trees, and partly visible from the nearby Hall. It was small and old, a chancel and nave only, with a good tower; flint rubble was the material with stone dressings, the traceries being village-gothic. There was a good old porch on the south side and a modern lychgate. Near the north door was a chest cut roughly from the trunk of a tree. The interior at that time was seemly, but without some old features of interest discovered a year or two later during a restoration.

"PASSING RICH ON ......?"

I stayed several days, and was pressed to accept the living. The gross tithe-rent was one hundred and eighty pounds per annum, which, based on the computed septennial average price of the chief cereals was worth little over fifty per cent up to 1914. Less than one hundred pounds per annum, therefore, was the income plus the house and glebe. From all these sources there were obligatory deductions of taxes, rates, repairs and insurance. There was also annual interest and sinking fund to be paid on a comparatively large sum borrowed by a former rector, John Harbord, son of Lord Suffield, from Queen Anne's Bounty, to build extra bedrooms for himself and family, which mortgage he left as a charge on the living to be paid off by his successors. This gentleman, Sir Edmund told me, always read other people's sermons, and made no pretence about it. One day Lady Buxton was over from Shadwell and said to him gushingly – "How clever you are, Mr. Harbord, I would love to have a copy of the lovely sermon you preached to us this morning." "Well, I'll tear it out if you want it," he said, "but it's a pity to spoil the book." This was funny, but I never found paying for his bedrooms equally so, nor saw any bountifulness in my share from Queen Anne. Out of my own pocket, later, I redeemed the mortgage, and so freed the living just before I left it. If I would come, the squire promised to pay to my account fifty pounds per annum additional, and they would help me to furnish part of the rectory. We drove with the agent to Thorpe hamlet, which, like Middle Harling, once had a church. Here, now, were only an old farmhouse and three cottages. What I saw on the way were sandy commons, with their gorse, bracken and pines, the slowly flowing little Thet, game coverts and woods. The whole parish was about five miles long, and had a population of only a hundred, simple, rural folk in nineteen cottages, three farmhouses, the rectory and the hall. I stayed for Sunday, took the services, and spoke to many of the parishioners in the churchyard afterwards.

Next day I went back to Portishead to think about it. Father said "If you go to West Harling you'll be like your favourite Vicar of Wakefield – passing rich on forty pounds a year!" He had accustomed us to the care of our small monies when we were boys, and to make our own little investments. I had now something under fifteen hundred pounds capital; not excessive, I thought, for my twenty-ninth year, and I resolved, if possible, not to break into it. To cut one's coat according to one's cloth was a rule with us all. If you limit your desires to your means you always feel wealthy, was another family maxim. These prudences have their own dangers, and I do not think I escaped them as life went on. But from the first I believed that "nest eggs" in every family in the land, would make for social stability, and the comfort of some measure of security from the uncertainties of life. Health was a chief consideration, and the house sheltered by the woods,"out there in the wilderness" – as the Bishop of Durham described it in a letter that I foolishly showed Lady Nugent – exerted a powerful attraction. I should have leisure for reading. The church and the cottage people were delightful. I hoped I should get on with the Nugents – so far in my life I had found the world friendly. I wrote accepting the living.

CHURCH OF ALL SAINTS', WEST HARLING

In June of 1899 I settled down at West Harling, intending to remain there for not more than two or three years. But life took charge of me in its own way, and I lived in two houses within three miles of each other for twenty five years, a third of my present span, and the whole remainder of my life as a parson. For a number of weeks I was the Squire's guest while the rectory was got ready. The Nugents were very kind and hospitable, and I always remember those early days with gratitude. But I was in an atmosphere strange to me. At matins-communion on my first Sunday, the squire and his lady came to the rail first of the congregation, and alone. I waited for other communicants to join them. None came. It dawned on me that this was the custom here, and I should not allow it. I have always been painfully nervous, but I think nothing untoward showed now. I waited quietly until Sir Edmund turned round and beckoned to others to come up.

Church of All Saints', and West Harling Hall.

The change was thus easily made, and was permanent. My hosts never spoke of it, which I appreciated, and I never mentioned it with anyone.

The wall behind the squire's pew was panelled in modern oak with brass plates let in, recording his father, whose wife, daughter of Lord Colborne, brought him the West Harling Estate. Other members of the family were likewise recorded. Armorial bearings were carved above the panelling. The seating throughout the church was of good simple English oak. the squire read the lessons at all services from a handsome brass eagle-lectern. He read them remarkably well, in a robust, manly tone that was pleasant to hear. He left out the final 'g's', said "Git thee behind me Satan," and used other East Anglian dialect expressions. He was a good man, at this time about sixty years of age, with a sense of religious duty that led him to conduct family prayers in his own household morning and evening, at which he read discourses written by himself. He and his family never missed any church service. He always discarded country garments for a top hat and tail-coat in which to come to the House of God. Invariably punctual, he glared at late-comers. He had lost his left eye by a shooting accident, and had a glass-eye in its place. The sound right eye enabled him to be a good game-shot.

The Gothic pulpit of English oak had behind it the ancient upper doorway to the rood-screen, that probably was destroyed by a fire whose scar-traces showed on the chancel arch. The entrance to a flight of stone steps within the wall, complete with door, was at the pulpit foot. A hymn-board on the wall told us it was a present to Lady Nugent from her son George – an inscription more domestic, if less devotional than Ad majoram Dei gloriam [to the greater glory of God]. On the floor of the nave were some small ancient brasses. One of these was a figure, full-length, in pre-Reformation vestments, of a former rector, Ralph Fulloflove. Other old catholic traces were a priest's door into the chancel, the holy water stoup in the porch, the aumbrey, lavabo, and a double pillared-sedilia in the sanctuary. These details were uncovered at the restoration two years after my coming. A Gothic plain oak communion table and rail, in keeping with the pulpit and choir stalls, superseded a heavy mahogany table with gilded pillar and claw feet. We retained this old table in the vestry. At the back of the new altar some ancient carved wood panels of the Nativity were framed as reredos. They were probably

Interior of West Harling Church, looking east, showing Johnny Cross's "graven image" on the right (p. 4).

Interior of West Harling Church, looking west.

Dutch or Spanish and were fine old work. The panel of the circumcision represented that painful operation with such minute exactness that it attracted attention. Our alms-dish was a satisfying large old brass platter, showing the grapes of Eschol carried by the spies, a bunch bigger than themselves. An oak barrel-roof, good for sound was over the chancel, and an oak hammer-roof covered the nave. The main door was rough old oak, with the original iron work and a huge wooden lock.

A peal of eight tubular bells was given by the squire, who also paid for most of the restoration work. Lighting throughout was by wax candles in brass sconces. Against the south wall outside, near the porch, was a long stone coffin, said to have contained one of the de Herlings, who held the manor of East and West Harling by gift from the Norman conqueror. My old clerk-sexton, Bussey, told me its skeleton was of a very tall man, the skull having a noble forehead, and the teeth were all perfect and beautifully white.

Guests

My father's first cousins, Ann Richardson and her sister Mrs. Walpole, were my earliest guests and spent the day with me. They told me of their sister who was the wife of Mr. Cavell, rector of Binham Priory, Norfolk, and hoped I would call on her. Next, Mrs. Howlett and Nellie came down from London for a fortnight. They had found me a housekeeper, a middle-aged Londoner, who said she longed for the country, but when a frog walked in at the back door, she changed her mind. Then father and mother arrived and helped me in many ways. Father and Aunt Carrie each now gave all four of us brothers a small half-yearly allowance. This enabled me to staff with a housekeeper-cook, a maid, and a lad for the garden. Financially it was a tight squeeze, but I could not do with less help. Father said "You should start a home for inebriates here, Poody. You could put them in all these little rooms and they wouldn't be able to get a drink anywhere in miles and miles."

I had only my faithful bicycle as a vehicle to begin with, and on it covered an annual average of six thousand miles for many years.

The Boer War Begins

The end of that year was the end of the nineteenth century. The date was more than a period of time. For the western world its actual limit marked the final close of an era of long established things. From this date nothing in England was ever quite the same again. It drew a sharp line. The past was forever past. How little we realised into what a tragic current human affairs would be drawn. Fate and free-will worked together as ever. It appears to me now that free-will drove us into the stream of fate. If a god, looking on past and future had then shown us the scroll, he would have put his finger on ten thousand converging streamlets, tendencies, causes, incidents, events, and showed them inevitably leading from human choices and decisions to consequences beyond our control.

Britons and Boers had for sometime past been increasingly angry with each other. The root of the trouble was money, as usual. Since gold and diamonds were discovered on the Rand and at Kimberly, a stampede of speculators gathered like vultures to a carcass. Cecil Rhodes, and a few like him, had minds that saw in money the means to great ends. But the outcrop caused inevitable fighting between those most nearly concerned, and set all the dogs of Europe barking. The chorus of hate was amazing. Britain was carried off her feet on a wave of jingoism.

"We don't want to fight, but by Jingo if we do

We've got the men, we've got the ships, we've got the money too!"

Rudyard Kipling wrote, and all Britons sang:–

"Twenty thousand horse and foot goin' to Table Bay,

Pass the hat for our credit's sake

And pay, pay, pay!"

The Duke of Cambridge took credit to himself for the existence of this "magnificent force that, unexampled in history, has been conveyed without loss of a single ship or a single man the length of the globe." George Nugent, the squire's eldest son, a captain in the Grenadier Guards, came home to say goodbye to the family. He was going out with the Brigade of Guards under the command of Lord Methuen. At dinner he told us how he disliked the khaki uniforms now first worn by the whole army. "I should like to see the Guards, in scarlet, advance with fixed bayonets on the Boers. I don't think they would stand against us long." His eyes shone, he twisted up his moustache. He was a gallant, witty fellow. A newspaper correspondent wrote home of one of the early batteries, "Captain Nugent could be seen galloping on his white horse." He was mentioned in dispatches. Jack Hanton the bailiff's son also went to the war, like the troubadour, leaving the lady's maid lamenting. Long before Christmas the eyes of the army and of England were opened – complacency, conceit and ignorance had received many rude shocks.

The Misses Nugent, Evelyn and Violet, with estate families in front of the coachman's cottage, stable yard, West Harling.

COUNTRY CHRISTMAS 1899

The Christmas Festival is the tenderest, most joyous day of the Christian year. It is the beginning of good things, the birth of new hopes for friendliness among men because of the infinite love of God. It is the children's day, and through them it is the parents' day, the day of the home, of old people, of gathering everyone homeless and friendless into the warmth and sympathy of those who are happy. The beauty of the Christmas story in gospel, liturgy and hymn, is the loveliest of life's flowers blooming in the dark wintry world. The Nativity, by all accounts was at a rare moment of world peace.

A war-time Christmas is like a forlorn stranger, holding out a hand in mute appeal. Peace and Goodwill? –

We were celebrating the last Christmas of a century nineteen hundred years later, at war with farmer-burghers whose only wish was to be left to enjoy in peace their own lands. We had our grievances and the Boers had theirs. I believed a just and friendly agreement ought and could have been made. Notwithstanding the cloud of war, I remember with pleasure my first Christmas at West Harling. I initiated a three o'clock afternoon service at which everyone could be present.

Afterwards everyone went to the Hall for the evening. Those were great occasions. The squire's relations filled every available bedroom. His sister, with her husband Sir Francis Boileau, their two sons and a daughter, always came over from Ketteringham near Norwich. They were known in the parish as "The Boilers." Sir Francis was a fine big man with a long beard. Maurice, the elder son, also was bearded. He was a little fou, but able to take his seat on the bench after he succeeded. They were a very delightful, friendly family, and all much attached to each other. Maurice was fond of finding names for his friends' horses, dogs and other animals, all suitable and unique, and he never forgot any of them. He had a remarkable store of knowledge upon many curious subjects, but was a difficult person to shift when he got into your easy chair. His sister Margaret took a medical degree. Several of the Bulwer and Gascoigne cousins likewise came, and two little, old French governesses, daughters of a painter. Every window was lit up, every room warmed by open fires. There was a great Christmas tree and presents for everyone.

Some clever people argued that the new century would not begin where the almanac indicated. However, the date 1 January 1900 was good enough for me. We all gathered in the church at 11.30 p.m. on December 31st, and celebrated the Holy Communion as our first act in the new century.

My Study

My house proved, snug, dry, and comfortable in winter. [Ed. Now the Dower House] The original study was a little room on the ground floor, opening out of the small dining room. It had a built-in bookcase and gun-cupboard. There was a side entrance to the garden. I preferred to have for my study the large bedroom that was above, and the same size as the drawing room. It had a pretty three-light sash window to the south, and a big semi-circular bow window to the west. No other dwelling was visible from my windows, but only grasslands and woods to a mile or two distant. This winter I often sat before the open southern window bathed in sunlight. After alpine snows, I enjoyed seeing grass and trees, with little snow or frost. The dry climate, and well-drained, sandy soil, and the wind-sheltered site did me good. I had the sun on my windows from rise to set every day of the year. The winter sunsets, seen from the study, filled me with joy. The great stag-oaks shone as frosted silver, and tall pines glowed red like burnished copper against their dark green foliage, and the smooth gray limbs of beeches.

Cuckoo

The incident of this poem occurred at my rectory. The pair of wagtails nested in the Seven Sisters rose, Monthly rose, and other creepers under my upstairs study window. I saw the cuckoo lay her egg which was in shape, colour, size and markings almost indistinguishable from the rest. I saw her, before laying her own, strike one of the wagtail eggs with her bill, apparently sucking the contents. She then tossed it out of the nest and laid her own in its place. Then she flew to the fence and chortled, being answered jubilantly by her husband from the oak on the lawn. The fledgling cuckoo soon kicked all his foster companions out of the nest where they died from the fall to the ground. The young cuckoo himself had to leave the nest when quarter grown. He was then so big that the tired little foster parents used to stand on his back in order to reach his bill with the morsels they so indefatigably provided from dawn to dark.

THE AGGRESSOR

Welcome, ye bridal pair , who seek a nest
Beneath my study window. Here find rest
Free from intrusion midst the climbing rose,
Jasmine and woodbine. Here shall ye have those
That will protect you, and show interest,
Respectful guardians of your happiness.
 Now smartly clad in black and silver coat
Your slim legs trip the lawn, and ye do float,
Tails and wings fluttering, in the changing breeze,
So do ye fly and every flight doth please.
Now with swift dart you tease my dog in play,
Nigh touch his head – he snaps – you flit away,
With sweet cadenced falls of tinkling laughter,
Whereat old Bob doth wag his tail thereafter.
 One May morn I, essaying to read a book,
Needs must more often from my lattice look.
The little dame sate neatly on her eggs
Her bright eyes on my face, as one who begs
A minute's respite from her hopeful care,
And would I guard her eggs while she's not there?
Scarce had she left when to the garden oak
A pair of cuckoos flew and neither spoke
But the she-culprit sped as in a race,
Sullied one speckled egg, and laid another in its place.
Then the triumphant male did loudly shout –
Cuckoo cuckoo cuckoo – all round about.
They flew off fancy-free o'er field and wood
Regardless save for pleasures and their food.
When missis wagtail came back to her nest
She found each egg exactly like the rest,
And my unworthy care was not confessed.
 Great poets have sung high praises of the bird
Whose voice when spring begins is gladly heard.
But I will make complaint for my poor friends
Sad, burdened and bereaved, without amends
From whatseover Power conjures the jest,
To wit the encroaching monster in the small bird's nest.

*   *   *   *

 Is here some semblance of the man or state
That by aggression studies to be great?
If I am told it is Dame Nature's plan,
This view I do most resolutely damn –
We're something more than beast, we have to grow up Man.

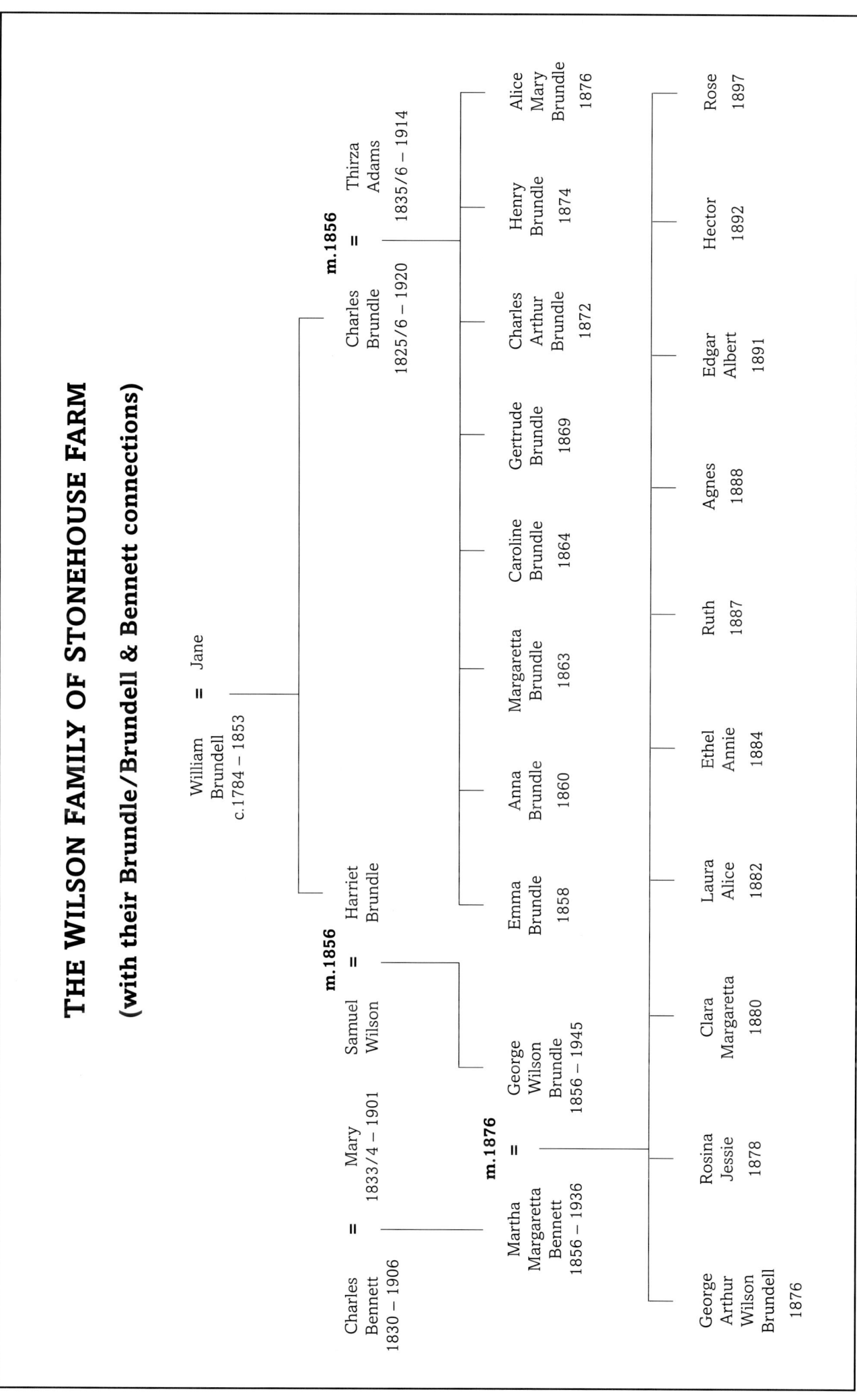

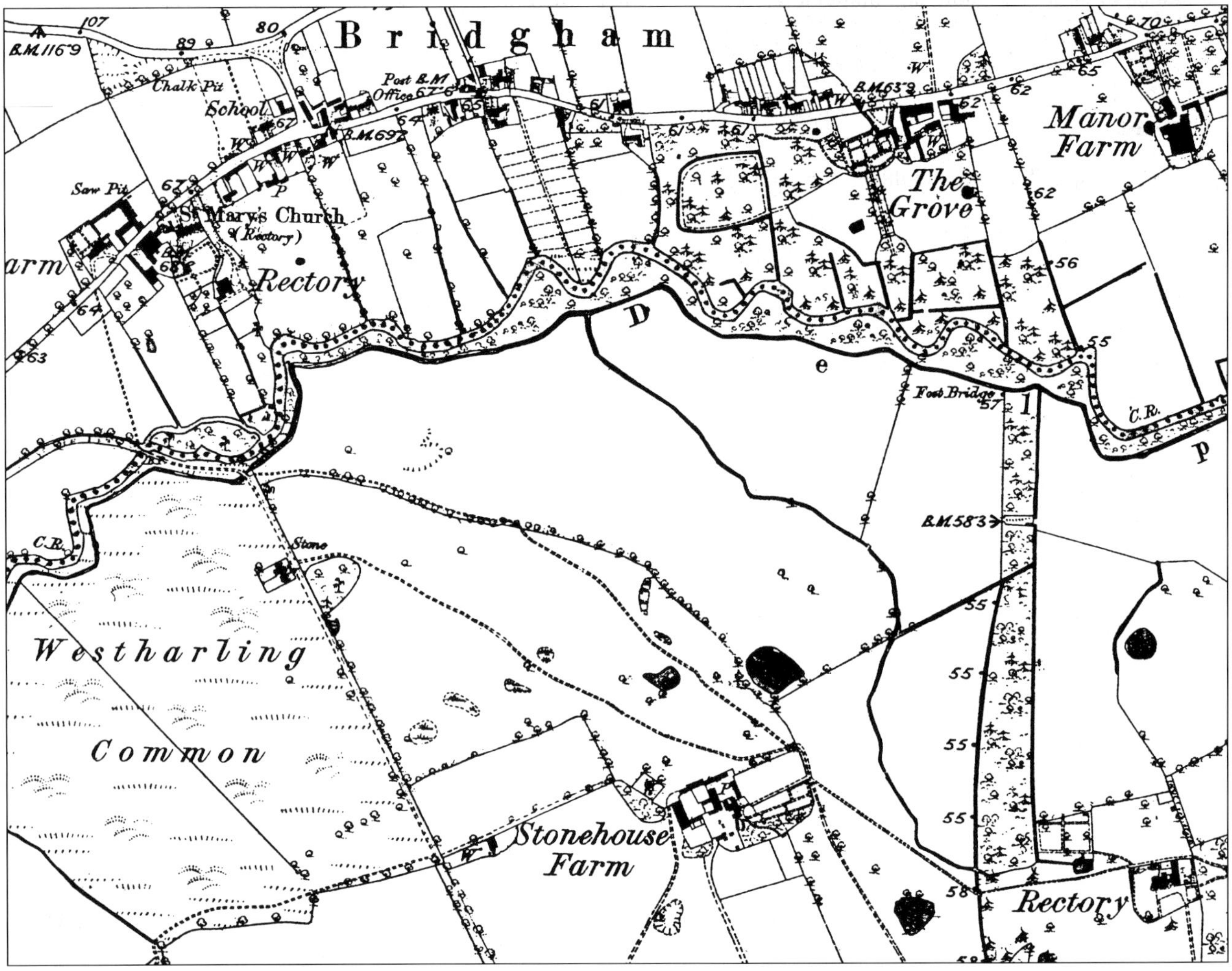

STONEHOUSE FARM

My nearest neighbour to the west was farmer Wilson of Stonehouse, only a couple of fields beyond my glebe. He was a working-farmer, employing no labour beyond his own family; a strong bearded

Stonehouse Farm.

man, and a sound sensible fellow. His son Hector was going to resemble his father, and was already useful. His wife Margaretta looked after the dairy and poultry, aided by a succession of daughters, who in due course entered life as ladies' maids. One of them went to Barbados. Stonehouse must have had history. It was a flint-built dwelling, with high-pitched roof, and a flight of steep, broken steps outside to the first floor front. The house was dilapidated, and incomplete, but had the appearance of greater days. To confirm this the main interior staircase was a truly magnificent example of Tudor oak, the great carved urns at the angles having a stately, solemn effect. I wonder what has become of it. It was silver with age. This small old farmhouse should have been properly restored, but I am afraid for it.

[Editor: Harper had good cause for concern: the farmhouse was demolished in the 1950's when the staircase was reputedly sold to Americans for £200. Margaretta was the daughter of Charles and Mary Bennett, of whom more later].

THREE AVOIDABLE DEATHS

Continuing our walk, we came to Pinner's cottage [Editor: this is still standing and known as 'The Oaks']. Poor fellow, he passed my house a few years later with a hacking cough. He was a healthy young man, but I told him he ought to go back to bed and keep warm. He said, "I couldn't do that, Sir," and went on to his work. In two days he was dead. He and his wife had come from Larling recently; his wife had

The Wilsons of Stonehouse Farm c. 1880. George, Margaretta, Arthur and Jessie.

been maid to the Atkinsons at the rectory, and he the gardener. He was now in the Hall gardens. Two other men died similarly in the next few years through neglecting chills, both in the prime of life, and farm-hands to John Lock of Thorpe hamlet. Fear of the loss of a day's pay was responsible for each of these deaths. I read the high spiritual words of the burial service, but felt much of it was as applicable and intelligible to these crying women as astronomic figures or statements of metaphysics. No-one could be blamed. The Hall surely would not stop the pay of outdoor servants during illness, nor wish them to undergo risks to health. A light-land farm like Thorpe, though let at a very low game-rental, scarcely kept the Lock family in the simplest necessities of life. Farmer Lock could not afford to pay sick men wages. Most of the arable had been fallow for years, bracken, brambles, and ragwort covering the land. The thin pasture maintained only a few heads of stock. The rabbit-warrening paid the rent. So it was, over a considerable area in the parish, that had only been cultivated long ago when corn had been at a high price. The top-soil of plow blew away in strong winds. Sheep, and marl top-dressing were a solution. The neighbouring parish of Riddlesworth shows light-land farming as it could and should be carried on. But farm produce prices were so low that few men dared risk the cost. Practically all of our men belonged to Friendly Societies, that gave sick-pay benefits, so the loss of wage by sickness was not serious if the necessary

Pinner's Cottage, now The Oaks.

doctor's certificate was obtained. The nearest doctor was six miles away, mostly by wood and field tracks, and patients normally had to go and see him. Naturally they felt they might as well go to work. Old Doctor Soffe was much trusted, but could not do impossibilities. His many horses were in constant work, day and night. Rabbit holes, gates and rough ground made walking almost as fast, and much safer, than riding or driving across our Brecklands. The bye-gone generation of farm labourers wore smockfrocks in summer, and over them "duffle" great coats in winter, when they might be had. This thick soft all-wool English cloth had long been out of fashion. Our parishioners formerly received such coats through Dame Dorothy Gawdy's Charity, with cloaks for women. These must have saved many lives.

My Friend Charles Brundle

In the next field from Pinner's was Charles Brundle's cottage. He was a tall slim old man, with white hair, and the ruddy, clear skin of a boy. In my first spring I was digging in the kitchen garden, and Charles came in to see what sort of a job "our Reverend" was making of it. He approved the spade father had lately given me. "That be all steel," he said, "not like they mucky ones wi' only a inch at t' bottom." He showed me how to lay-out the work better, and after some weeks gave his "verdic'" that I was going to be "a master good digger".

Charles and Thirza Brundle.

His gay, old, chuckling laugh, cheerful blue eyes and simple respectful manner, with his store of rural knowledge made him a desirable friend. I frequented his cottage and garden to my great advantage. His little, old wife was as perfect a lady as he was a gentleman. Considerateness, attention, naturalness of manner, with quiet directness of friendly speech, made half-an-hour in their clean homely living-room a restful experience. I don't suppose Charles ever received a pound a week during his whole life on the land. The standard agricultural wage in Norfolk at that time was approximately fourteen shillings. It had been lower. Yet this good couple, like Wilson of Stonehouse, had brought up a family that had gone up in the world, and the old people had always had regular employment, a comfortable home, and security of tenure. How was it done? Charles used to tell me that when he was a little boy he had a shilling a week for "crow-scarin'". From dawn to sunset in seedtime, and before harvest, he walked the cornfields with his rattle, singing out – "Away goo my clappers! I'll knock 'ee down backards – Ahoy – O!" A turnip, a swede, a handful of grain or berries helped to stay his little belly. He said he was sometimes cold and wet, but missis at Bridgham farm was kind to him, and often gave him a hunk of bread and bacon or cheese, or a plateful of rabbit pie. "Ah," he said, smacking his lips, his eyes shining, "she wor a kind woman, she wor and master he wor none so bad neither."

On the great estates in and around Breckland, long-resident labourers had sound, small pretty cottages for the most part, with good gardens. Although wages were low, families could keep a pig and fowls, and it was understood they could have a rabbit when they wanted as they were so plentiful. Hares, and of course other game, were strictly preserved. Wholesome home-brewed ale was commonly and sparingly made and drunk in most cottages. Dried gorse faggots provided fuel for the week's bread-making. "Sticking" was allowed from dead fallen wood plentiful everywhere. The cottage women, from having been in good service, knew and practised all the arts of simple housekeeping, making jams, apple-drink, plain cake. Very little was bought beyond flour, sugar and tea, all cheap then. The farm provided milk and a little butter. A big can of strong soup was fetched each week from the Hall kitchen by all the cottagers.

Charles remembered the stage-coaches, and when the first train from London to Norwich crossed Roudham Heath, he was there to watch it pass by. But he had never gone by train in his life, and had never seen the sea. Before I left for Riddlesworth, Charles' eyesight failed, and he could no longer see to garden. At the same time he suffered a painful affliction known as "bad leg". He could not stand, and young Dr. Cooper, who had bought Dr. Soffe's practice, told him he thought the leg must be amputated. Then strangely, suddenly the leg healed. He could get into his garden again, and his sight too became a little better. He and his wife had a lovely little spell of renewed happiness. When I was leaving, he said "I don't want no one else to bury me but you who've been our shepherd." He was anxious lest I might be too far away. I promised him I would come and bury him from any distance. And so it was.

I think this old couple showed human life of a very perfect kind. Like the Thet flowing under its nearby bridge, their lives together had gone on quiet and unchanging. Nature, often so cruel and unheeding, had been kind to them in relenting. In the infinite variety of man's existence, with its conflicts, ambitions, strivings, excitements and changes, all needful for interest and growth, a tenure like that of Charles Brundle appears futile and empty. But one glance at his face showed it was worthwhile.

THE GAWDY CHARITY

I have mentioned the Gawdy Charity. This family held several manors in the district at a much earlier date, and one of its ladies, Dame Dorothy Gawdy, left parcels of land in several parishes in trust of the rectors and churchwardens, for the poor. West Harling and Riddlesworth both received her benefactions. I administered these during the whole time I lived in Norfolk. Owing to the low value of agricultural land since many years, the sum available annually for West Harling was small. I wrote to the *Guardian* and other papers asking for information regarding schemes for the use of charity monies in other parishes. I had some useful replies, with the result that we evolved a method of contributory self-help that yielded the maximum pecuniary benefit to the parishioners without any loss of their self-respect. In brief, they held cards that showed their monthly subscriptions to a coal and clothing club. Before Christmas each year, they received in cash the total of their year's subscriptions, plus interest added from the Gawdy charity doubling the amount paid in. So each winter from their own prudent savings the members had a nice little sum in hand to buy boots, garments, and fuel or anything else, that came "very acceptable" in the cold season. Our Gawdy land was at Kenninghall, near the Guiltcross Institution. When the old workhouse was sold a good offer was made for our land, that the trustees accepted with the consent of the Charity Commissioners, Whitehall, and invested in Consols, more than doubling our former income. With these added resources we were able to improve our medical services. Hitherto some cottagers got far behind in paying their doctor's bills, and this would result in his not being called in when needed. Now, whenever they brought me his bills receipted as half paid, I paid the balance to the doctor, and gave back the fully receipted bills to the owners. The working of this scheme proved satisfactory to patients and doctor alike. It was of course a small matter in our case, but I think the plan could be carried out for a much larger population if the funds were available. I used to remind our people to hold in their memory the kind intention of the good Dame of long ago for those who would live in after-times on the lands that she undoubtedly had loved.

West Harling Church – Gawdy Family Tree.

It has been the fashion in recent time to decry "Charity" and to substitute "Rights" for the word that the New Testament has placed in highest honour. The ideal I know has been abused, and the duty neglected or mutilated. Nevertheless love is eternally the highest goal in the evolution of man. The beautiful ancient alms-houses to be found in all parts of our land may be out-moded now, but they are an honour to our past, and a lesson and example of the spirit that should animate possessors of wealth whether private or governmental. It is likewise a habit to speak of the great landowners of Britain with abuse. Our social history is a chequered and often painful page – as also in other countries. But the tradition of *noblesse oblige* has, I submit, been better observed in this happy isle than anywhere else. Feudalism and the old conception of monarchy's right divine have passed away, but respect and affection still go out to those who truly care for and serve their less privileged fellow-beings. This reality has been behind the notable clanship of British blood in many crises of our race, unifying the most bitter oppositions of divergent interests.

THE BRIDGE

Just beyond the Brundle cottage was a grass road, one of the old routes across Breckland that dated long before the existing metalled highways. Southward it went straight to a ford over the Great Ouse, here no bigger than the Thet, but marking the boundary between Norfolk and Suffolk. Northward it soon crossed the Thet by what must have been for long a bridge, because the village was named from it Bridgeham. This bridge however was modern. On the West Harling side were two cottages in which lived a woodman, and the second a gardener. These cottages faced a common across which was my shortest way home. In spring it was glorious with clumps of May-blossom and lakes of golden gorse. It was now enclosed, but had once been common-land. I always stole quietly to the bridge parapet, and, looking over, would see a pike headed up-stream lurking in the shade of the arch, or a silver cloud of dace leaping for flies in the ripples over the shallows. For this was evidently a ford before the first bridge was built. A yellow wagtail often bathed here, and the turquoise arrow-streak of a kingfisher would be seen as he darted away straight and swift downstream. On the other side, in late spring, before the weeds were cut, the water was starred by little ivory flowers, with iris, bugloss, meadowsweet, fireweed and foxgloves nearer the bank. The river came round a sharp double bend above the bridge, and a bed of osiers was backed by tall poplars and aspens. In the angle of the bend was a deep pool, and a rustic boathouse at the garden end of Bridgham

New Bridge, Bridgham.

Church of St Mary the Virgin, Bridgham.

rectory. To reach the house I had to cross a water-meadow to the Harling-Bridgham-Thetford road, or in flood go by the lane. Bridgham church was alongside the road by the rectory gate. It was a strange building – ancient flint chancel and nave, heavily buttressed, with some good window traceries, and a lofty porch, were cut short at the west end, that was blocked to the roof-ridge by plain masonry. There must once have been a tower, but now an ugly, square, wooden box like erection, containing a single bell, and known locally as "the Reverend's Game Larder," topped the roof angle.

BRIDGHAM RECTORY

A dark avenue of limes almost concealed the pillared porch of the square Georgian rectory house. It was a solid, old building, with the good shaped rooms of its period, but too surrounded by trees and bushes, and only a few feet above flood water from the river that was but fifty yards away. There was no lawn or flower garden to speak of, but the kitchen garden sheltered by the church and the limes, and protected on three sides by brick walls, and gently sloping to the south, was a little paradise for vegetables. Amos Cutter, the lean,

Bridgham Rectory.

phlegmatic handyman, who for so many years had tilled it, produced such peas and other succulent green things as my soil could not rival. I could only beat him with my asparagus that likes sand. His strawberries and wall fruit were perfection. The little orchard was full of choice apples. The riverside meadow, entered from the drive, had coach-house, stabling, fowl houses and pig-sty on the higher end. The fat, rectory pony, a billy-goat on a chain, some nannies and kids enjoyed the rich grass. A stack of good hay was near the stabling. A row of beehives was on the south side of the wall near the rector's pathway to the chancel door.

HENRY WILFRID BLUNT

My nearest clerical neighbour and first caller was the rector of Bridgham. Henry Wilfrid Blunt was short and heavily built, clean shaven with bushy eyebrows, ironic eyes, granitic features, abrupt in speech. He wore a white, lawn tie, ill-cut gray tweeds, and ungainly boots. I had been warned by Sir Edmund – "He's a very dry feller." But I liked him from the first, and although we sometimes sparred we never lost touch in thirty years until his death. He was about twenty five years my senior, and his former red hair that must have been fearsome was now gray. He had an iron constitution and died in harness at Bridgham. He came of a clerical family, his grandfather being rector of Chelsea, and his father of St. Andrew's Holborn. Others of his family later became bishops. Wilfrid had held a London living, but rather soon exchanged with the incumbent of this country benefice who wanted town. The village straggled untidily for about half a mile from the poor, maimed church, on the road towards East Harling. Yet in this aloof, unmarked place he remained for nearly fifty years, apparently undesirous of any change. We soon got into the way of having supper with one another on Sunday nights.

Rev. Blunt fishing.

It was less than a couple of miles between the two rectories, and still less if he ferried himself across his fishing pool, or I hailed him from the bank for a passage.

FISHING THE THET

The Old Bridge at Bridgham.

We almost always fished together. There were no trout in slow moving Thet, but many pike and smaller jack, bream for which we groundbaited, perch, roach, dace, eels and occasional chub. When gudgeon were troublesome stealing our baits we put on a small hook and quickly caught platefuls of these delicacies for tea. Before the weeds grew we used the flat-bottomed boat to take moorhens' eggs from the nests among the reeds, with a kitchen-spoon lashed to a bamboo for those we could not get near. If they floated when tested in the river we returned them to the nests. Fresh, they are almost as good as plovers' eggs. The other riparian owners had no interest in fresh-water, course fishing, and we had five or six miles of river with many small pools to our two selves the year round. The charm was not in the quantity of the fishing, but in the complete seclusion of the little river, the bird life, the wild plants and flowers. I had my early copy of Izaak Walton's *Compleat Angler* and other old fishing books of my boyhood. This was the very scene in which to read them again. On summer evenings I would go down through my lower glebe-field to the river bank, and spend an hour with pipe, rod and book. On a winter afternoon, if a strong warm sou'west wind blew upstream, lashing against the slow current and stirring up the silt, Wilfrid and I would walk the banks trolling for pike, he using the old-fashioned live bait in the pools, and I spinning an 'indestructible phantom' everywhere that looked likely. It was a deadly bait, new to these waters.

MORE OF WILFRID

Then we would come to an open fire for tea and talk. He had read some history, travelled on the continent, perused the new *Daily Mail* that he admired, and the *Westminster* or *Pall Mall Gazettes*. He was a Cambridge man but never returned. He liked books with an historic background, and memoirs, but read little. He was singularly characterised by what in time appeared to be an obsession that was, I believe, cultivated and enjoyed by himself. He had the invariable habit of looking for, seeing, and pointing out the flaws in people – not with acerbity or bitterness or savagery, but with a caustic, acrid and sly humour. He loved to prick the bubbles of conceit, of pomposity, of shams. I did not know him young but now, past middle age, his apparently convinced view of human beings was not the duality of mixed good and evil in them, but an almost complete unbelief in any virtue in man or woman. It was not a religious point of view nor a Rabelaisian, nor of any urgency, but just in the nature of things – all men are liars, often very funny ones. In his methodical matter of fact way he looked after his parish, and his duties as a guardian. He

Rev. Blunt in his study.

understood country life thoroughly, and knew everyone high and low for miles around. He was, and he was not, a welcome guest in many houses; everyone liked to hear his racy gossip about their friends and neighbours, but each had an uneasy suspicion, fully justified, that in other houses they were themselves the objects of his shafts. By the time I knew him, he had long held a local reputation for almost brutal candour and devastating cynicism. No one and nothing around him escaped the corrosive acid of his criticism. When we first shook hands he said, "I am blunt by name and blunt by nature." He liked to be spoken of by ladies as, "that dreadful Mr. Blunt." He got on famously with some of them, especially the pretty ones. But he was the complete, old bachelor. He told me some scathing stories of feminine attacks on his fortress in his earlier days at Bridgham. The living was a fairly good one, in the gift of the Lord Chancellor. Wilfrid also sold the considerable produce of his land to a circle of relatives and friends in London.

His sisters told me they had never dared to suggest a single domestic alteration to their masterful brother. One of them was married to the Mr. Sheepshanks who had a beautiful place near Bolton Abbey, in Wharfedale, with a grouse moor. He was the head of the family of which the then Bishop of Norwich was a member. They used to walk over and have tea with me, and gave me an open invitation to stay with them in Yorkshire. Blanche the elder and unmarried sister sometimes gave a lantern-travel-lecture at Bridgham, and it was amusing when Wilfrid interrupted it with flat contradictions – "That is not so, Blanche," followed by her equally determined retorts – "Yes, it is so, Wilfrid." The parishioners were quite used to the battles of these elderly children, and stolidly watched their betters behaving badly. I fear that I have not shown the best side of Wilfrid Blunt. He was a naughty, a *very* naughty old man, this wilful Wilfrid. All the same he and I foregathered of necessity, and also of choice for a great many years, and he wrote me long letters to the end of his life. His hail, "Well, fisherman!" was his usual greeting to me, and I know he missed my company dreadfully when I could no longer see him often, and this I too felt. I hope Styx has given him sport like that day we each in the same minute landed a fine tench from Great Ouse.

Bridgham School – 1920.
Back row, L to R: Edith Cole, Pearl Forman, Elsie Baker, Doris Kenny, Ivy Smith, Lily Large, Evelyn Stammers.
Middle row : John Reeve, Agnes Baker, Olive Ward, Sally Alderton, Ethel Smith, Doris Ward, Mabel Stammers, Cyril Peeks, Fred Trumpess.
Front row: Jack Smith, Billy Baker, Ray Newson, Bob Copeman, William 'Peter' Reeve, Jimmy Alderton, Tom Garnham, Stanley Kenny.

Rev. Blunt with Bridgham Church Choir.
Back row, L to R: Myrtle Betts, Edna Ward, Mabel Burton, Hattie Cutter, Marjorie Chapman Florrie Crook, Audrey Waller.
Front row, L to R: John Alderton, Agnes Baker, Doris Ward, Rev. Blunt, Nancy Porter, Ivy Ward, Sidney Burlingham.

"From Eastern Daily Press." Government Office Letter Bag.

To the Editor.
Dear Sir,—The enclosed quotations come from letters received in a Government office from wives asking for separation allowances. They are genuine (not faked), and I do not think have appeared in print.
Yours H. W. Blunt.

"I have not received no pay since my husband has gone nowhere."

"We have received yours truly, I am his grandfather and his grandmother. He was born and brought up in this house in answer to yours truly."

"You have changed my little girl into a little boy. Will it make any difference?"

"My Bill has been put in charge of a spittoon. Will I get more pay?"

"I have not received no pay since my husband was confined in a constipation camp in Germany."

"I am glad to tell you that my husband has not been repotted dead."

"I am paying attention to a nice young man. How do I go about my money?"

"If I don't get my husband's money soon, I shall be compelled to go on the streets, and lead an immortal life."

"I should be glad if you would tell me that my husband is dead, as the man I am living with does not know whether his wife is dead and it is awkward. What had we better do about it?"

"In accordance with instructions on ring paper, I have given birth to twins, enclosed in an envelope."

"Please send my money at once, as I am in need of it, because I have fallen into areas with my landlord."

FEES AND IMPOSITIONS

The Bishop of Norwich (Sheepshanks) had instituted and inducted me in June '99 whilst he was staying at the Hall for a confirmation. Owing to Middle Harling being styled a separate parish, I paid double fees for a living worth under one hundred pounds per annum, twice the fees paid by a neighbour just then, whose Tithe Rent Charge was over fifteen hundred pounds a year. Such inequalities and even injustices were still calmly accepted in the Church of England, as being among the natural dispensations of Providence. In this view Church and World alike agreed regarding life in general. At that time, too, in our rural deanery, the widow and children of a poor incumbent were mulcted [i.e. fined] more than the whole amount of money the clergyman left behind, in order to pay for outgoing repairs to the parsonage house. They went out penniless – a widow and four children. Bishops and 'the superior clergy' for centuries had lived in comfort, and had done nothing efficient to help their poorer brethren. Bishop Sheepshanks had been a missionary, and prided himself on having crossed the desert, I think from Baghdad to Damascus, on a donkey. His long gray beard would have given him a patriarchal appearance on such a journey. After the beloved Bishop Pelham his short tenure was not very noteworthy. His evangelical dean (Lefroy) was a thorn in his high church side. I was seldom in Norwich. Sir Edmund offered to propose me as a member of the Norfolk county club, but I could not afford the expense.

HAIL AND FAREWELL

In my first three years at West Harling, I preached rather widely in country churches, not only in the neighbourhood but further afield. I was beginning to be known in the 'dead see' of the Norwich diocese as one who would freely come and preach if asked. But the long bicycle journey in all weathers over rough roads tried me severely. Then came a blow. In the spring of 1902, I had a letter from father asking me to go down to Folkestone to see my brother Roger, who was there with his wife and baby son, Geoffrey. He was now curate-in-charge of a mission parish in Streatham, and had suddenly become ill. I found him in a bad way under a doctor who, as it turned out, had wrongly diagnosed. Next day was Saturday, and when I left by the night mail for Thetford, Roger was sleeping peacefully and we hoped would recover. The eight mile ride home after midnight was very lonely. Next morning, before I went to Church, a telegram came saying Roger was gone.

After the funeral, passing through London for West Harling I saw doctors, and was told to go very slow for some long time to come. They put me on a diet in which raw beef juice and raw eggs were the most tasty components. Alone, I tried now to make up my mind about several matters that were important to me. I concluded that a live dog was better than a dead lion. I have never since been sure that I was right. I resolved to draw a sharp line behind me. I would give up old hopes and plans for an active clerical life. I would stay where I was, live upon my land, and if possible maintain myself thereby. I gave up the idea of marriage. I confess I felt bitter – the cruelty of nature oppressed my thoughts. Though she wounds she also heals. I would spend no more long mornings reading and writing. Like Dean Swift, I threw up my study window to "glorify the room," and drive my dismal dumps out of doors.

I began slow enough indeed, with six hen-coops on the grass along the drive sheltered by the wood. Every two hours I fed those golden chicks with a little breadcrumbs mixed with chopped hard-boiled egg, later a handful of wheat and so forth. Never were mother birds so studied, and their offspring so waited upon. I learned intimately all their varied conversations, and became acquainted with the eternal habits and customs of motherhood, so exactly alike in every living creature. Of those seventy nurselings I lost not one.

The cockerels came to plump early maturity, and the pullets began their laying at the dearest season. At first I was as shaky on my legs as they were when hatched. I used to lie on a cane chaise-longue against my porch, and entice a pair of wagtails to take crumbs from my hand.

Birds, common and rarer, were all about. Redstarts, or fire-tails as they were called locally, displayed their brick-red backs as they flew away. Snipe towered and drummed incessantly above the lower meadow. A pair of wild duck nested in the hedge bottom against the pond. The drake, magnificent in purple blue and green sheen, sunned himself on the lower step below the gate. In due time the quaker-brown little mother emerged complacently, launching her ecstatic fleet upon the water. Gold-crest wrens, long tailed tits, garden warblers, flitted about. Fly-catchers perched on the fence, making dipping flights over the lawns. Doves cooed, and wild pigeons called incessantly "take two cows Taffy… you great fool you," from the deep woods. With evening, the cock pheasants crowed loudly as they settled in the trees for the night. A solemn great white owl sailed, silent and majestic, weaving and turning among the violet and darkening shadows. Nightjars patrolled the long avenues, emitting a constant flow of sound exactly like a watchman's rattle. I would sit snug and warm in the thatched summer-house against the wood, and listen to nightingales' songs, such as I never heard the like elsewhere. Reluctant, I stole in to my bed. The scent of white jasmine, and of the free flowering Seven Sister and monthly roses, came through the open window.

KITTY

To help my recovery now, father gave me a horse. She was a three-year old bay mare, rising fifteen and a half hand, bred at Chilcompton by my brother Alan on his small farm that he rented at his marriage after giving up the sea. The sire was a thoroughbred hunter, and the dam a useful hackney. I called my mare 'Kitty,' the pet name of my sister Helen. Kitty arrived in a horse box from Somerset, and with her a set of new harness made specially for her. She had a fine, satin coat all dark bay, a flowing tail, and no marks save one white sock on the near hind leg. She was perfectly sound but out of condition when she arrived. Alan was giving up the farm, and she had been overworked recently. With the mare came a fox terrier, of whom more anon.

Market Street, East Harling.

LUCK

Just before this time I had engaged as groom-gardener, to sleep in, a tiny man with a hump. He came to me under rather curious circumstances. He had been a drover up and down the country for many years, a waif and wanderer, with occasional spells of settled employment on farms and in stables. At Harling Spring lamb sale he heard at the Nag's Head that I might be wanting a man, and came to the rectory to see me. He was dressed neatly in tweed jacket, breeches and buskins. In his peaked cap he looked like a dwarf jockey. He had no references, but he spoke straightforwardly about himself, and I liked the dog-like expression in his candid brown eyes. He certainly understood horse-flesh, was very strong, and in spite of his lack of inches could do most garden work. I touched his hump for luck, and luck he brought me during the year and a half I kept him. Everything outdoors prospered. We had a good haysel. 'Polly' my Alderney cow had a fine heifer calf that I proposed to keep. I bought a half score bullocks cheaply that autumn. They cleaned up the pasture, and had just finished my stack of hay by the end of March, when an almost miraculous spell of warm rain and sunshine brought out such a rush of spring feed, three weeks before sale, that the beasts were in splendid order and sold well, not having cost me a penny for fattening. Sir Edward Bulwer, who, like his brother, stayed at the hall, was much interested in my dwarf. He told me he once had a valet, the spit of James, and like me his luck had been in all that time. Likewise the little men had the same failing. About once every three months James had a fit of restlessness, like an aborigine's itch for a walkabout. He would take himself off for a night, and not return till well into the next day, looking dishevelled and ashamed. He confessed it was drink he had gone for, and could not resist. Finally I had to get rid of him, with regret on both sides, and I had occasional news that he spoke with gratitude for his happy time with us.

DOMESTICAL

Pollard's Shop in East Harling.

My housekeeper, Ellen Pollard, thoroughly understood the little man, and did her best for him. She was nearing seventy, and had been in good service all her life. In a kind of way I stole her from my neighbour the rector of Banham, who had just married the daughter of Bishop Earle, now Dean of Exeter. Mrs. Pollard came to Norfolk with the bride, and came on to me. Her father had been an innkeeper in Cirencester, and Ellen could speak the tongue twisting dialect of her native Cotswold town. She was a tall, slim, fresh-faced old woman, very active, healthy, and strong for her age. She ruled her department justly and consistently, and looked after my house faithfully until she was over seventy five when she retired to a niece's home. For twenty years after that Mary Ann Alderton house-kept me in Norfolk, and for some years later in Devon. Even more than Ellen, Mary was a good cook and a great character. Her parents lived in their own pretty cottage, with its barn and large garden, at Bridgham.

When James had gone I took into the house a tall thin lad, Reggie Barrett, the son of a farm labourer at Middle Harling who had lost his wife. This boy soon grew into a strong young man, who served me for twelve years, until the first world war took him away.

The hamlet of Roudham, with a ruined church, was part of Bridgham parish. There was a sale at Roudham Hall just when I wanted to buy a vehicle. I secured very cheaply a neat light London-built dog-cart, with lancewood shafts, and first class axle and fittings, together with old squire Mornement's comfortable saddle, riding bridle, martingale and a lot of other etceteras thrown in. Kitty stepped out with spirit carrying the whole outfit home. She was beginning to like very much her new surroundings. From Pollard, the enterprising ironmonger at East Harling, I bought a new combined chaff-cutter and corn-mill. This last, kibbled oats or any other grain, also dry beans or peas. Looking back now, the low prices of those days are amazing. A coomb of oats cost well under ten shillings. A set of shoes all round for my mare at Pollard's forge was half a crown, including twopence to the smith. Kitty shied at first at rabbits and pheasants popping out suddenly on the road in front of her, but soon showed a whimsical appreciation of all her neighbours.

Roudham Church.

A Bad Dog's Diary

I told of a young fox-terrier that came with Kitty in the horse-box from Chilcompton. I had not invited this guest which was a gift from my brother Alan. One should not look a gift-dog in the mouth, so I received 'Bobs' with hospitality. Field-Marshal Lord Roberts, in spite of his lack of success in South Africa where his only son was killed, never ceased to be beloved by the British public, and many dogs were named after him. This soldier disliked cats and so did my terrier. I had a favourite cat, whose life Bobs rendered miserable from the outset. But he was young, full of life and spirits, beautifully shaped and marked, and I hoped would learn better ways. His first morning was not an encouragement to optimism – he chased and killed two of my laying pullets, and had all the poultry flying helter-skelter from the moment he set eyes on them. We put mustard and pepper on a mangled body, and rubbed his nose in it, with a taste of stick to emphasise its educational significance. But all our attempts to cure the ill habits from his lack of training were in vain. If he was off the lead going walks he chased everything in sight – sheep, cows, poultry, game. Once off he would obey no whistle or order of recall. I was in butcher Solly's shop when Bobs espied some young turkeys in the yard. At the moment I was paying a bill he broke away dragging his lead. He had four of those five birds dead within seconds, and my bill was increased accordingly. Another time he got among Hanton's fowls, kept for the Hall in a field near the church, and killed several of them before he was stopped. Riding my bicycle I had him on the lead, when a hen flew in front of us from a cottage garden hedge. In a flash he broke that hen's neck, while still on the lead and I in the saddle. I saw him snap a sparrow off the gravel before the front door, where he was apparently asleep on the mat. I drove, with him in the cart, twenty miles to lunch with a friend, in whose stable I tied up Bobs with Kitty. Someone must have loosed him for he was gone when I was ready to return home. Arriving home I found Bobs on the hearthrug looking as innocent as could be. I trembled to think of letters I might be receiving in the next few days. He had his own troubles owing to an enquiring mind. He found a hornet's nest in a stump on the rockery – a gentleman in amber gold and bronze sallied forth, and stung Bobs on his tail stump. "They sort ha' wholly got hot feet when they sits down" – and so Bobs found out. Poor little chap, he came howling to me with the sting sticking out on his tail. I put half a bottle of ammonia in a soup plate, and sat him down in it. He was trembling and weak with pain and shock. But next morning he was himself again.

THE HORNETS

My sunny peaceful garden
  Was nice for work or rest,
Until one year inside an oak
  There came a hornets' nest.

These hornets were prolific,
  Next summer nests were three,
And soon in woods around there seemed
  A nest in every tree.

For some long time I left them
  Alone, to wait and see,
Then my poor dog Bob playing round
  Got stung upon his b.

At that I joined the neighbours
  With cyanide of p.,
And tar and straw and oily rags
  We killed them in each tree.

Another time he put a paw in a rabbit trap, and I was well bitten before I could release him and bandage the foot. For these and other attentions he began to show some little signs of affection. But we could not cure him of his killing propensities. His life was threatened by gamekeepers, and he was too dear a dog for me. I put a label on his collar, paid his fare, and sent him back to Somerset.

THETFORD

Privet Lodge: Coote Family.
L to R. Back row: William, Henry, Florence.
Middle row: Percy Lake, Nellie, Reginald.
Front row: Bob and Wilhelmina.

I marketed at Thetford each week. From my house I drove south through the coverts, past second keeper Coote's lodge. Beyond this the park drive crossed the Harling-Thetford highway. Turning right, the road was narrow, straight, sandy and unfenced, with occasional woods alongside. It was a lonely track, across uncultivated moorland, except for a small patch of arable belonging to Thorpe Farm on the Shadwell border. The next mile or so to Rushford corner was tree shaded. Thence, turning again to the right, passing fine beeches and the entrance gates to Shadwell Court, in about another three miles Thetford was reached.

Few country towns are less noticeable than this ancient grouping of squat, flint-built little dwellings, clustered at the ford where my Thet, and later my Great Ouse in its infancy, met and meandered in a just navigable stream to Brandon and the Fens. From the surrounding Breckland low summits the town was scarcely visible, lying in its hollow, and matching in dull colour the wide expanses of its environment. Since I knew it, perhaps brick erections and red tiles have spoiled the uniform gray of flint walls and slate roofs. Small Thetford has three parishes with their churches. But long ago it had abbeys, monasteries and nunneries, and was the ecclesiastical centre of East Anglia, and the seat of the bishopric before Norwich. The collegiate church at Rushford, and the numerous ruined churches in the district, showed the hold religion once had on this now sparsely populated countryside. Stone coffins of dignitaries, and foundations of church buildings, have constantly been unearthed. The castle mound with its steep sides, saucer top, and ditch surround, tell of the early battle of Snarehill. The grammar school, an old foundation, still carries on its good work.

Shadwell Lane.

Castle Hill, Thetford.

The London-Norwich high road has long crossed the Thet by a narrow bridge in place of the ford. Travellers over the Breckland wastes from Newmarket, and onwards by Roudham Heath, were glad to put up at the Bell Inn, when night fell, and highwaymen were abroad. So lonely was the road, and so long the miles, that the King's House was built at Thetford for the use of his majesty on his journey, and lodged also judges and other public personages. Not only religion, but free thought and advanced, liberal ideas came from, even if they never remained in Thetford, for Tom Paine was born in a humble dwelling here. I could return by taking the Norwich road and turning to the right, past Admiral Lord Fisher's house at Kilverstone, and Brettenham's church and manor, to Bridgham. Or I could continue the longer route straight across open Brecklands to Roudham Heath, where a gibbet once stood, and where a parson of Larling, according to tradition, was hanged as a warning to other highway robbers. Kitty made light work of the sixteen or twenty miles journey to Thetford and back, for there were only easy gradients, unless I came by the Kilverstone road and up a steep pitch to the Shadwell-Thorpe corner. All these roads were still flinty gravel and sand, untouched by tarmacadam, for the twenty five years I lived on the Norfolk-Suffolk border. They were being modernised just when I left.

Guildhall Street, Thetford.

MENTAL ARITHMETIC

When I first went to West Harling, Middle Harling farm was occupied by a bailiff, Charles Bennett and his wife. This old couple, like the Brundles, were a beautiful example of the type of human character that not seldom has grown on English soil. They too were illiterate, never having had opportunity to master the three 'Rs'. But Charles' memory was so trained by use that he went to market for his master, Timothy Colman, of East Harling, with many commissions to execute, involving sometimes considerable sums of money. Timothy, who for the last two years of his life, sat in the front pew under my pulpit, himself told me that Charles always came back from market having sold and bought exactly as ordered, stating and accounting for to a halfpenny the details of each transaction, and able to tell his master that day's prices of corn, sheep, bullocks, pigs, with weights and prices per stone or cwt., and all the news of the market. I knew a similar example of good memory in an unlettered man in Di Harvey, well known as a horse and cattle dealer in the district. He was a self-made man, and knew all the tricks, but he never let me down in our many transactions, whether in selling to or buying from me. Di could carry in his head all the prices and details of however large a market or sale, and quote them weeks afterwards. Both were short, brown-bearded men who chewed straws, and had quiet ruminative eyes. Both could tell at a glance the weight of any beast to a few ounces. Each could estimate its value exactly. But though neither could do a sum of arithmetic on paper they would calculate with rapidity and perfect accuracy mentally.

Inmates of Thetford Union Workhouse.

Di, like Timothy, had the faculty for acquisition. He wanted things for himself, to be master in however small a way. Money stuck to both these men and they stuck to money. Both died rich but Charles Bennett just as capable, never managed to make or hold anything for himself, though he handled not a little business for his master. When Mr. Colman died he left five shillings weekly to one or two old servants, but left nothing for Charles, who was old and in ill-health. For a time the couple lived in a two-roomed cottage, just outside my parish, and I often saw them. The old man loved to talk about farming days. Though there was interest and good sense in his conversation, he had the curious habit of ending a sentence with one or other of three irrelevant tags – "as the boy said," or "that'd make a difference," or "that's where't comes in." After a few months their little savings were exhausted. Their family could not, or would not maintain them, and they had to go to the workhouse. I was asked to soften this blow to the old people who trusted me, and to try to avoid a scene by going with them in the cart at least part of the way. This I did. It was a sad business, specially as the sexes were separated in the wards. My duties as guardian of the poor enabled me to see them twice monthly when I would take a little tea and tobacco.

Charles Bennett.

They became happier soon, for we had a good master and matron. I thought when I watched their beautiful faces that they had a better treasure than had Timothy and Di. Everyone had a nickname in our part of Norfolk. Perhaps Harvey's stood for 'Dives.' At least Charles and his wife found Abram's bosom, and the peace of God was in their heart.

THE WORKHOUSE

Guiltcross Workhouse, Kenninghall.

I have read in books many terrible descriptions of conditions of life in workhouses under the British Poor Law. I have little doubt that miseries and wrongs can be substantiated as historical fact over a considerable period. But I believe there were many exceptions, and that generally there was marked improvement as the nineteenth century advanced. I have only had experience of the two rural workhouses of Guiltcross and Thetford, and I can speak well of them. In our joint capacity as members of the rural district council and guardians of the poor, our board had only one paid servant; he was a solicitor, and acted also as clerk to the magistrates' court of Petty Sessions. For the rest, squires, farmers, a few leisured people and capable ladies were the unpaid management. Many of these were persons of experience, high character and genuinely interested and devoted to the welfare of their poorer neighbours. Squire Molyneux-Montgomerie of Garboldisham and Prince Frederick Duleep-Singh who now, in comparative poverty, lived at Blo' Norton Hall, and was respected and loved by everyone who knew him, were men of fine ideals and knowledge of affairs. Wilfrid Blunt never missed a meeting of either boards, and kept such complete and accurate records in his notebooks that he could, and did, confound lawyer Clowes whenever that unfortunate functionary slipped

Staff of Thetford Union Workhouse.

up in his facts. When Wilfrid later was made a magistrate he could pursue his victim also from the bench with his unerring records – if he said "You're wrong" it was so. When, very seldom, someone got back on Blunt there was general cheering. The ladies were invaluable on the house committee and in the women's wards. Much concerted and individual work was done to make the settled inmates happy and comfortable. Tramps, vagrants and casuals, seeking only supper bed and breakfast, if able-bodied, had to do an hour's morning-work for their keep. But infirm and old people and the sick needed to perform no tasks. The hated name 'workhouse' was changed to 'institution', though the

Garboldisham Hall.

dislike and sense of degradation to pauper rank remains inevitably, until the causes can be removed. It was not true in our case that we were there to keep down the poor-rate. The few who had that point of view were always out-voted. When Mr. Lloyd George carried his old-age pensions bill large numbers of old people were enabled, through their weekly five shillings, to find homes with relatives or friends. It was a heaven-sent boon to thousands of respectable poor people, who had worked hard all their lives, and yet had no money for old age. Lloyd George was the saviour of such, and I remember Charles Brundle saying to me with tears in his eyes – "he gie'd us our pensions."

LANDED PROPRIETORS

Hundreds of square miles of Breckland are a rolling plateau of sand and gravel, overlaying deep chalk. Since the last ice-age, much of this locality cannot have changed materially. Conifers, some oak, beech and other English hard woods could establish themselves in the coverts.

Many of the proprietors were keen agriculturalists, and had the capital necessary for light-land farming. The Dukes of Grafton, in their ancestral seat at Euston Hall close to Thetford, always did their best for the very light land around them, maintaining fertility by Coke of Holkham's roots and sheep plan. When Mr.

Euston Hall.

Admiral 'Jacky' Fisher.

Vavasseur of Armstrong Vickers bequeathed Kilverstone to his friend Admiral Jacky Fisher's son; Cecil, who had been a judge in India, came home and devoted himself to farming the estate. He married an American, and wisely made new farm buildings instead of enlarging the moderate-sized hall. The land was some of the lightest close to Thetford, but he improved its productiveness. The Breckland estates at Croxton, Thetford, Major MacKenzie's near Brandon, with Lord Walsingham's at Merton, and many others towards Swaffham, were largely uncultivable, beyond providing a little corn to keep game in the coverts. If a poor man were given fifty or a hundred such sandy acres, let alone Jesse Collins idea of maintenance on three acres with a cow, he could not earn a living. The district was ideal for sport, that circulated money to some extent among the population. I gather that a good deal of Breckland, since my time, has been taken over by the government for its afforestation schemes. However valuable this may be as a use for the land, I doubt if even the former small number of well-housed, interested, healthy and contented people remain in these state forests. I hope that Euston has not succumbed. When the old Duke of my time, who was revered and liked by all his neighbours, died in his

Alice Musker (1848-1929).

John Musker (1846-1926).

nineties, his son and grandson each died soon after their succession, so that this family three times paid death duties within a few years. Another disaster was the destruction of Euston Hall by fire early in the century. The house was at once rebuilt on exactly the former plan, but it seems impossible that the estate could withstand the later burdens of taxation.

There were two, very wealthy men whose estates likewise bordered the borough of Thetford. Lord Iveagh, head of the Dublin Guinness Brewing family, bought Elveden from the Maharajah Duleep-Singh. The shooting here was some of the best in England. Queen Victoria's son was the Maharajah's guest every season, and King George followed his father by yearly visits to shoot Lord Iveagh's coverts. The Maharajah's family were impoverished when they sold Elveden, and it is common knowledge that they needed the sum they claimed should have been paid by the British government for the Koh-i-noor diamond and others of their splendid jewels.

Elveden Hall.

Almost as large as the Elveden property was the thirty thousand acres of the Shadwell estate, that a newcomer, Mr. J. Musker, bought from the widow of Sir Robert Buxton, just at the time I came to West Harling. Shadwell Court was one of the most successful large modern Gothic houses I have known, with its graceful carving it looked a flower, set in emerald parklands, against a wooded slope, with a mere, fed by the Thet, in the distance. A private drive to Thetford went past Snarehill Hall, where Harold, the eldest son lived. The second son Herbert, lived at Rushford Hall, and the third son Percy, dwelt at Roudham Hall. So the parents had all their sons, with their wives and children in dower houses round the patriarchal mansion. I think they could walk, if they wished, twenty miles in a straight line without going off their own land. John Musker made his fortune in a comparatively few years in the chain-grocery stores, known as the Home and Colonial . He was a handsome, tall, slim man, none of his sons approaching him in good looks. When the manager of Marshall Field's great stores in New York decided to found Selfridge's stores in London on his own account, soon after the commencement of business he found himself in serious need of working capital. Neither in America nor in England could he obtain the necessary credits. There followed a rescue of the undertaking that was almost a romance. For a gentleman quietly offered to lend Selfridge's £300,000 pounds sterling for a term of years at a low rate of interest under the circumstances. The offer was accepted with gratitude, for Mr. J. Musker's immediate single draft for the amount was ready cash on the spot. The great Oxford Street stores flourished thereafter, and the loan was duly and punctually repaid. There was a fifth good house on the Shadwell estate, Shadwell Manor, where dwelt Mr. Popham, a solicitor, whose whole time was taken up by Musker business.

John Musker's chief hobby was the breeding of race horses, and to a great extent everything on the estate was influenced in this direction. As a beginning it was planned to kill off all the rabbits. On Breckland no one can ride horseback safely, from the innumerable rabbit

Shadwell Court.

burrows. Everyone said it was impossible to clear Shadwell of rabbits, but John Musker did so. He put down scores of miles of first class fencing, with fine mesh wire netting properly installed, and employed many warreners to kill off the bunnies. In two years, at haysel, harvest, and shooting parties, scarcely a white scut was seen, and henceforth they were soon finished with. Ranges of stables for brood mares, with grooms' cottages, were built in suitable spots about the estate. Many thousands of pounds were spent for the finest bloodstock. Lovely foals, yearlings and two-year-olds appeared in their own paddocks. On the tan exercise rings the three-year-olds ran, and were timed before an experienced trainer. John Musker did not bet, and did not race largely under his own colours at Newmarket and elsewhere. He would walk the green slopes near his house, admiring the glorious horses paraded for his inspection. Then, one after another, they would be galloped over the measured course. It was a scene for a picture by J. Munnings, the Norfolk painter. The Shadwell horses did not win many of the classic races, but I think their owner felt he had a good return for the enormous sums of money he spent on them.

On the Snarehill-Thetford border of the estate, where the Thet flows near the Castle mound, site of the ancient battle, was an old house still called 'The Nunnery,' from its former religious use. Here were racing stables, and the residence of the trainer. Within view on the other side of the river were the buildings of the workhouse. Charles Bennett lodged there after his life's labours. He had gained nothing of earth's wealth, though he was an able and honest good man. John Musker, in a much shorter life, had heaped a pile of gold higher than the Castle mound. He had done so honourably under the laws and customs of his country. It is regrettable that the country had shown so little regard for poor Charles Bennett

POULTRY

The grass of my upper and lower glebe meadows showed improvement in a few years. We wire-fenced against rabbits from the wood, and along the upper portion of the glebe. Barrett cleaned out all my ditches, and dug 'grups' across the lowest ground. In winter I occupied myself making movable fowl-houses, and all my coops, runs and poultry appliances. I had a large size incubator, and made my own hot water brooders which were very successful. Thus, my poultry-keeping outfit cost me little beyond the materials. I crossed pure strains only – Orpingtons, English Game, Leghorns or Minorcas and Rhode Island Reds. I aimed at early hatching, and kept on a hundred laying pullets only. By moving all the open-bottomed fowl-houses on to fresh ground every week, all the grassland benefited from the droppings. At the same time the acreage was much more than ample for the head of poultry carried. Besides Kitty and a cow or two, there was generally something or other in the way of stock to feed off and improve the pasture. In two years we had exterminated the thistles, nettles and ragwort on the land by frequent cutting. Moles were trapped, and their workings bush-harrowed. We repaired the fences. My neighbour and friend, the squire of Riddlesworth, sent me enough green larch poles to make a quarter mile new fence along the ditch of my lower field, beside the alder covert.

BEES

I planned to keep bees. An old roadman at Bridgham offered me a couple of skeps, and brought them over, and installed them with all the mystic ceremonies tradition required for so important an undertaking. It was late autumn. He washed himself well, put on a clean shirt, and his Sunday best clothes. Then he paid a visit to his bees, and whispered to each hive what he was going to do, saying, "I'm taking two of yous to a good master, work well for him and he'll take care of you." Slinging a skep to either end of a shoulder yoke he carried them without jolt to where the bridge goes over Thet. Here he paused to utter the incantations requisite for bees crossing running water. He told them they were now leaving Bridgham for West Harling parish, that was bounded by this stream, and to which they would henceforth belong. When he reached my door the medicine man's enjoyment of his peculiar rites and mysteries was in full flow. He went into the kitchen and melted brown sugar, and anointed with it the floorboards nailed to oak posts on which the skeps were to be placed, facing south under the shelter of the kitchen garden hedge. Carefully adjusting them, he said – "Look what yar new master ha' gied ye. Now nivver yar imitate that yar wants to goo back to Bridgham. This is yar home this is, and this is yar master standing by." He told me to "say a ward" to them, which I did. Puddling some clay, he moulded it round the bases to the bits of wood laid for the entrance, and made occult passes to keep off tits, death's head moths, wasps and other marauders. Two earthenware pans were superimposed to keep the skeps dry. We were then able to return to the kitchen, where, by the fire, he spent a joyous evening that he never forgot. If I saw him at his road-mending he always wanted to "pass the time o' day an have a ward about them bees." I gave him a gold piece, and he spat on it, saying "Tha's th' right colour, tha'll bring luck to both on us." Though these skeps were good and heavy with winter stores, I fed them in early spring, and they gave me three swarms each. Within three years I had an apiary of half a hundred frame-hives every one of which I made during winters. These, with a neat shepherd's hut on wheels, all painted white and numbered, made a smart show. We worked a large geared extractor, and other modern apparatus in the hut. We had a honey-room, and storage for bottles and cans. Until the first German war I wrote a monthly bee-keeping article for the agricultural page of the London *Daily Telegraph* newspaper. Mr. Cowan the editor of the Bee-keepers' Journal, and president of the British Beekeepers' Association, wrote kindly and gave me a new edition of his book.

Work Sacred and Profane

What with one thing and another there was plenty to interest one and keep one employed. In winter we saved logs, for there were dead trees to be felled, and branches to be lopped, providing abundance of firewood. I had two cross-cut saws, axes, mawl [mallet] and steel wedges, and we became adept woodsmen. "That du wholly warm yar twice over, that du, when yar cuts it, bor, and when yar kindles it," was a common saying. I did most of my carpentry on winter nights, and, after making things, the annual painting and repairs took much time. If bees do little in winter it is not so with the beemaster – he has a thousand jobs. So has the poultryman if he wants early chicks and winter eggs. Horse, cows and stock, like children, must be fed and cared for every day. The rectory had a cool dairy to the north, with slate slabs and stone floor. I bought a new Hathaway churn, and had a glass bottle-churn for smaller quantities, or when supplies of cream ran short.

West Harling Sunday School Picnic.

One afternoon a week I had a homely Bible class in my dining room. I don't say I taught the good folk much, but at least they liked to come, and not for the reason the parishioner came to John Harbord. One of them told him she was in anxiety about her soul. "I didn't know what to say to her," said the rector, but he gave her a bottle of sherry and a bottle of port and told her, "If you're feeling low perhaps this will do you good." This was another of Sir Edmund's stories about my predecessor. One evening a-week in winter our boys and young men came to see me. We had a big, wood fire in the gun-room, and a few tables for games. The rest of us made a ring round the fire, and I read to the company a book of adventure. They were keen not to miss any chapter of these stories. Sometimes I read a short

c. 1898 West Harling Sunday School and Bible Class.
Back row, L to R: E. Bussey, Johnny Cross, B. Blackburn, S. Wilson, ?, ?, W. Endley;
Middle row, L to R: Lizzie Riches, Mabel Wiggett, H. Riches, Nellie Coote, M. Hanton, ?, ?,
M. Bussey, May Wiggett, B. Blackburn, Kate Bussey, Ella Wilson, D. King;
Front row, L to R: ?, Reggie Coote, B. Blackburn, W. Endley, Walter Wiggett,
George King, S. Bussey, ?.

poem, and strangely enough some of them liked bits of Robert Browning – such as "How the good news came to Ghent," "Up at a villa down in the city," and "The bishop orders his tomb." I lent the previous week's papers to the Coote brothers. One of these boys went into the Navy, and the other became a keeper on one of the royal estates. Both were intelligent fellows, and when the Dreyfus case was on knew more about it than I did. Round the fire my dozen or so boys would talk animatedly, ready to be interested in anything that turned up for conversation. In summer they played cricket near the church. I had some bowls with which our choirmen played matches from time to time on my lawn. We had a choir supper in summer in the coach house, when songs of many varieties were indulged in. The poignant-sentimental was chiefly admired, with tremolo vocal effects. One favourite told of a General, asked "Who is that man?" "Tis our hero, said the Capting." The chorus was – "Break the news to mother. Tell her there is no other to take the place of mother for I'm not going hoome." The squire's two daughters gave themselves wholeheartedly to Sunday school, choir and later, the Boy Scout movement. They were almost never away from the parish.

St. Valentine's day, the fourteenth of February was supposed to bring daylight for farm working from six a.m. to six p.m. Along the whole length of my oak paling fence under the wood, the daffodils and jonquils in their thousands came through the grass in silver and golden processions. In front of them were violets and primroses also in the grass. On the lawn under the old oak, crocuses pushed up their yellow and purple heads. In the alder covert were acres of snowdrops with some daffodils. This profusion had resulted from a few bulbs thrown carelessly over the hedge from the kitchen garden in past years. Hundreds of bunches were sent from this patch each spring to the Norfolk general hospital. Sometime in April my asparagus bed began to be productive, and boxes of juicy heads went off by rail. Like Wilfrid Blunt, I had a clientele of friends in London and elsewhere eager to buy my produce – honey in bottle or section, jams, fruit, all kinds of vegetables, rabbits, a little butter, with bunches of flowers as gifts. Our light land grew splendid potatoes, and we had several tons to dispose of every year. The G.E.R. sold useful boxes for packing, charged special low rates for agricultural produce, and delivered the goods to the customers' doors. I don't think state railways in any country offer such facilities. I had special boxes for eggs, hampers for dressed poultry, strong bags for potatoes, and steel cans for honey in bulk to wholesale chemists. Returned empties were charged very low rates. All this packing and despatching meant a lot of work, and most days my car went to the Harling or Thetford railway stations with goods.

I bought my corn and offals through the Riddlesworth estate office from Mr. Gooding the agent. The mill was at Knettishall, on the Suffolk side of the Ouse. It was a pleasant drive of about four miles from my house, going out by the Coote's lodge and straight across the Thetford-Harling road to the Riddlesworth border. Here the differences between West Harling wilderness Breck, and Squire Champion's great areas of well-farmed plough and grasslands were most significant. Here our rabbits were guarded against by miles of lasting and adequate fences. The woodlands were maintained, hedges were cut and up-kept, gates painted and well hung, park roads gravelled and neat. Passing the good buildings of Riddlesworth Home farm, where the agent lived with his pleasant young wife and in due time four, bright children, I drove by a woodland track down to the beautiful little modern bridge over the county river boundary. Here was a fishing and bathing pool, with an eel trap in a dam that held up the waters of the lake below Riddlesworth Hall. Nearby was the good house and fine modern buildings of Knettishall farm, at that time occupied by a bailiff. Here I would find cheery Lacy Gooding, with my sacks of corn ready for me at the store. He was a light-weight trim figure, gaitered, ruddy cheeked, with blue eyes and clipped, fair moustache, honest as the day and always friendly.

Kitty knows the Points of the Compass

Kitty now had two coomb of corn to pull in addition to my twelve stone, up the gentle slopes. She always knew which way her nose pointed, and her free stride was more marked when homewards bound. She seemed to know the points of the compass, and in which direction her home lay, even when several hundreds of miles away. Her marked animation and gaiety when we turned south, though on a different road, after fourteen days driving north was unmistakable testimony to this assertion.

We "Learn and Labour Truly……"

I kept complete accounts of outgoings and receipts during the years that I engaged in petit culture. I had to buy my experience, but made fewer mistakes than I might have done because of good friends around me, poor and rich. Net balances varied, but not greatly, because when one thing turned out worse another would be better. The biggest uncertainty was the honey harvest, that depended largely on the year's weather and the strength of colonies. Sometimes the flow of nectar and the vigour of stocks would quadruple receipts. Other years, cold wet and windy conditions dwindled everything in the apiary – honey, stocks. Pigs are always a gamble – "gold or copper" according to the old saying. In matters of luck I am a pessimist – defined by someone as "a man who wears a belt as well as braces." But mischance makes "the best laid schemes of mice and men gang aft agley." Thus, coming from church one fine spring evening, I found forty or fifty golden ducklings massacred by a stoat or rat. Before leaving, I had myself put them in a run, with small mesh wire underneath and overhead. No possible entrance I thought could be made. And yet their feet and heads lay all about with little puffs of down when I returned. Or again, our hay, would be in perfect condition for carrying, sweet scented with seeds on the heads, and sap in the stems, just enough moisture to beget the desirable moderate heat in the stack. The East Harling farmer, who always cut and helped cart my hay, would be on the field as soon as the dew was gone, with his horses wagons and men, to make a single day's job of the stacking. Then, into the blue sky, would crowd up companies, battalions, brigades of black clouds, followed by divisions and army corps, with thunder of artillery and missiles of hail and pelting rain – all directed at my little patch. The wagons and men went home. I would shake my fist at the elements – "Be damned to you fellows up there, do your worst, I'll be even with you yet!" Day after day, sometimes week after week, Barrett and I would turn over the cocks, shake out the windrows, and half dry the now musty and blackening grass, only to have it again and again rained on interminably. Its aroma, its colour, its food value could never be recovered. Our haysel was a washout.

THE TITHE BARN

Our haymaking usually was a time we enjoyed. All the household turned out with rakes or forks to tidy up after the wagons, or to bring us our meat and drink. Against all advice I built my first haystack within the tithe barn, that was large enough to allow plenty of space all round it, with a clear threshing floor and ample room beyond for chaff cutting, wood storage, and heap of mangolds. Even my biggest crop of hay left plenty of room beneath the rafters. We were always careful to avoid danger of overheating, and of course lost no precious hay from wet.

West Harling Rectory (now the Dower House) & Tithe Barn.

The great four-fold doors were high enough to admit a loaded wagon, and we continued to stack here in after years. The walls were clay-lump with old brick foundations, and the long thatched roof was upheld by oak timbers. In the parish registers, that were complete from the earliest date – I think in Elizabeth I's reign – there was an entry, when Oliver Ridley was rector (1855-60): "An unknown stranger man was this day found dead in the rectory barn, the cause of death being apparently from cold and starvation." This Ridley was fellow of an Oxford college and was succeeded by another of his family, younger members of which, including a Somerset parson, I entertained during my tenure when they came to see the graves of their parents. Old Oliver had at least his fellowship to augment his income.

"MINE OWN HANDS..."

My books showed on average that I made enough from the glebe to pay rates, taxes, repairs, insurance, wages and our food. I had no rent to pay for house or land and did not charge the account with a hypothetical wage for myself. We produced almost all our food except groceries, and some butcher's meat. We used a good deal of honey for sweetening. Roughly, putting increase value of livestock against capital expenditure, I arrived at the conclusion that, even on such poor soil as West Harling, a man with a little capital could just about maintain himself if he was content to live frugally. Sandy soil is hungry. We managed to have a good supply of manure from stable, cow house, pigs, poultry, wood ashes, soot, leaf-mould, lawn

Brundle gravestone, West Harling.

cuttings, beet tops, pond and ditch silt and so on. Dung, which all East Anglians like John Bunyan plainly called 'muck' is the salvation of light lands. We treasured this precious commodity as our most valuable asset.

When all goes well life on the land is, I think, the happiest possible. The brown faced men and rosy women, jogging in their traps to a country town on market day with baskets of eggs, poultry, fruit and vegetables, are a heartening sight. On Sunday afternoons in summer, when parents and active youngsters and friendly neighbours walk around to admire the growing crops and promising livestock, their faces and talk manifest enjoyment. It is life as nature meant it. "Our mother earth" Charles Brundle used to say, "is gude to us du we take care o' she." I have seen this health and contented happiness in many lands, as well as in most parts of our own country, where it can be seen best of all. The picture has often been more than threequarters destroyed by men's sins and infirmities. but it is the substance of truth that "God gave the earth for our bread, gave it to all not to few." I want to see in England, and in the world, countless more millions of its inhabitants enjoying the fruit of their labours, each one on his own piece of land. For the ills of mind and body there is no cure like the anodyne of handicraft. You are troubled, but you go and do a job of work, and behold you are relieved. There is a rhythm of the seasonal year that, for the country dweller, brings subtle harmonies to body and mind in the progression and variety of necessary tasks. For the country parson and his parishioners, there is added the solemn earnest and lovely rhythm of the Church's year. Many a time, I, like everyone else, was soothed and uplifted as the recurring seasons of pastoral life unfolded.

CYCLES AND MOTORS COME TO BRECKLAND

Lambert's, Thetford.

At the opening of the new century the bicycle had not yet come into general use among the working classes of the community. This was particularly the case in country districts, where bicycles would be most valuable as means of communication. At West Harling only the squire's two daughters and I had bicycles. Wilfrid Blunt had one, and the vicar of Rushford was also a cyclist. At Thetford there was a carriage-builder named Lambert, whose son had just left the grammar school there. This boy like all others, was interested in bicycles, and persuaded his father to let him have a small window in the next door cottage to show a few oil cans, spanners, bells and suchlike articles connected with cycling. He greatly admired my Beeston Humber, and was thrilled by its adventures in Morocco and Grand Canary. As a tremendous commercial venture he bought half a dozen new cycles, and displayed them in the living room of the tiny cottage, the whole of which had become his place of business. Soon they were all sold, and a dozen was his next order. The history of the rise of this moderate-sized country business to an established position was, doubtless, like hundreds of others at that time. In four or

Motor accident, Kilverstone 1913.

five years, in this case, the young cuckoo had kicked his parent out of the family nest, or rather they had to build new and much larger premises in the vicinity, of which the carriage-building occupied an ever diminishing portion. Almost every family in our neighbourhood in time had at least one bicycle. The cottage women at first grumbled, using the direct East Anglian speech – "I telled 'un he'd better off wi' a bastard child" – for flint- gravel roads were hard on tyres, and part payment instalments had also to be met. But soon, mother was on wheels too, and even grandparents sometimes emulated the youngsters. This new use of the roads was the beginning of something even greater.

About 1903 I was in Bristol, looking into Willway's shop near the old drawbridge, as I loved to do in my boyhood. Among the bicycles was one propelled by a motor, a very strange looking contraption. They had been shown in action at the Crystal Palace, and newspaper reports for some years past, told of queer motor vehicles journeying from London to Brighton and back, since the red flag restriction against locomotives was repealed. Squire Montgomerie was dead. He had crippled his estate by building Garboldisham Manor near the old hall, that was now let to the Freres whom I had known in London. The Manor was let to a certain Count Zborowski, if that was the name, a young man who was a pioneer of this new motoring. The most that people saw of him was a cloud of dust on the high roads. He

Percy Musker, behind the wheel, at Roudham Hall.

had two or three of the first racing cars – Benz, Mercedes, De Dion Bouton and other foreign makes. A few years later he was killed by running into the rocks when cornering during a race on the Grand Corniche. The Muskers had some of the early cars, that I studied admiringly when opportunity offered. I read all the literature devoutly, but bided my time before making a modest trial for myself. The first motoring was far too expensive for me. It was horribly uncomfortable behind the wheel, and if you did twenty miles without having to lie on your back under the car you were lucky. I remember John Musker saying enthusiastically – "We have just come from Newmarket without having to stop." People dressed up like Polar bears in furs. Helmets and goggles kept out the tearing winds and swirling dust. But it was chic to look like that – in the first years only. An attempt was made by the best people to ultimate the accent in motór. They did not succeed for long, but it sounded well while it lasted. One hostess' opening conversational gambit was always – "How did you come?" I used to listen delightedly – "We drove," "We bicycled," "We came in the donkey cart." And then, with enormous self-importance – "We motóred." This last was almost as consequential as one lady's story of "my fourth footman."

During my time the motor car hardly affected Breckland's wide spaces, and even up to 1925 there was no alteration in the flinty narrow roads. Tarred macadam began to arrive at that date. Except that our part of the London-Norwich Highway was tarred just before the first world war. One other portent of things to come was a humming drone in the sky one evening about 1906. The pheasants flew out of the coverts in terror, and birds of all kinds in the woods uttered cries of alarm. Kitty galloped about the meadow snorting and whickering. Polly blared, and all my livestock were running about in consternation. Over the tops of the trees appeared a great bird, as they thought, emitting a trail of smoke, and making indescribable whirring noises. It had flown from Boulton and Paul's in Norwich, and got as far as Brandon, which was thought a fine performance. I saw no more of these birds until the German war, when Breckland saw Zeppelins, airplanes, and the very first tanks.

CAR VERSES

[Ed. Rev. Blunt was a notoriously bad driver. He made fun of his own inadequacy:]

I rattle over bumps and ways
She bumps and toss and pitches
I sometimes have my banking days
And sometimes visit ditches.

Rev. Blunt in his Rover 9 H.P. (2 cylinder).

The poet, Alan Haig-Brown, contributed the following for Blunt to use in his Christmas card:

New Year's Wishes

May your road be broad and smiling, fringed with honey-laden flowers,
And the sun on every milestone as you travel down the hours;
May you take the hills that meet you in the newly opening year,
With a bright and happy freedom and without a change of gear.

If the floods cross your going and fill you with despair,
I pray you come to Bridge'em and be here with time to spare;
If the flints should look forbidding, keep your courage to the front,
And you'll generally find them (like your good friend) kind and Blunt.

May life's engine run with smoothness, never clog and never toil,
Keep it well supplied and charity grand lubricating oil;
And if you find a traveller who has somehow got adrift,
Don't be too proud to stop awhile, and offer him a lift.

So fare you well, my greeting o'er, I leave you with regret,
I can hear the gentle throbbing of my eager Humberette;
But I hope that we shall often meet throughout the coming days,
At every turn and corner new but never at cross-ways.

Ice House and Pigeon Cote

Walking over the sedgy ground on the Thet bank near the hall I came on a sandy mound, having a few bushes at the top. Among these was a circular hole, and the remains of a wooden cover, like a well-head. Looking in, I saw a ladder, which I descended carefully, and found myself in an egg-shaped chamber, beautifully built of bricks. A door near the bottom on the north side led to a short tunnel, the end of which was earthed up. There were drain holes at the bottom of the chamber, that plainly had been used in

East Harling Church and Pigeon Cote.

former times to store ice from the river and flooded ground. Another old brick erection of domestic utility was on the north side of East Harling church. It was a circular pigeon-cote, having a pantile roof, surmounted by a little wooden and metal cupola, and a weather vane. The walls were rose colour brick, pierced by apertures for the birds. It was of considerable age, and as good an example of the sort as I have seen. It stood as a reproach beside Timothy Colman's pretentious, red-brick villa.

Timothy Colman's Eastfield House.

Timothy Colman.

More Neighbouring Parsons

Inside the finely proportioned East Harling church, with its beautiful window mouldings, were some tombs of the de Herlyngs, a Norman family that received the manor in grant from the Conqueror. There was no rectory house attached to the benefice in my time. The rector, Baseley Hales Grigson, lived in his own dwelling somewhat grandiloquently styled East Harling Hall. It was a good house built of small, white bricks that weathered to ivory shades. A fine example of a classical, palladian mansion built of this brick was at Redgrave in Suffolk, the property of Rowland Wilson, a relative of Grigson. East Harling Hall and gardens, sheltered by trees from cold winds, faced south across a park like meadow. The living was a fairly good one, and the parson had land of his own as well as the glebe for shooting over. Altogether it was a delectable spot, and Baseley enjoyed it hugely. It came to him through his first wife, whose parents bought it for the young couple as

East Harling Hall.

> **DEATH OF MRS. B. H. GRIGSON.**
>
> A gloom was cast over the parish of East Harling when it became known that Mrs. Grigson, wife of the rector, died early on Wednesday morning. The deceased lady had been in failing health for some months, and a change of air was tried in the hope that it would prove beneficial, but as no good result followed she came home. Latterly it was known that her medical attendants had pronounced the complaint from which she was suffering to be incurable. The Rev. B. H. Grigson became rector of East Harling in 1889, and from that time Mrs. Grigson has taken an active part in the work of the church and other parochial matters. She trained and instructed the church choir, and for several years acted as organist at most of the church services, and also worked hard in promoting the success of the Sunday School. She was secretary to the local technical education committee and was instrumental in the formation of classes for nursing and ambulance work. In the arrangement of concerts and parish entertainments she was an indefatigable worker. The deceased lady was very kind-hearted, and by her cheery manners and invariable courtesy to all she had gained the respect and esteem of the whole parish and much regret at her removal in the prime of life.

well as the advowson. He was hospitable with a jolly laugh, more fond of the pleasures of the dining room than of the study. Cricket, tennis, shooting and other active exercise did not lessen his girth with increasing years. A close-clipped beard, a hearty manner, with a few more inches he could have played Falstaff. His son, Pawlet, had rooms next to my old staircase at John's, and looked after teak forests in Burma until his father's death, when he followed on at the hall. His sister Olive married Shearme a naval lieutenant.

Baseley's adventures in search of a wife in the years after Mrs. Grigson's death amazed his friends. As a start he became engaged to a spinster lady near Diss – "plentifully endowed with this world's goods" – as he told us with a candour that was disarming. She was of a suitable age, genuinely pious and settled in her quiet ordered existence. Baseley had a way with him, gallant and persuasive. But when his legs were under the mahogany, and a good dinner inside him, he might have appeared a little too highly flavoured for maidenly timidity. Whatever was the cause after some months we learned that a marriage would not take place. He took the rebuff very much to heart, and went as winter chaplain to a Swiss resort. Here he met a daughter of Sir George Wills, the chairman of the Imperial Tobacco Company. Baseley was old enough to be her father, but his winning way led her into an engagement. Next summer father and daughter came on a visit to Baseley. Again the poor man was thrown overboard, perhaps mercifully for both. There being more fish in the sea than ever came out of it, Baseley, with heavy heart and heavier purse, decided on a voyage round the world. He quartered his horse on me, "meat for manners". Kitty was due to foal that spring, so the arrangement suited us both. I had sent her to a sire belonging to Lord Fisher, and Admiral Jacky himself supervised the nuptials, and said to Barrett – "Tell your master if that hasn't fixed her up nothing will". It did, and Kitty safely dropped a lovely filly foal the image of herself. Meanwhile Baseley visited Ceylon where he had a sister, and Burma to see Pawlet. He went on to the East Indies, China and Japan, and crossed the Pacific to California. In the romantic West he fell in love with a comely widow of the late governor of Arizona. We heard nothing more until the news that he and the belle of Arizona were married in London, There was a joyous homecoming, and they had a great welcome, for his parishioners genuinely liked their rector. The new Mrs. Grigson was in every way a good companion to her spouse, handsome, fond of society, bright and interested in her new home. So all was for the best in the best possible of worlds. They looked down upon us all from a giant Minerva car, the windows of which I have no doubt were rose-tinted.

> **FUNERAL OF THE REV. B. H. GRIGSON.**
>
> The funeral of the late rector of East Harling, the Rev. Baseley Hales Grigson, took place yesterday, the magnificent church of the parish being well filled with a congregation representing more or less the whole of the Harling and Thetford district. The committal was performed by the Bishop of Thetford, who, in the prior parts of the service, had the assistance of the Rev. C. A. Sturgess-Jones, rector of Garboldisham, who read the lesson, and the Rev. Leonard Wilson rector of Redgrave. Miss Pole, who was at the organ, rendered some suitable introductory music, including the air, "O Rest in the Lord," as the congregation were assembling, and the "Dead March" in "Saul" as the coffin, borne by ringers and men of the choir, was taken to the grave. "On the Resurrection Morning" was the only hymn sung. The Psalm and Nunc Dimittis were chanted. The mourners were: Mrs. Grigson (the widow), Mrs. Shearme (daughter), Commander Shearme, R. N. (son-in-law), Mrs. Pawlet Grigson (daughter-in-law), Mr. Jack Grigson (nephew), Mr. J. B. T. Hales, and Dr. R. T. Hales.
>
> Thetford Board of Guardians and Rural District Council were represented by Mr. J. Henry Cronshey (Vice-Chairman of the Guardians,) the Rev. J. C. Wilson (Vice-Chairman of the District Council), Mr. W. West, Mr. W. D. Dixon, Mr. E. Cross, Mr. N. J. Barker, and Mr. W. J. Haywood (Clerk).
>
> Also in the congregation were Lord Fisher, Sir Hugh Beevor, Miss Nugent, Miss Violet Nugent, Capt. T. H. Foster, N.R., Mr. Edmund Beevor, Mr. W. J. Barton (East Dereham), The Rev. R. Jones, R.D. (Banham), and Mrs. Jones, the Rev. C. L. Norris (Blo' Norton), Mr. Murton-Webb (Knettishall), Mr. and Mrs. J. N. C. Ray, Major Denny, Mr. H. Freeman, The Rev. C. H. R. Harper (Riddlesworth), The Rev. C. J. Eastwood (Lopham), Major Edward Mornement and Mrs. Mornement, Mr. W. R. Pollard, Dr. and Mrs Adams, Mr. and Mrs. Edwards, Miss Spellman (Norwich), The Rev. J. T. Poole (Wilby), The Rev. R. W. Pitt, The Rev. H. S. Rowley (Wretham), Mr. and Mrs. Walter Kerridge, The Rev. J. J. Morgan, The Rev. W. E. Tourtel (Norwich), The Rev. G. W. Watson (Shropham), Mr. and Mrs. John Hall, Mrs Coldham and Mr. Henry Hewitt. Canon E. S. Garnier, who should have taken part in the service, was kept away by illness.
>
> January 1924

Garboldisham Street and Church.

Unfortunately he did not live long to enjoy these added comforts.

Another of the five surrounding parishes that touched West Harling was Garboldisham, whose rector, Charles Lewis Kennaway, was even more of a sportsman than Grigson, and also a good painstaking parson. Wilfrid Blunt said of him – "In spring he's away fishing, he plays cricket all summer, he shoots and hunts through autumn and winter" – which was perfectly true. He and his wife kept several hunters in the stable, he shot at least three days a week in season, guns, bats, rods and pipes were more evident than the books in his study. All the same his church, schools, and parish, were competently and efficiently worked. He was a nephew of Sir John Kennaway the patriarchal squire of a parish near Exeter. He once drove four-in-hand to see his nephew in Norfolk. Later he paid me a visit, taking back a sack of my potatoes to Devon for seed. He was chairman of the C.M.S., (Church Missionary Society) and said to me "I hope you'll get my nephew to support it instead of the S.P.G. (Society for the Propagation of the Gospel).

I think today the English parsons who farm their own glebe and share in the work, the interest and enjoyments of country life, must be few in number. They had their weak spots, but, all the same, they had an influence and understanding of their people that the more cloistered type could not possess.

Riddlesworth with Gatesthorpe (Gasthorpe) and Knettishall, west of Kennaway's parish, further along the West Harling border, had an elderly rector, John Robinson Wells, whose father had been rector of the same parish before him. He was a gray-haired, quiet man, who kept a good horse, and gardener, but read little of his father's large library. With wife and three daughters, I found them kind but rather dull. After his wife's death Wells seemed to need any little help I could give him.

My last bordering parson neighbour was Thomas Robinson, vicar of Rushford with Brettenham. His house, that belonged to John Musker, was the partly modernised remainder of the mediaeval Collegium placed here against the ford over the Great Ouse, now crossed by a picturesque old bridge. A stately tower, and a high pitched aisle, were all that remained of the Collegiate church, but they made a seemly sanctuary. The Robinsons loved their charming house and grounds, that they both had beautified during years of happy work. But when she became an invalid, most of the labour fell on him, for they could not afford much outside help, and he hated her to see uncut lawns and fewer flowers. He was a cultured and sympathetic man, not really strong enough for all the cycling and manual work he must needs do. He died suddenly, little past middle age, after I had gone to Riddlesworth.

Rushford College, used as the Rectory.

Brettenham Church.

East Anglian Humour and Dialect

Bridgham was an 'open' parish, having no resident squire before John Musker bought Roudham for his youngest son. I think it can justly be said that the housing and general amenities of cottagers in the 'closed' parishes of the large landowners were a good deal better than the open localities. The comparatively small farms and other holdings resulted in a different type of population, and Bridgham for long past was backward and primitive. Some housing was bad, with consequent deterioration in the inhabitants. The coarseness of language and blunt directness of habitual speech, upon subjects never alluded to in polite society, was not so much a mark of decadence as of earlier English custom. The older among these remote village people, in the end of the nineteenth century, had much of the speech and point of view of at least a couple of centuries earlier. Their sense of humour was nearly always associated with natural functions, in which they saw nothing to be ashamed of. Conversation up and down Bridgham village street, and bandied across the road, was always flavoursome, but often hardly printable. But it was so honest and revealing, that it would be a pity to lose all record of these sayings. Chaucer and Shakespeare did not hesitate to portray the candours of English vulgar speech, and I shall shelter my puny pen behind these great masters.

Maeterlinck in his book of the bee, I think describes a village seen from a hill, and then goes down into the street for a further picture. The first portrayal is full of romantic beauty, the colours, the shapes, the sounds, the sight of labourers in the fields, and figures in the doorways. He conjures up a score of charming sentiments. And then he tell us, as a bitter jest, how vile and cruel are these peoples' words, how drab and futile their narrow lives. It appears to me to be a false comparison; that worth and even beauty are down there in the village street, and among the people, as well as from the artist's eyrie on the hill. Rancour and ugliness are to be found among all sorts and conditions of men, and to my mind they are more unpleasant when covered by the veneer of cultured manners.

In East Anglian villages, when intermarriages were chiefly from the immediate locality, and anyone from the outside 'sheers' was dubbed a 'foreigner', names of families recurred in the church registers for centuries. Among the Anglo-Saxons were a few Norman, Scandinavian, Huguenot and Low-Country types. The common speech of all was not the slow deep utterance of the west, but quick, often rather jerky explosion of short sentences, with a rising inflection in place of the dropping tones of elsewhere. Unlike the cockney, aspirates were never dropped. This rising intonation is well illustrated by the old story of the balloonist calling from the air to a Norfolk labourer in the field – "Where are we?" "Whar are ye?" "Yes,

The Street, Bridgham.

where are we?" "Whoy, y'are up in a balleune!" – ending on a high note.

"Thar goo old doctor Soffe agin to see Lady Flatt" – the wife of the squire, rector, or big farmer had this honorary title. "What be t'matter wi' she? "Happen she've got a fart gone crossways agin, I expec' ".

"Marnin, Missis Cutter." "Marnin, Missis Meek." The latter's greeting is not cordial, so the former utters a loud aside – "Garn wi' yar, sometimes yar all honey, an' sometimes yar all turd."

"That there mawther be a dawdles. A man's wages wou'dn' goo nowheres wi' she. She's too fond o' tardries."

"I don' racken nothen o' yar groceryman. He sawdles everythin' he sells yar."

"Marnin, Missis. Hop' yar slep' well. "No, I didn'. Everythin' fare to'be contraversary t' marnin'. A flea kep' bitin' my arternune all las' night." "Yar sh'd drive 'im inter bushy park, Missis, an' I'll come an' catch'm for 'ee. Ha! Ha!"

One man's wife was thin and bony. He was hoeing roots in the small piece of arable glebe on the further side of the road, when a passer-by hailed him jocularly – "Thee'd best be gittin' home, an' look arter tha missis. That's a packman up thar'll be sellin' she more'n thee'll wanter keep." "I an't worryin' nothen, bor," he said. "Taint no matters du he goo thar he'll get cut. Well I knows it. Let'm goo."

Sir Robert Buxton of Shadwell, newly wed, came to Larling for a political meeting. He was late, and farmer John Steggles was in the chair. "Good evening ladies and gentlemen," said Sir Robert, "I must apologise for being late. The fact is I got out of bed late this morning, and I haven't caught up all day." "Don't yar apolergize, Sir Robert," said Mr. Steggles. "If I had a loverly lady to lay along o' me like yar hev' I would'n git up all day, danged if I would." "Thank you Mr. Steggles, thank you very much indeed for the compliment", said Lady Buxton delightedly.

The education of wives, and a woman's last word, were matters of importance and humour to husbands. 'Happy Meek' had lately married, and came back several mornings from his early work for his breakfast to find his young wife had 'laid late'. He complained when he found no fire and no breakfast ready for his return. She made excuse that "I could'n fare t' make it burn." He said to a friend – "That thar fule, Jack Seaman, he allus made hes fire hesself, an' took hes wife up a cup o' tay in bed. But I war'nt agoin' t' hev sech monkey tricks along o' mine. I've on'y half an hour t' git my brekfus, an' due I means t' be comfurabul, that got t'be ready when I comes in. So when tha's happen' three times, I ketched her a master crack o' t' skull, an' said t' her – Tha'll larn yar ter light a fire! I sez, an' so t'did (complacently) an' I don' wanter better wife than mine's bin sence. She howled gude tidily at t' fust goo off, but we was soon right as rain agin'.

A woman's persistence in having her 'say' is shown by the frequent jest – "she had to tell 'm tho' she comed t'm wi' har t'roat cut." Jimmy Alderton used to tell 'Lisbeth the following as a warning – "There was a man so dunted by's wife's tongue that he ducked her i' t' pit. Twice she comed up hollerin' at 'm, an' t' third time she said "ssss – scissors –" (sound of expiring breath). She didn' come up no more, but she had the last word!."

On the Broads, up and down the reaches of the Yare and Waveney rivers, there sailed at the end of the century many tall-masted wherries so familiar in the pictures of Crome, Cotman and Stark. The single great russet-tanned sail , with the mast stepped right forward in a tabernacle enabling it to be lowered for bridges, made close pointing into the wind and quick handling easy. The greeting was invariably a chanted musical – "Thar yar goo, bor!" answered by "Ah! thar yar goo!". Often gaily painted in reds, greens, blues and yellows, with a bright pennant for vane at the masthead, these craft on a background of silver stream, woods and reeds or old houses, made Broadland a painter's dream. The wherry man's salutation from passing boats, is also commonly used among other greetings by people meeting on the roads. "Thar yar goo, bor!" "Yes thar yar goo, bor!" A newcomer to a circle seated on the settle before the fire at a public house would say "Thar yar sett together bors!" "Yes, hyar we sett, bor!" There is a station on the Harling-Norwich line named Hethersett, and countryfolk passing through in the train often make a joke as the porter calls out the name of the station – "Ah bor! tha's right, hyar we sett."

Chaffing questions and remarks were frequent especially from older to younger – "Du yar mother keep a dicky, bor?" To which the correct riposte was – "Yes, and if she'd had yew she'd ha' had tew."

Jokes at the expense of neighbouring localities are found among all people in all ages. Norfolk spoke of "silly Suffolk", that the county antiquarians said meant Anglo-Saxon *saelig* (holy) but the commonalty riposted with the nickname "Norfolk dumplings." East Harling said West Harling was nothen but flies, fules an' gates." Or another – "What' yar goin?" "Harling Heath, after a faggit, come an' help me drag it." and again – "Whar' yar from?" "I come from Swaffham, whar they doos a day's troshen for nothen."

A few more words in old-time use in some districts of East Anglia, that was an isolated Anglo-Saxon kingdom, are – "spaffle" for babble, "lannock" for romp, "buffled' bothered, "holl " hedge, "duller" lament, "dother" a row. In some places a scarecrow is called a "boggart" instead of the more usual "mauken". "That wholly fare t' be a right master bit, that that wholly du" was East Anglian praise for anything they approved. I hope not one of them would give me a 'verdic' like the above.

VISITORS AND VISITS

From time to time I had a friend or two to stay, but I was a long way from everywhere. Two interesting men from the British Museum came each for a night or two – one looking for traces of Thomas Nashe, poet and pamphleteer in the reign of Elizabeth, the other seeking information about Philip Gawdy, whose Letters he was editing on behalf of Lord Amherst of Hackney, for a volume to be published by the Roxburgh Club, founded by Lord Rosebery. I enjoyed these two strangers so much, that on both occasions I persuaded my caller to stay. Nashe lived at the rectory, probably the old one near the church. Philip Gawdy, like so many men of family of his time was more concerned to marry an heiress than to serve his country. Both men afforded certain sidelights on history though of minor importance. Lord Amherst sent me a copy of this privately issued volume.

My schoolfellow Tucker after his mathematical honours at Balliol went as headmaster to Trent College. He came to stay with me, and during his visit asked if I would care to look after a young fellow who, with his brothers had been at Trent. Guy Cutforth, in his last term at school, had become epileptic after an attack of typhoid caught in Switzerland. His parents wanted to find a country home for him, where he would be away from the dangers arising from his condition. With the boy and his father I interviewed several specialists. There seemed little hope of cure. After talking it over with my household I agreed to let him come for a time. The open air life, gardening and simple interests were all helpful. I kept charts for his doctors, and there was improvement but not final. Off and on he stayed with me a good many months during about fifteen years. Mary Ann was always very good to him. At other times I coached Musker and Popham boys for Eton entrance exams.

Absent Minded Horseman

In our part, before motors and telephones, a custom existed and I hope may still obtain, of open house welcome and hospitality to all and sundry. People dropped in to lunch or tea without any formality. Pot-luck was the accepted menu. In the country there is always something to eat and drink, if not fine yet sufficient. One's unexpected visitors were usually from a little further afield than the next parishes. Rev George Dennis of Hopton often rode or drove across for lunch. He had been a chaplain in India retiring with a pension of one

Croxton Village.

pound a day, that, doubled by his rectory and some private means made a comfortable man of him. He loved a beautiful horse and smart turnout, and was an accomplished horseman. Notwithstanding, on coming through the wood into my garden, I once found him seated on his horses head in the middle of my rosebed. He was quietly smoking his pipe waiting for someone to turn up. Around him was the wreckage of my gate post and of a beautiful four-wheel cart. No one had seen him arrive and he started to take his horse out in the yard by himself, as he was perfectly competent to do. But by some momentary forgetfulness, he slipped off the bridle before undoing the traces and taking the horse out of the shafts. The animal moved, got agitated, and being under no control pulled the cart against the gate post, turning it over and coming down on his side on my lawn and rosebed. Dennis was the only skater around, and always let me know when Riddlesworth lake bore ice, when we would make a day of it.

Hentley Curtois, vicar of Croxton, and I exchanged occasional dine-and-sleep visits. He was fond of books and we exchanged volumes. Still more interesting was picturesque old Mr. William Chas. Green, rector of Hepworth, beyond the Suffolk border. He arrived on a tricycle, puffing and blowing from exertion over our loose sandy gravel road. He was a fellow of Eton, a senior classic and an Icelandic scholar. His hobby was the 'cello that he played with great facial expression, his long gray hair about his ears and brow, his lips pursed, his eyes rolling, his short arms and legs all moving. With a bottle of whisky at his elbow he could be persuaded in his eighties to sit before my fire and talk till midnight, coming down next morning fresh as a boy for his long ride home. His rectory had not been painted inside or out for half a lifetime, from its appearance. But he and his sweet old wife hospitably and graciously received their appreciative guests.

John Sikes Sawbridge

I fished the lake of Livermere Park, which like that of Redgrave held large pike. With John Sikes Sawbridge my first catch at Redgrave was a nice fish that he got stuffed for me in Norwich. 'Old John' as he was affectionately known was loved far and wide. He was a gaunt, tall, ruddy-faced man with a big nose and fatherly manner. He was truly religious, earnest, simple-hearted, charitable. At the same time he had the fullest appreciation of every aspect of country life. With his humble parishioners he loved to speak the genuine Suffolk dialect, to their delight and without in the least losing their respect. His rectory at Thelnetham close to the good church was a family house as indeed it needed to be, for he had, I think, ten children. I once saw a photograph of the whole family on horseback. They made a line that must have been twelve riders including those on the pony and donkey. Jack, the eldest son was at Eton, and became a parson. His brother Bartle went to Winchester. We three did a good many things together, and I look back on their friendship with many happy thoughts. Old John's enthusiasm for his church festivals was tremendous. He was always trying to rope me in for special occasions. To see him presiding at a 'hawkey' was a subject for a painter's brush or for serious study by a radical reformer. His children enjoyed their home and countryside as much as he did, and, remarkably, they were just as keen on the church services. Father was again the nightly dispenser of little cigars and port to the elder boys, with chocolates and other dainties for the girls. Merry stories and laughter went around. Mrs. Sawbridge was, alas, an invalid, but very charming when able to come downstairs. In my earlier years I often spent a week with them, and I still have a garden spud, a walking stick, pencils and other little gifts that Old John loved to shower upon his friends.

PEDDARS WAY

Of the many ancient tracks that crossed Breckland, the one nearest my house crossed a bridge over the Thet, separating West Harling from Bridgham parish. Southward this track led to a ford over the Ouse at Riddlesworth, passing on the Suffolk side a lonely cottage known as 'America', perhaps so called from its far off position. Northward from Bridgham it crossed Roudham Heath, and could be traced for a great many miles to Swaffham. Its name may have come from the pedlar who long ago, according to the story, found a treasure or acquired some wealth on his journeys to and fro between London and Swaffham. He became a benefactor of Swaffham church, where an old oak pew-end carving shows him with his dog at his feet, and his staff and pack over his shoulder. I have spent whole days along Peddars Way and not met anyone. There is a mere called Thompson's Water and near it a beautiful old church. Like other Breckland meres it has many shells that are said to yield fresh water pearls. The black-headed gull nests in thousands at Scoulton Mere beyond Attleborough, where I have seen them rise from the island in winged clouds that obscured the sky. To me there was a great attraction in the solitudes of Breckland. I felt a pull towards these wastes, the desire to get away from everyone, to walk under the high sky, over the wide expanses, to feel the wind and the sun, strong clean and invigorating.

Peddars Way.

GRIMES' GRAVES

Flint artefacts were everywhere in this county. Once I arrived at Grimes' Graves not far from Brandon, at the very hour that an archaeological excavation of one of the pits was completed. Only the scientist with his labourers were present, and he invited me to descend the ladder into the chalk. I had joined others in a small subscription towards this enquiry, and now I saw several low tunnels made by stone-age man, and boulder flints excavated ready to be hauled to the surface, the marks of the deer-hide thongs still visible on the chalk walls. The ashes of a primitive man's fire were on the floor, and further off in a gallery lay many antlers used as picks, left there just as they were dropped by the ancient diggers. Everything was photographed with care and microscopic examination before the pit was refilled. At Brandon flints were still made for guns used by Arabs and West African natives by a family that had been flint knappers for many generations. The flints of different sizes from pistol to elephant gun were packed in barrels for export. The knapper made me a

Flint-Knappers at Brandon.

set, and included some arrow and spear-heads sharp and skilfully made. They had not the polish of old artefacts, but nevertheless required great skill to make, as I found when I tried my hand at knapping. I expect this industry has now passed away for ever.

TREASURE TROVE

In my garden I once dug up a beautifully-finished, golden-coloured, little adze of the flint-age. There were plenty of scraper flakes all over the parish, and the much later gun-flints occasionally turned up. My garden also yielded a little cylindrical pierced object of fire-clay that was used in curling wigs on a block. I dug up several very early types of clay tobacco pipes, always broken, and an old, silver spoon much battered. These, with a few coins, are about all the treasure-trove my garden digging yielded.

GHOSTIES AND ECCENTRICS

At Rockland, from which our rural deanery took its name, was a wood, said to be that where the bodies of the babes murdered by the wicked uncle were covered with leaves by the robins. No one who has heard at night the eerie voice of the large brown Norfolk plover, now getting rare, like the cry of a lost soul, out of the blackness of the heath, will wonder at the queer fancies of the Brecklanders.

Solitary cottagers in out-of-the-way spots sometimes developed strange antipathies and exhibited eccentric beliefs and behaviour. Two old women I used to visit, who lived next door to one another in a very secluded part, I found had not spoken to each other for many years. When I came up to the honeysuckle covered porch of one of the pretty dwellings I caught sight of a hand placing something behind the pots of geranium in the window. "What a nice aroma of tobacco," I said as I entered, and feeling behind the pot I pulled out the warm pipe, saying – "Ah, here is the smoker," and persuaded the old lady to resume her pipe, at the same time lighting my own. We became friends, so much so that she made me various herbal concoctions for small ailments from time to time. But she would give me no clue to her animosity against her neighbour, who was an equally well-conducted person, and her cottage similarly well-kept and comfortable. The most she ever said to me was – "I don't hold wi' her principle – she frame," [pretends]. Greatly daring, I invited them both to tea at a slightly different hour. Their natural good manners prevented their showing surprise or ill feeling when confronting one another at my table, but they spoke only to me, and I thought it best to respect this convention. However a year or two afterwards the 'framer' fell sick, and the 'wise woman' next door was so pleased with an opportunity to show her skill that all of a sudden they became skilful nurse and grateful patient. The medical qualification of my friend may be judged from what she told me about the cause of the rector of Blo' Norton's deafness. "When t' Reverend Norris he wor called on to see an atheist what wor a'dyin', an' fared wholly frighted o' t' divvel, nex' day t' reverend come he fared t' be dead. But Mr. Norris he ask for a piece o' glass, an' put 't hes mouth. He's not dead, there's damp on't. Then t' man shruck an' bruk t' glass t' smothersends, hollerin' out Save me! 'an ketched t' reverend round's neck so's he swallered t' dyin' breath. T' reverend git' troat bad, an' had t' be operated, an' wor deafer an' deafer ivver arter." Norris was a little bird-like bright eyed man with a delightful winning smile. He had several children and a poor living. He was an excellent clergyman who deserved a better paid benefice that, so far as I know, he never obtained. His father had been rector of Blo' Norton before him. Prince Freddy Duleep-Singh lived at the small old hall, and was a friend to them, but could not be a benefactor.

GYPSIES AND POACHERS

I was driving once with old John Sawbridge, who stopped at a tiny bridge under which was a streamlet. "That," he said playfully, "is the Great Ouse. This side is *sealig* Suffolk, the other is not so holy Norfolk. Our noble river is well described by the name of this village on its banks – The Belles Eaux of Norton. (Blo' Norton)." A strip of land opening into this same lane was used every year by gypsies wintering in their caravans. It sloped to the south and was sheltered from the north. The mother of one family sometimes called at my house, and Mary Ann bought a few clothes pegs, and gave her pots for her husband to solder. She was a remarkably fine specimen of a woman, straight, brown-faced, slim, agile, trim ankles and wrists, tireless, walking erect like a princess. She looked not more than five and twenty yet had twelve living, healthy children. These gypsies were not liked by landowners and farmers for they helped themselves to game, rabbits and roots as opportunities offered. Nor did the cottage folk ever make friends with them. They always have been, like the Jews, a race apart.

We had living in our district some members of a family, not gypsy, who were hereditary poachers on the great estates upon and

"Squire" and gamekeepers: Bob Coote, Charlie Riches (?), Sir Edmund Nugent, Jerry Riches, ?, ?.

surrounding Breckland. Every week in autumn and winter consignments of game were sent by these people to London, under the noses of landlords and their gamekeepers. Very rarely did one of these skilful fellows get brought up before petty sessions, but in that event any fine was cheerfully paid from their ample funds. One night a fracas took place near my rectory at Riddlesworth. In the darkness the under-keeper got hold of his man. The head keeper said "Hang on to him Jim whiles I gits his gun and bag." The younger keeper mistook this for an order to catch hold of the game bag and gun, and loosed his grip of the poacher who escaped. Unfortunately for him, his cap fell off in the struggle. He was charged and put in an alibi that he slept that night at his brother's house near Newmarket, but the cap bore his name, and gun and bag were also recognised. He was a fine upstanding fellow, and John Musker thought it a brilliant notion to offer to make him a keeper on one of his estates at a good wage. "No thankee, Sir. 'Tarn yar manny thanks all t' same, but I've a better job on me own." I knew this member of the poaching family who showed deep pleasure in his unlawful calling – "'tis my delight on a shiny night in the season of the year." But they overreached themselves when they bought a fast motor lorry, and collected game in one night from widely separated estates, and were in London by daybreak. This was getting beyond gamekeepers' control, and the police came heavily into action and nipped this hopeful industry in the bud.

Canon Sawbridge, for he got a well deserved stall, though without fodder, at Ely, rented mixed shooting for his sons over commons and marshes where, if you walked far enough, you were pretty sure of something turning up for the pot. Parsons and poachers have fellow feelings, Jack used to say. Sir Edmund told me of an old parson who, whenever there was a big shoot, used to get his man to put a comfortable armchair from which the rector could pot every bird that came over the glebe from all the drives. Wilfrid Blunt was just such another. At nightfall he would sit on a camp stool in his willow beds or other shelters waiting for the pheasants to perch for the night in the trees on the West Harling side of the river. Bang, and down they would tumble for him to pick up in the punt. On the other side of his glebe he had John Musker's birds to shoot at. At our Sunday night meals he would point to a dish of roast pheasant saying, "That one bears the badge of the bloody hand," i.e. of a baronet, and, " this one won't go to Selfridges." In snow we sometimes donned white sheets to await the wild duck or geese flighting over after sundown. I had a double-barrel twelve bore of no great value, a collector's gun, and a .22 rifle. The last was a weapon of precision. The bullets, long or short, of the tiny copper-cased cartridges would kill a rabbit at two hundred yards. Once, by luck, I got three rabbits with one bullet and several times had a brace. The little rifle was always a pleasure to use. It was sighted up to five hundred yards, and had wind-gauge allowances. At night it was deadly against pheasants roosting high in trees. Aligning the bright sight tips against the dark object backed by a star, a click not greater than the snap of a finger – and the heavy bird fell stone dead at your feet. This sounds reprehensibly like occasional poaching, but I was in my legal rights on my own land, and though I had not bred the pheasants they had lived on my brussel sprouts and other winter vegetables. Ground and other game were an important item on our table. Most of the year I could shoot a few half grown rabbits for a pie, whenever they were wanted. With some slices of bacon, I know of no pleasanter dish, hot or cold for a picnic.

RABBIT VERSUS STOAT

One Christmas Eve a stoat killed two rabbits and laid them on my back door step. On a summer evening I once saw a buck rabbit defend himself against the attack of a stoat in the open field. Again and again the stoat tried to get round to the rabbits front in order to fasten on its throat or neck. But the rabbit, wheeling about, threatened it with its powerful hind legs that could break its back. Until then I did not know that a rabbit could defend itself against a stoat or weasel.

THE HERO

> On summer eves I'd wont to roam
> In the glebe pastures round my home,
> And there with pipe and book I'd sit
> And watch the sun setting o'er it.
> Then from the covert near would steal
> Many a rabbit for its meal;
> A doe with young did nibble and frisk,
> And a bold buck his scut did whisk.

> Once from a tree root crept a stoat
> To seize the coney by its throat;
> And now began a wondrous sight,
> For the jack rabbit stood to fight.
> When all the rest popped into burrows
> He held his stance to save his morrows;
> He stamped his hind pads on the ground,
> That gave out a repellent sound
> So fierce it made the varmint pause,
> Sheer off a bit to learn the cause.
> Then, edging round, the wily stoat
> Sought place to spring at t'other's throat;
> But jack, as quick as lightning, he
> Turned his back on 's enemy,
> And as the fellow sprang he kicked
> With legs that hit and claws that slit
> The throat of the voracious sinner,
> Who thought to have jack for his dinner.
> I think not in a century
> Would anyone such a fine fight see.
> Yet there are good people who say
> Jack shouldn't have acted in this way,
> But when his enemy drew near
> He should have turned the other ear,
> And not have smitten him with his rear.
> And what about good Missis Doe
> With her young family below?
> If Jack had showed himself a craven
> They'd have been murdered in their haven.

Hares were scarce at West Harling but plentiful at Riddlesworth where I often got a leveret. I have said it was dangerous to ride horseback off the roads at West Harling, the ground being so burrowed by rabbits. Once or twice every year a stag of the drag-hunt came in our direction, and invariably made for the rectory. He would cool himself in my pond, sniff round stable and cowshed, and when the hunt came down the drive leapt the yard gate light as a feather, and went down to the river where he was hard to recover. He used to live on the root crops till he was caught again, sometimes months after.

A BITTERN PASSES

Red squirrels, the great green woodpecker called yaffle, and jays – all colourful creatures – loved the great beech trees against my garden. In several trees the drooping branches had rooted themselves to grow up big and strong round the parent stem, like the banyan. Wilfrid Blunt and I were keen to preserve the rarer nesting and migrating birds. At one winter sunsetting, Jack Riches was walking the river bank, when a strange bird flew over. He brought it down with a shot, but stooping to lift it from the reeds, it struck him near the eye with its sharp beak. It was a bittern, whose boomings were once frequently heard on the Broads, but not often now. The long dagger-like beak is a formidable weapon, and Jack was lucky not to lose his eye. He took the bird to Sir Edmund, who, much pleased to add it to his collection, sent it to London to be stuffed. Wilfrid stirred up the ornithologists, and, in atonement, the bittern was sent to the Norwich museum in the castle, where there is a magnificent case of bustards. These great golden birds were once native in Breckland. What a meal one of them would make! I fear few are left in the world today. But bitterns have returned to the Broads to some extent.

*Shooting Party at West Harling 1893-4:
Brig. Gen. George Nugent, Bob Coote, Jerry Riches,
Charlie Riches, George Barnard, Sir Edmund,
Fred Hanton, Charles Endley.*

COTTAGE WEAVERS

In the pre-machine age many rural parishes in England supported some particular industry in addition to agriculture and the arts and crafts necessary for local life. To East Anglia French Huguenots brought their weaving industry, and taught many of the inhabitants this craft. When I first came to Norfolk there still existed in North and South Lopham parishes of our rural deanery, linen weavers with their looms in their cottages, who wove linen tablecloths and napkins of the finest quality. They worked for a Mr. Buckenham who lived in a pretty, old, small house near North Lopham church. I got to know him, and several times spent a few hours in his parlour, where one felt to be back in the eighteenth century. The Lophams, like so many of our Norfolk-Suffolk remote parishes, seemed completely

untouched by modernism, at the beginning of the twentieth century. Mr. Buckenham told me his family had been weaving linen there for generations. He had a few looms in buildings near his house and in other cottages. Latterly, everything he could produce went to one of the great London clubs. When he died a few years later, this village industry finished for ever.

The Magic Carpet

By now I had in my coach house a little machine that enabled me to cross England in a day's ride, and traverse all the roads and lanes of the country as easily as turning the pages of a lovely illustrated book. I was always fond of bicycles, and judged that from most points of view this type of motor vehicle would suit me best. All the early motors were ugly, inefficient and expensive, and in short supply to the public. But we had the joy of seeing Britain when the roads and countryside were quiet and almost unchanged from coaching times. In those early years I have ridden a whole day without meeting another motor. I had written a little account of travels on my old Beeston-Humber pedal-cycle, that the makers published. In return they gave me a new machine, and also let me have one of their latest motor bicycles on favourable terms. From time to time I wrote touring and semi-technical articles on the new motoring for the Press. 'Great are the uses of advertisement'. British manufacturers were now learning from U.S.A., but I drew in my horns when I found my name one day printed large on the advertising pages of the London morning papers; and again when the *Times* printed a short letter in which I commended its edition of the *Encyclopaedia Britannica* I had just bought. However I did enjoy one little bit of notoriety, when a small boy seeing my motor-cycle numberplate that I was using as a nom de plume for a series of touring articles, called out – "Look Bill, here's the bloke what's riding round England." I certainly found great interest in the constant improvements in motor-cycles, and in a small way suggested various details and gadgets from my own experience, particularly for greater silence and cleanliness.

Rev. Blunt on his Dyson Motorette, with wall autowheel engine attachment.

Until the war I took delivery of a new motor-cycle each spring. It was my magic carpet for in an hour or so I could be fifty miles on my way to anywhere I liked. A few pints of what looked like water, costing at first well under a shilling a gallon, and so well refined it would clean your handkerchief, yielded power enough to carry me and my luggage over two hundred miles without having to stop the engine or get out of the saddle. I did not often make these long, non-stop, quick, cross-country journeys, but my route from West Harling to the West Country became so familiar that I could almost have followed it blindfold – Cambridge, Oxford, Bath, Portishead – any day I could make that leap and have an evening with the parents. Duty did not often allow, but the power to cover the miles was mine, by means of this little machine. I was fascinated by thinking what the motor was going to do for the world. I saw chiefly the plus quantities of the equation. The minus were to become visible to later generations.

Apple Pie Bed for Jacky Fisher

Quidenham is the seat of the Keppel family. King Edward stayed with Lord Albemarle two or three times when I was at West Harling. Mrs. George Keppel [Alice] was often 'commanded'; for her wit and charm made her a great favourite of the King. The countess, heiress of Lord Egerton of Tatton was by no means so fond of Mrs. George, who did not often appear at Quidenham for unroyal occasions. She once told a very

King Edward VII's visit to Quidenham, October 1909.
Back Row, L to R: Viscount Bury, Hon. Col. George Keppel, Canon Edward Garnier, Sir George Halford, ?, ?.
Middle Row, L to R: Earl of Derby, Lord Haldane, Earl of Albemarle, Earl of Leicester (Lord Lt. of Norfolk).
Front Row, L to R: Lady Chelsea, Viscountess Bury, Countess of Albemarle, King Edward VII, Countess of Leicester, Hon. Mrs. George Keppel, Lady Elizabeth Keppel.

King Edward VII.

Mrs. George Keppel.

funny story at the dinner table, and when Queen Alexandra, rather deaf, saw everyone laughing and asked what it was about, Mrs. George instantly told her a quite different story, but equally funny, that amused the King and everyone even more than the first. The King and some of his guests drove over to Kilverstone to see Admiral Fisher. "Let's go and see how Jacky Fisher does for himself in his new house." And I was told the King also said – "Let's go up and make Jacky an apple-pie bed," that took the Admiral completely by surprise when he turned in. Thus 'the captains and the Kings' disport themselves in their lighter moments,

Kilverstone Church.

by all accounts ancient and modern – and why not? They have enough grave anxieties to bear them down at other times. I was driving in the lane at Quidenham just before the King's last illness, and as I came up to the road near the hall gates, the King's motor car drove past taking him to Norwich for the last public occasion of his life. I saluted him with crossed whip that he acknowledged with a friendly and gracious smile. Kitty and I returned home much gratified. The King left for Biarritz after his Norwich duties, and returned to England ill, and died soon afterwards.

The Colonial and Continental Society asked me to take the perpetual chaplaincy at Homburg and later at Biarritz when the King favoured those places. At the former I would have met Kaiser Wilhelm, and his royal uncle at both places, but I was not to have such honours. A Norfolk parson, Fellow by name, according to his own account was noticed by King Edward at Homburg, who said to his equerry, "Who is that handsome parson over there, like a cavalry officer?" The correct version of the King's question was – "Why is that damned parson wearing a moustache? Go and tell him to get it shaved off."

Facing Old Buckenham common, near Quidenham, lived Major Keppel, uncle of the earl, and brother of Admiral Sir Harry Keppel, the beloved and life-long friend of most of Queen Victoria's descendants. The Major, also a very small man, had all the great charm and humour of his family, and his wife was equally delightful. Living quite simply in their pretty rural house, they were kind and good to everyone about them high and low. Lunching with them before a garden-party, I found the major finishing cutting a lawn with his gardener. He was

Banham Village.

stripped to shirt and flannel trousers and sweating profusely. "I shall be finished in a minute, and then we'll go in and drink a bottle of beer before lunch." I congratulated him on his ability to drink beer as a septuagenarian. He said – "It's the only medicine I take and it keeps me out of my coffin."

This portion of our rural deanery was well outside Breckland, lacking its charm but more productive. Two parsons here I sometimes stayed with, Jones of Banham, and Upcher of Besthorpe. The former married Bishop Earle's daughter, who told a story of having once been kissed by Bismarck, and of another kiss she gave to Lord Chancellor Halsbury when thanking him for giving the valuable living of Banham to her Robert. The walls of Upcher's small drawing-room were hung with some of the most glorious landscapes Crome painted.

St Mary's, Kenninghall.

On the southern side of Quidenham park was the parish of Kenninghall, a compact village sheltered from north and east, its square towered old church dominating the little valley below. Tyler, its vicar, knew Charles Wood of Clapton-in-Gordano, my old friend in childhood. The lords of the manor of Kenninghall were the Dukes of Norfolk for centuries past, and to their palace here Queen Elizabeth paid more than one of those visits so heavy on the purses of her loyal subjects. Atkinson, rector of Larling, also in our deanery, was another link with Clapton, for his sister was wife to Mr. Horne who succeeded Charles Wood as rector on the latter's death.

Larling was a sandy breckland parish on the edge of Roudham Heath. Its old church stood on the north bank of the Thet near Larlingford, where now was a bridge that carried the high road from Thetford to Norwich. The tithes of Larling amounted to almost nothing, but Atkinson, out of his own pocket, built perhaps the best rectory in the deanery on a slope of glebeland well above the damps of the river meadows. The material was the same small, fine, white brick of a few other local houses, the rooms being lofty, opening on a pleasant garden. Atkinson welcomed me with open arms on my first coming, and the old couple were always most hospitable. They were child-like in their

St Ethelbert's, Larling.

simplicity and there was a story that Atkinson once took off a new broadcloth coat and gave it to a tramp. I was asked to take his funeral. The little church was packed as well as the churchyard by the poor cottagers from far around. They said to me, "He was a good man", which was exactly the text of my sermon. A world of Atkinsons is unlikely, but a few more simple, good people here and there would be an undoubted advantage. Major Keppel, carving beautifully the pulpit of Wintle's little church at Snetterton with his old gnarled hands, and John Sawbridge, affectionately gathering his people together for church services and village frolics, were only two of many lesser but still good examples in that remote countryside.

If anyone should ever read these annals they may well ask of what possible use were the parsons of Breckland and the Norfolk-Suffolk border? That question must needs include all rural England and all the quiet leisured people who for generations have lived in our villages and country towns. They were comfortably secured in their modest affluence, enjoying happily the sports and beauties of their environment, with some endowment of culture and education, traditional and acquired. Black sheep appeared here and there, but by and large the others set an example and made a standard that was looked up to, respected and sometimes even loved by those less fortunately circumstanced. Their sons and daughters carried on the record of good service in the community and abroad. Their religion was not often on their lips, but observable in kind actions and fair dealings.

Gandhi, who lived two years in England, said he came with the belief that Christianity was the highest type of religion in the world, the best suited to India. But, he declared, that he never found a single Christian in England, and went home to teach a different creed.

Einstein, I think, saw deeper when he said that kindness and just dealing have an element of eternity about them. Our shortcomings are many, but a love of justice, with a softening of kindliness, is found among all classes of the English speaking countries.

HAWKEY

Mrs. Mann, whose son rented Middle Harling farm for a few years, was accustomed to give a hawkey after every harvest in her husband's time, and continued to do so for her son. John Sikes Sawbridge, rector of Thelnetham, farmed some land there and at Coney Weston, that he inherited from his mother who was a Woodhouse. He was interested in preserving good, old customs and kindly intercourse among his parishioners. Where farms were small and poor, three or four generations would join together for a hawkey, the labourers as well as masters contributing. Both sides profited by a quick harvest. But if the weather turned bad, weeks might go by, and only the agreed sum accrued to the harvesters. In mitigation, piecework hoeing and singling of turnips was given if possible. The ancient word 'largesse' was always used for gifts in money or kind received by the 'lord of the harvest' (elected by fellow labourers) from the master, the men, friends and neighbours, towards the expenses of the 'frolic'. The 'lord' bought and distributed the daily beer ration for the harvesters. He arranged and portioned out the course of operations – the order of crops to be cut, the varying hours for starting and ending work according to weather and the condition of the corn.

At the end of the hawkey itself the 'hold ye' boys came forward for their competition. These were the envied lads chosen to lead the horses in the harvest fields, along the lines of stooks when the wagons were being loaded up. Immediately before each frequent re-start the boy's duty was to sing out "Hold ye" as a warning to the men on the top of the load to secure themselves from falling when the horses went forward. These clear ringing calls can be heard miles away in still weather, telling the whereabouts of harvest operations. The boys vied with each other in the clarity and strength of their shouts. During the hawkey frolic a grave circle of elders judged a contest of voices, and the prizewinner was patted on the back and felt like an Olympic champion. The farmer noted him for next bird-scaring, and the parson sighed for the top note of next Sunday's Te Deum – but then reflected that at least we could make a joyful noise to the God of our salvation.

[Ed. The following poem by Harper connects the role of the 'hold ye' boys of ages past with the Allies fighting to save civilisation in the second world war which was when he wrote both poem and autobiography].

HOLD YE

From the far harvest-field the boy's voice rings
Brilliant and brave as song of mounting lark –
'Hold ye.' Each loadman to a safe stance springs
As the wain's horses make their sudden start.

'Hold ye.' The golden aisles, the columned sheaves,
The ordered stooks in splendour richly stand.
Each pitcher to his wagon deftly heaves
The heartening bounty of our native land.

'Hold ye.' A richer harvest hence has grown,
Men valiant-wise, and women fair and good,
Who in a score of savage lands have sown
High freedom's seed that shall not be withstood.

And all the littler men – God's praise be theirs —
How have they lived, endured, and dumbly wrought,
That the new states, in their few hundred years,
A nobler life and future might be taught.

Hold ye the virtues of those earlier years,
That were the living bread of living men.
The world, through pride and greed, lies drowned
  in tears,
Having scant hope of peaceful life again.

Hold ye the hand of friendship to thy friend.
Hold ye the scales of justice for thy foe.
Hold forth the gift of mercy at the end.
And hold the sword to ensure it shall be so.

Hold ye the truth that life is more than gold.
Hold to the link of all men's brotherhood.
Hold to the faith 'tis splendid to grow old
And see the harvest of the Eternal Good.

THE FLOODS OF 1912

The summer of 1912 was very wet with much flooding. Evelyn Nugent recorded in her diary:

August 26th A continued downpour from morning to night.

August 27th Terence and I tried to get to see the cricket in Norwich, but found we could not get further than Wymondham. Norwich is under water, many bridges broken etc.

August 28th Floods out everywhere. I bicycled this morning to Mrs Wilson on the common, could not go by Mr Harper's because of the floods.

September 3rd A lot more money and parcels. Went with Sybil Montgomerie to the rectory and their working party for the flood victims.

September 5th Busy all the morning packing up and sending off five books for the Flood Relief Fund.

BRIDGHAM HARVEST'S PAST – 1912

[Ed. In Bridgham, Rev. Blunt was none too pleased to lose his fowls and hay-cocks down the flooded Thet. He upset the village by refusing to have a Harvest Festival, saying there was nothing to thank God for! Some of the villagers retaliated with the following poem].

There's a little village by the River Thet,
That have had no Harvest Festival yet,
The Rector has given as the reason
That this has been such a disastrous season.

The men have had to idle stand
While the crops be nothing on the land
or what is enough to make one shiver,
Are floating away down the flooded river.

Now we'll all admit that it's been a bad season,
But cannot say that is sufficient reason,
For withholding our thanks for what we have got.
It might have been worse had it all gone to rot.

Although the quality is not very good,
It's not all washed away with the flood.
Though it took a good while to gather together,
Most people have finished, in spite of the weather.

And now its complete, there's been plenty of growls,
Which must have been caused by the loss of the fowls.

A DOOMED TREE

The greensward on which the lychgate of West Harling churchyard opened was used by the village lads for their cricket. It extended from the ha-ha that crossed the vista, to the garden fence fronting the hall. About it at varying distances were a number of fine English forest trees – oaks, beeches, elms, and one magnificent chestnut. In this open position they had grown freely to great height and girth. The space for cricket was reasonably large enough for the game, boundary hits being

The Doomed Tree, West Harling Church and Hall with tree to the foreground.

counted for the trees, the nearest of which was the great chestnut. At all seasons this tree was a fine spectacle, towering high and spreading wide, in spring a mountain of snow, in autumn a cascade of gold, in summer a depth of cooling shade under which village spectators sat to watch the cricketers. In winter its branches shone in the sunset, glistened in the frosts and snows, vibrated with multitudinous notes in the winds. Alike from the hall, and from all around, the tree composed into the picture with a perfection of harmony and dignity. Its splendid benignity seemed the friendly patron and guardian of church, house, and surrounding pleasures. The green, open space could never be large enough for serious cricket, and for long the squire resisted his grandsons' appeal to have the tree removed. Then the younger boy had a place in the Eton eleven, and his grandfather at last yielded his consent that the tree should be cut down. It was done in high spring, flowers and young leaves wilting, and sap spurting at the axe strokes – a bloody spectacle. Late one night I passed the great trunk, loaded, chained between wheels for dragging away. I got off my bicycle, and went to stand close by the dismembered body. I was grieved. I put my hand on the trunk and said –

"Tree, I am sorry for you." I thought I felt a pulse, and heard a groan from the spirit of the tree. Unexplainable mysteries perhaps. I had no ill-will against those who had wrought this ruin. It was understandable that youth must be served. But I had a conviction at that moment that troubles would follow.

DEATH OF MR. CALEB BARKER.

The public, especially those who are concerned with the organised affairs of local agriculture, will learn with painful surprise of the death of Mr. Caleb Barker, which, as our obituary column records, took place at East Harling on Friday. Mr. Barker had been for many years the secretary of the Royal Norfolk Agricultural Association and the Christmas Fat Cattle Show Association. He thus came in contact more or less with everyone concerned in the exhibitional work of those societies, and being a man of marked capacity he wielded much influence among them. It will be noticed that he has just survived the show at East Dereham, which was held on Wednesday and Thursday last.

Mr. Barker was an example of the type of man who by force of character and native ability is able to overcome the adversity of early circumstances. He obtained his start in life by being taken into the office of the late Mr. Samuel, who then lived at Rudham. Having quickly shown his fitness to carry responsibility he next went to Taverham as agent to Mr. Micklethwaite. Then he went to Shadwell and took up the agency to Sir Robert Buxton, which he retained till the estate was sold. By this time his reputation was so well advanced that he was justified in setting up a business at East Harling. There he received the agencies of the late Mr. C. T. M. Montgomerie, Mr. Harvey Mason of Necton, Captain Adlington of Bradenham and Holme Hale, and others. On the retirement of Mr. James Bacon from the secretaryship of the County Agricultural Association Mr. Barker was elected to the office in a spirit of utmost confidence, which he early managed to justify, for the society's financial stability is certainly to be attributed to his careful management as a man of cool head and sound business views. Under his secretaryship, also, the Christmas Show Association has grown in national weight and prestige. Several years ago, after a serious illness, Mr. Barker became afflicted with blindness. But by this time he had come to enjoy the right hand support of Mr. Walter Kerridge, whom later on he took into partnership with the happy result that he was able to retain both his secretaryships, without diminution of efficiency in either case. In his state of blindness his wife attended him with utmost devotion. When some ten months ago death took her from his side the effect upon him was crushing. Thenceforward he failed seriously. On Wednesday, the opening day of the Dereham Show, his illness took an acute turn, and it at once became plain that the end was at hand.

CHAPTER OF ILLS

The squire and his lady had celebrated their golden wedding recently, and received, as was their due, congratulations from the parishioners and tenants. Our village tribute took the form of an address illuminated on vellum, in a carved frame of Irish oak. This was carried out by the Oxford craftsmen of my old parish, and was a fine example of their work. The church, the hall, Sir Edmund reading from the lectern were painted in miniature within initial letters in the manner of the Book of Kells, with ornamentations in the border, and carving of Celtic designs. Torrents of rain came down after the presentation in the racquet court, preventing the outdoor fixtures. With a characteristic gesture the hall doors were flung open, and all the muddy boots and wet garments were made welcome without regard to spoiled carpets and seats. It was in the best patriarchal tradition and it was pleasant to see the glory of happiness on the faces of this worthy squire and lady, good representatives of standards of character that have built up much that is valuable in the fabric of England. But troubles of many sorts were not far away. Some did no more than irritate or depress. But others were serious griefs. When the cook one night jumped into the mere behind the hall in lovelorn despair for young Jack Riches who was courting another sweetheart, and the butler going to the rescue found more mud than water, laughter mollified displeasure. But late one night the butler, riding his bicycle across the park, did not arrive at his cottage. Upon search his dead body was found lying on the road beside his bicycle. Ice and a little snow covered the gravel. Meeting the keen east wind over the open

Caleb Barker's tombstone.

THE DEATH OF MR. CALEB BARKER.
FUNERAL AT WEST HARLING

Amid every manifestation of respect and sympathy, the funeral took place yesterday at West Harling Church of Mr. Caleb Barker, for many years secretary of the Royal Norfolk Agricultural Association, whose death occurred somewhat suddenly last Friday. There was a large gathering of agriculturalists and personal friends, who had come from all parts to pay their last tribute to the memory of a gentleman who for a considerable period had closely identified himself with the agricultural life of the county. The mourners were Miss Tapper, Mr. Walter Kerridge, Mr. J. N. C. Ray, Mr. G. O. Read, Dr. Cooper, Mr. E. Mornement, Mrs. Ray, Mrs. Mornement, Miss Turner, Nurse Shaw, and the maids. The body, which was encased in a shell and outer coffin of oak, was met at the lych gate to the pretty little churchyard by the rector, the Rev. C. H. R. Harper, and as it was borne into the church Lady Nugent, who was at the organ, played, "O Rest in the Lord." The service was of the simplest character, the hymn sung being "Abide with me," and the procession left the church to the strains of the "Dead March" from "Saul." The interment took place in a brick grave, in which Mrs. Barker was laid to rest last August, the sides being tastefully lined with moss and white flowers.

park in thin clothes after the warmth indoors, he had skidded and fallen on his head. He was stunned, and the cold stopped the heart. The estate agent, Caleb Barker, who owned a very good house at East Harling, suddenly became blind. He was remarkable from the fact that, unaided by anything beyond his own talents, he had built up one of the best estate agencies in the county. The Shadwell, Garboldisham, West Harling, Larling and Quidenham estates were in his office, more than fifty thousand acres and he had other estates to manage. He was a tallish man, slightly built, very dark, pale and nervous, a good shot with fine hands and feet, but with a harsh voice and hard manner in business. His house and garden were kept very smart, his wife being fond of flowers. He had good horses, and later a motor. He perhaps was under sixty when he lost his sight and his wife died soon after – a further shock for the poor man for they were an affectionate couple. He did not survive her long. They were both buried near the wicket gate of my little church. Sir Edmund, who had lost his left eye from a shooting accident in youth, now had the misfortune to cause a newcomer, named Paget, to lose an eye from a stray pellet. Upon this Sir Edmund gave up shooting, and soon afterwards his good eye failed, and he was unable to see to read Sunday lessons. These things were great grief to him. The West Harling and Larling shootings were now let to a stranger, a Mr. Ker from the north. The fine old gray horse had died, and carriage horses were hired for the small amount of work now required. At this time I had gone to Riddlesworth after the death of John Robinson Wells, whom I was asked to succeed as rector.

In the first years of the great war, 1914-1918, more sorrows came to the West Harling house. Two sons, Charles and Claud, had previously died in 1887 and 1901 respectively and another Frederick, had become a Roman Catholic priest. The eldest son George, now brigadier, was killed by a stray bullet in France.

[Ed. The following information is largely inaccurate time-wise. This makes one wonder how much else is 'out of time', but can no longer be checked].

His mother died about the same time. Prue, my successor at West Harling, died after only a few months tenure of the living, that was then joined to East Harling. Sir Edmund died soon afterwards, and West Harling Hall was pulled down, when the whole estate was then sold to the Forestry Commissioners for inclusion in a state afforestation scheme.

[Lady Nugent died in 1922, seven years after George. Rev. Prue died in 1924 nine years after becoming Rector and Sir Edmund died in 1928].

The Gainsborough portraits, and most of the contents of the Hall were sold by auction. The Misses Nugent went to live in the rectory [Ed. now the Dower House] that the Ecclesiastical Commissioners sold to improve the income of the joint living. In my last years there, before I knew I was to have Riddlesworth benefice, I redeemed the mortgage to Queen Anne's Bounty, on the rectory. I am glad of this, because I shall never cease to have an affection for it. It must now be almost unrecognisable, buried in plantations of conifers. So ended a long history of small village life, that went back for more than a thousand years. The church will still stand, I hope, for many centuries more, with all its memories of aspirations and shortcomings, of joys and sorrows, of vanities and strengths, that bring us all humbled and grateful before the presence of God.

THE END OF AN ERA.

From West Harling Estate Diary –

1915, Sir Edmund Nugent writes:
This has been the most terrible one [war] in all history. This was perhaps only to be expected because of all the inventions of late years in the way of submarines and aeroplanes; but it has been rendered far worse by the utter disregard of fair play. We have lost our dear, brave, eldest son in action on the 31st May. He had been visiting his Brigade accompanied by his staff, and was shot by a stray bullet or by a 'sniper' and died ten minutes after he was struck. He is buried at Bethune. He was a splendid soldier and devoted to his profession, and we have had innumerable letters from all classes of people testifying to the high esteem in which he was held by everybody who knew him.

1923, Evelyn Nugent writes:
Owing to my father having become totally blind, this book has been neglected in the last few years. Of course the property has been very much let down owing to the war,–we have found it very difficult to meet the very heavy taxes arising from it and the very considerable rise in wages, and we have been forced to make great reductions in the number of people employed on the estate.
The principal events that have happened in the last few years are first,
My mother's death in January 1922. She is a great loss to us all, especially to my father after 59 years of married life.
Rev. C. H. Harper resigned the living of West Harling in 1915 after 16 years tenure, and Rev. A. E. Prue, who was already Rector of Larling was appointed to West Harling.

1924, On February 7th Mr Prue died, and in consequence both the livings of West Harling and Larling became vacant. The Rev. Edgar Reynolds was appointed Rector of Larling. In October the living of West Harling was joined to that of East Harling and the Rev. Leonard Holt Wilson was appointed Rector over the two.

1925, West Harling Rectory was sold by the Ecclesiastical Commissioners and bought as a Dower House and given to the Misses Nugent.

1927, Terence [Nugent] went on a tour to Australia and New Zealand as equerry to the Duke of York [Ed: later George VI].

1928, On December 4th my father died at nearly 90 years of age.

The present Lord Fisher recalls: In 1928 I was taken to West Harling for the funeral of Sir Edmund Nugent and heard the "Last Post" sounded for the first time in my life.

THE LATE GENERAL G. C. NUGENT. M.V.O.

Memorial service at West Harling.

On Thursday memorial services for the late Brigadier-General George Colborne Nugent were held in the parish church at West Harling and St. Paul's Church, Knightsbridge, London. Since it became known that on May 31st this gallant officer was killed in action in France, when in command of his brigade, very general sympathy in the parish of West Harling and for miles around has been manifested towards Sir Edmund and Lady Nugent and the family in their great bereavement, deceased being the eldest son. A large and sorrowing congregation attended the service at West Harling Church, which, with its peaceful surroundings in the park, adjoins the hall, the seat of the Nugent family. Close by is the Red Cross Hospital, where, under the kind care of Lady and the Misses Nugent and a staff of nurses a number of wounded soldiers are being comforted and treated. There were present Sir Edmund and Lady Nugent, the Misses Nugent, Miss Boileau, and Sir Maurice Boileau, and among the congregation were the Rev. B. H. Grigson (East Harling), Rev. H. Jones (Banham), Dr. and Mrs. Adams (Kenninghall), Mr. W. N. L. Champion (Riddlesworth), Messrs. Edgell (Thetford), Steggles (Larling), Lawrence (Harling Road Station), Miss Marshall (Bridgham), Mr. W. W. Kerridge (the estate agent), Messrs. G. Wilson, N. Barker, and other tenants, and the employees on the West Harling Estate, Miss Lock, Mrs. Prue (Larling), while from East Harling there were also present Mrs. Ray, Mrs. Everett, Messrs. Pollard, Dewhirst, Coldham, Warby, Hanton, Nebbett, Hewitt, and others. The West Harling Boy Scouts, whose training has long been under the care of Miss Nugent, lined the church path, and several of the nurses from the Red Cross Hospital attended the service. The Rector of West Harling (the Rev. C. H. R. Harper) officiated, assisted by the Rev. E. A. Prue (rector of Larling). As the congregation assembled, "O rest in the Lord" was played on the organ, and the choir effectively rendered the Nunc Dimittis and several hymns, which included "The Women's Hymn in Time of War," the words of which were composed by the deceased when he ranked as captain, and are set to the tune of Sullivan's Jubilee Hymn. After the singing of the National Anthem the "Dead March" in "Saul" was played.

THE LATE LADY NUGENT.
FUNERAL AT WEST HARLING

The funeral of Lady Evelyn Henrietta Nugent took place at West Harling on Monday afternoon, the very large assembly at the church and at the graveside testifying to the great respect and esteem in which her ladyship was held, and to the general and widespread sympathy with Sir Edmund Nugent and the other members of the bereaved family. The homes of the villagers of the quiet parish of West Harling lie mainly in and around the well-wooded and spacious park in which the hall, and the church which adjoins the mansion, stand out. The ivy-clad church of All Saints', with its peaceful churchyard and surroundings, formed a most fitting resting place for the body of the departed one, who, with Sir Edmund and the other members of the family, was a constant worshipper there, and where at the organ she shared the responsibility for the musical portion of the religious services with her two daughters, who lead and train the voices of the choir. The church possesses stone and brass mural tablets to the memory of past generations in the line of owners of the estate from the family of Baron Colborne to the late Sir George Nugent, Bart., who married the second daughter of the baron, and who was the father of the present baronet, Sir Edmund Nugent. More recent brasses, fixed near the family pews, record the death of sons of Sir Edmund and the late Lady Nugent.

At the morning service in the church on Sunday the rector, the Rev. A. E. Prue, made feeling allusion to the sad event to a sorrowing congregation. The seating accommodation in the church at the funeral service was quite inadequate for the large assembly, and had to be temporarily supplemented. The ceremony was conducted by the rector, who was assisted by the Rev. J. W. Knight (Illington), and Canon Pelham read the lesson. Mr. Kingston Rudd, of Attleborough, was at the organ, and played "O Rest in the Lord" and "I know that my Redeemer liveth" as the coffin, covered with wreaths, was borne into the church on the shoulders of the principal employees on the estate, Messrs. Wiggett, Petch, Kent, Elener, Wilson and Barnard. The service was choral, and the hymns, "Just as I am, without one plea" and "On the Resurrection Morning" were impressively sung. As the cortege left the church the "Dead March" in "Saul" was played. The Rector read the committal prayers, and the coffin, which was of old English oak, with brass inscribed shield and fittings, was lowered into a freshly-dug grave near the tomb of two of the departed sons of Sir Edmund and Lady Nugent, namely, Lieut. Charles Henry Nugent, who died in 1887, and Claud Nugent, who died in 1901.

DEATH OF SIR EDMUND NUGENT.

We regret to announce the death of Sir Edmund Charles Nugent, Bart., which took place on Tuesday night at his South Norfolk seat, West Harling Hall. Born on the 12th of March, 1839, he was in his ninetieth year. There could hardly be a more striking confirmation of the theory that length of days is usually a matter of heredity; his father, the previous baronet, died in his ninetieth year, and his grandfather attained the age of ninety-one. For the last three or four years Sir Edmund had been confined to the house, and from further back than that he had borne the sore affliction of blindness. His other faculties, however, were all well preserved, as may be judged from the fact that as late as 1923 he edited and prepared for publication a volume of his collected verse.

Sir Edmund was the second son of the second baronet, and his mother was the Hon. Maria Charlotte, second daughter of Lord Colborne. Educated at Eton, he entered the Army in 1857 and retired from a captaincy in the Grenadier Guards in 1862. His succession to the baronetcy, in 1892, brought him into possession of a beautiful estate of about 4500 acres in Norfolk, in addition to some other lands in the Irish Free State and some town properties in Bath. In 1863 he married Evelyn, a daughter of General E. F. Gascoigne, by whom he had a family of four sons and two daughters. Lady Nugent died in 1922. The eldest son, Brigadier-General Nugent, was killed in France during the Great War. The only son now surviving is the Rev. E. F. Nugent. The daughters are Miss Evelyn Lilla Nugent and Miss Violet Nugent. The heir to the title and estate is Mr. Guy C. Nugent, elder son of the Brigadier-General.

Sir Edmund was an admirable type of the country gentleman, fulfilling all sorts of duties, magisterial, administrative, and other, appropriate to a man of active and large-minded disposition. The affection felt for him in the West Harling and Larling parts of the estate was enthusiastically testified on the 30th April 1913, when he celebrated the 50th anniversary of his wedding. An address presented to him was couched in the warmest terms. "We are grateful," it said, "for the solicitude you have ever shown for the welfare and highest happiness of the parish. The church has been restored through your generosity, and its worship helped for more than a generation by your personal services. Worthily following the examples of your family, who in bygone years preceded you in this place, you have taken every opportunity to aid, with kindness and wisdom, those who are dependent upon you, and to add to their comfort and happiness. Benefits like these, conferred throughout many years, induce feelings towards you of more than formal respect. It will interest you to know that everyone living in West Harling, from the oldest to the youngest, joins in this address."

To record all that Sir Edmund did in his prime would make a long enumeration. In 1905 he was High Sheriff of Norfolk. For a few years he held an Aldermancy on the Norfolk County Council. For a long time he was chair-man of the East Harling Bench of Magistrates. He was a trustee of the Norfolk and Norwich Savings Bank. He was chairman of the Norfolk and Norwich Soldiers' Institute, and of the branch Association for the Employment of Discharged Soldiers. He was a member of the National Patriotic Association, the Canterbury House of Laymen, the Queen Victoria Clergy Fund, the Norwich Diocesan Fund, and the Diocesan Association of Schools. He was a director of the Burlington Hotel Company, and in 1897 was chairman of that body. Sir Edmund travelled extensively in Canada and on the continent. The principal event of his military career occurred in 1861-2, when, with the 1st Battalion of the Grenadier Guards, he bore his part in the Trent Expedition.

It cannot be questioned that Sir Edmund had a considerable literary gift. As appears from the preface to his volume of "Military and other Verses," published when he was in his 85th year, he made a habit of writing "this sort of thing" all his life and had derived considerable interest and amusement from thus occupying his leisure moments. Some of his verse appeared from time to time in "All the Year Round," "Once a Week" and other magazines; and he was a pretty constant contributor to "The Household Brigade Magazine" when his son was editing it. He had the gift of almost instantaneous improvisation. When his eyesight had departed he still found solace in reeling off lyrics that were always metrically well finished and correctly rhymed. A young lady who at this time acted as his typist mentions that his dictation was so facile that she had all she could do to keep abreast of it. Hardly had she punched down one line ere another was tripping on his tongue. As a specimen of his easy lilting style, the following is worthy of recall: he entitled it "Philosophy" and it appeared in "The Household Brigade Magazine":

PHILOSOPHY

We were schoolboys together, were Billy and I,
Two extremely unpromising urchins,
And we shared the same "grub," smuggled in on the sly,
And endured the same consequent birchings.
And he copied my paper, he did, line for line,
With a really remarkable cunning;
Then he dropped a big blot in the middle of mine,
Which of course put me out of the running.
Well, I argued the point at some length, with my fist,
And we both went to bed rather battered,
But Billy came out at the top of the list,
So I don't think it very much mattered.

We were pals, I and Billy, yes, down to the ground;
For you see, we were birds of a feather,
So it's not very odd, when the sergeant came round,
That we both took the shilling together.
Then I met with a girl (the old story, you know),
And we talked to each other as "Mary" and "Joe,"
And were hoping some day, to get married.
Then Billy came by, with a cock to his cap,
And perhaps she was easily flattered,
But Billy was always a good-looking chap.
Well! I don't think it very much mattered.

It was hot work, no error, for Billy and me,
When the "Fuzzies" were thirsting for slaughter.
We were both of us hit, and cut off, don't you see.
And it looked like a case of "no quarter."
But I stood across Billy, and kept them at bay,
While their guns went on roaring like thunder,
Till some of our chaps came and got him away,
Then I chucked it and nearly went under.
I am out of it now, as you see, with the loss
Of an arm, and health hopelessly shattered.
But Billy – he got the Victoria Cross,
So I don't think it very much mattered.

RIDDLESWORTH

The name of my new parish, in full, was Riddlesworth with Gatesthorpe and Knettishall. These were three separate parishes, each with its church and glebelands. Nothing remained of the church at Gatesthorpe beyond a ruinous tower and a chancel wall and window standing in the churchyard still enclosed by a fence. Knettishall church still remained complete, much as it had been a century or more earlier, when it was last used for worship. It had a very simple chancel and nave with tower. Inside were some rough benches, deal box-pews, three-decker desk and pulpit, twisted Carolean altar rail, communion table and two chairs of the same period – all worm-eaten. The roof tiles were maintained, and the windows boarded to keep out wet. Two cottages of clay-lump thatched and whitewashed, in large gardens, adjoined the road on the slope below the church. They belonged to the rector, together with about thirty acres of light arable land surrounding. With two other cottages opposite, they contained the only population here, and were not above a mile distant from Riddlesworth church. The small total population of under three hundred, and the central position of Riddlesworth church, had led to the disuse of Knettishall except for burials. The name may derive from 'neats' e.g. 'neatshouse' a cow-byre. This hamlet was in Suffolk. Gasthorpe was earlier called Gatesthorpe, from gates that once barred the road at the Ouse river boundary here, between Norfolk and Suffolk. Riddlesworth may derive from the reeds in the same river. Gatesthorpe glebe was a rich heavy loam, nearly thirty acres, surrounding the ruined church. If there ever were parsonages on these two glebes no traces remained. The good loam soil extended along the slope on the Norfolk side of the river between Gatesthorpe and Riddlesworth churches. The distance was less than half a mile, so that within one mile there had once been three churches. If there ever had been population to fill these it had long ago vanished.

At Riddlesworth the venerable, low, square tower of the little gray flint church, standing in the grounds of the old rose-brick Georgian rectory, great oaks and elms sheltering gardens, orchard and paddocks, the whole snugly facing south across grassland sloping towards the gleam of water, where the Ouse widened into a lake, crossed at its narrow end by a wooden trestle bridge, made a picture of sunny peace as perfect as can be found anywhere in our land. A rustic school with teacher's house was just visible at the far end of the green, and, rather nearer the arable glebe, was a pretty two storied modern cottage.

RIDDLESWORTH HALL

Riddlesworth Hall, though only a stone's throw from the rectory gates, was almost hidden by giant elms on both sides of the park road that passed the church. The old hall was totally destroyed by fire a few years before I came to West Harling, and on its site was built a larger and handsome house, with classical decoration on the south side fronting the slopes to the lake. The front door was on the north side, reached by a flight of wide steps. On the park lawn opposite were a number of great Cedars of Lebanon, noble trees that gave dignity here. No flower gardens were near the house. A park road going west for about a mile led towards Shadwell and Thetford. Another went north toward West Harling, and at Riddlesworth church turned east to Gatesthorpe and Knettishall. The new hall was designed by Mr. Green the diocesan architect, whom I knew well. He had to his credit several mansions and public buildings in East Anglia. From the

Riddlesworth Hall.

front door one entered a large furnished hall with great open fireplace, a most comfortable room in all seasons. Out of this opened the library, with the dining room to the left, both facing south with beautiful views over the lake to rising ground with clumps of trees among bracken and gorse heathland. To the right was the great drawing-room facing south and west, and on the north the billiard room and the squire's study. All the chief rooms were spacious and lofty, with beautiful ceilings the work of modern Italian craftsmen, the doors of polished mahogany, the floors of oak. The chief bedrooms were on the floor above and a wing at an angle to give shelter from the east contained a large number of bachelor rooms.

W. N. L. CHAMPION

On my coming to West Harling the squire of Riddlesworth, W. N. L. Champion, called on me. He was then living at Coney Weston while the new hall was building. We had a picnic lunch, and went over the nearly completed Hall with the architect. That day began a long friendship, to which I look back with pleasure and gratitude. The squire was acknowledged as one of the leading agriculturalists of East Anglia. Although he had a capable agent and bailiffs, he competently understood and controlled all of his many farms, giving the requisite orders and visiting them continually. He had large flocks of sheep, herds of cattle, celebrated Suffolk Punches, and Berkshire pigs. Every now and then I would spend an afternoon with him, walking many miles to inspect crops and animals, or plantations and woods, and to interview keepers, for he was a large preserver of game. He had much knowledge of trees, and was interested in all country things. Slim, weather-tanned, with a notable nose, bright dark eyes, clad in beautifully-cut, serviceable country clothes, with a walking-stick spud [small spade] in chamois leather gloved hand, he could be seen any morning or afternoon striding across field and furrow, eternally smoking a special choice brand of cigarettes. Though he was twenty years my senior he could tire me out in walking, but I was never tired of his company, for his quiet genial but shrewd comments on men and affairs, and his invariable welcome, made me feel he was a true friend. Born in Edale, Derbyshire, where he inherited a considerable landed estate, including the Blue John mine, he had textile mills in Lancashire, a brewery and a coal mine in Yorkshire. He was fond of books of travel and adventure, but not *belles lettres,* nor was he musical. He was a good shot, and played a sound game of billiards after dinner into old age. He early joined the ranks of motorists, owning a succession of big Rolls-Royce cars. He never drove himself, but was fond of making what he called 'expeditions' to see historic houses, abbeys like Crowland, or Nelson's rectory birthplace (Burnham), or visit agricultural shows and trials of new implements. He used to drive to his home in Edale to visit his sisters, and shoot over his grouse moor. Although not formally a religious man, in my time he regularly attended Sunday morning service, and supported me wholeheartedly in the parish. While dogmas meant little to him, he believed in the Church of England as a cultural and unifying influence, steadying and humanising social relations in the community. His brother was an excellent parson in the north of the county. Mrs. Champion was witty and vivacious when well enough to come downstairs, but her health was impaired and she died soon after I became rector. Amy Oakden, who, for a great part of her life has been the friend and acted as hostess of late years,

---

THE STEPS AND RAIL OF THE PULPIT OF
THIS CHURCH WERE ERECTED BY
DELIA GRIFFITH-WILLIAMS TO THE GLORY of GOD
& IN MOST LOVING & GRATEFUL MEMORY of

AMY ELIZABETH OAKDEN

of RIDDLESWORTH HALL
FOR OVER FORTY YEARS THE DEARLY LOVED FRIEND & HELPER
OF EVERYONE IN THIS PARISH
BORN 1 JANUARY 1860 – DIED 6 APRIL 1939

'LOVING ALL, SHE WAS BY ALL BELOVED'

continued her invaluable help in house and parish. She was loved and respected by everyone, the kind of woman incredibly patient and self-sacrificing, who freely and quite simply give their whole lives to make other people happy. The squire's daughter, who married Colonel Follett, and granddaughter Delia, adored Amy who had cared for them from babyhood. When she died many years later the squire, then a very old man did not long survive her.

Riddlesworth Rectory

Although the distance between my old and new homes was not great, my removal was extremely leisurely, in all more than six months. I kept on the Riddlesworth groom-gardener, and he and Barrett, with a light wagon drawn by Kitty, gradually carted my belongings, after Riddlesworth rectory had been completely overhauled for repairs and decorations indoors and out. Although it had not so many bedrooms most of the rooms were larger and lighter. Dining room and drawing-room had each two tall windows to the south. Between them was a good sized hall, York stone flagged, with a wide handsome old staircase that went right up to the attic floor. A study facing south adjoined the dining room, that had a built-in bookcase extending the whole length of the room from floor to ceiling. It made a fine showing filled with all my books. The front door had a Georgian porch in keeping with the simple solid dignified front of the house. I had the beautiful weathered, pantiled roof new lathed and pegged to last for centuries more, and its dormer attic windows new-leaded. Two pantries, a big kitchen, scullery, dairy and bake-house were on the west and north. As at West Harling the drinking water was drawn by force-pump from a well deep down in the subsoil, and rainwater filled tanks in the roofs. These primitive supplies were pure and unfailing.

Our lighting was by oil lamps and candles - of late years much improved. At West Harling Hall a dozen or more candlesticks with glass cylinders were set ready on a table, and family and guests lighted themselves to their bedrooms. The lamps were one man's whole time job in that house.

There were three large cellars under the rectory, bone dry, and useful for many kinds of storage. Two drives from the road led to the house, one passing the churchyard and orchard and going through the flower garden to the sweep before the front door. The other passed the barn, stable, coach house and yard to the back door.

The first Derby Winner 1780

The outbuildings were a picturesque group, the old barn chiefly built of timber, with the stable block, reed-thatched, transversely at the end. Above this was an eighteenth century wrought-iron weather vane. It represented at full gallop the First Derby Winner, 1780 which was bred at Riddlesworth by Squire Thornhill. This family lived at the hall for several generations, where they were visited by Horace Walpole and other celebrities. One of these Thornhill squires was so rotund that his dining room table was cut at the end in a semi-circle to accommodate his person. Another, having lost heavily at cards, was said to have put up his wife Sarah for sale to the highest bidder in the company assembled, with what result I do not know. When a later member of the family died, his coffin was brought from London to be deposited in the vault under the nave, and I took the opportunity of going down to inspect the rows of lead-lined coffins on brickwork shelves – a gruesome sight.

A Fine Pear Tree

A width of beautiful, smooth lawn fronted the rectory, surrounded by herbaceous borders and rose beds, all sheltered by clipped yew hedges, interspersed with pink chestnut against a white cupresses, tall holly and other sheltering trees. Two grape vines, white and black fruited most summers on the south front of the house among forsythia, honeysuckle and climbing roses. The west front had a finely-trained espalier pear – or rather three varieties of pears grafted on one parent stem. This tree, quite old, and covering the whole expanse of wall from ground to roof angle was, in its way, a masterpiece of skilful pruning and care year after year. In my time its splendid early, middle and late fruit never failed. On a leaded pane near it, was clearly cut with a diamond the name of Charles Wake, once rector of Riddlesworth, a descendant of Hereward the Wake.

A pretty walled yard at the back of the house was entered by high wooden doors. Here were neat flint-built potting and firewood sheds, and the door to the kitchen garden that contained about an acre of rich loamy soil. It was enclosed on three sides by high flint brick topped walls, and on the fourth by a close-clipped beech hedge, very lovely at all seasons, impenetrable by winds, and so dense one could almost walk along its flat top. My gardens here were truly a paradise of flowers, fruits and vegetables. The walls held peaches, nectarines, apricots, greengages, figs. Cherries, with white, red and black currants, were on the shady side. All these I covered with nets in season, for we had birds of all sorts. In a wire cage there were raspberries, gooseberries, strawberries and more currants. Here and in the orchard were apples, pears, plums, damsons, bullaces, quinces, medlars – such quantities of fruit I had difficulty in giving them away, besides what we used or sold. Our asparagus, seakale and rhubarb under pots covered with heaped leaves were particularly early and good.

Riddlesworth Church.

Riddlesworth Church

My way to church, the tower and length of which were visible among trees from the rectory windows and garden, was a hundred yards down the front drive, and then by a little gravel path edged in spring with aconites, snowdrops, daffodils, primroses and violets. There were more of these flowers along the churchyard path to the porch. Inside the oak wicket-gate were the tombstones of the late rector, his father and their wives. Following these there were some ancient headstones with beautiful carving and lettering. Riddlesworth church, like West Harling, consists of only a chancel and nave with massive buttressed square tower. It was smaller and less lofty, but likewise had some nice old windows all of plain glass. Its furniture was plain but seemly in an old style, and there were a few wall tablets of about the same period, with earlier floor stones in the aisle. One of these last told of a young lady 'whose soule took its flight to heaven in ye furious hurricane' of one night in the eighteenth century. What happened was that a chimney in the hall fell and crushed the poor girl in her bed. The communion plate consisted of a large flagon, chalice and paten and alms dish of heavy silver, and also a very small chalice and paten of beautiful simple design of Elizabethan or pre-Reformation date. These last came from Knettishall church, and I took great care of them for they were thin but quite perfect. Like West Harling there was only an American organ in the chancel. I got a grant of one hundred pounds from Andrew Carnegie, and at the end of my first year had enough subscriptions to have a good little pipe-organ built by Norman and Beard of Norwich and London in suitable oak case. It had but one manual, with pedal and swell organ, but the few stops were good and musical, and it made a great addition to our services. Old Andrew was so fond of organ music that at his Scots castle he had hymns played on an organ in his hall when he was getting up in the morning and on going to bed, and he loved to give organs to churches. Our organ was the last pre-war grant made by the steel-trust millionaire who did so much for Scottish education, and for public libraries in Britain. At this time I wrote suggesting that the Carnegie Trust could, in addition to municipal libraries, usefully extend its grants to the foundation of lending libraries for country districts. The reply I received welcomed the suggestion but stated that nothing could be done until after the war. In after years county libraries with branches have been started with great benefit to rural areas.

> *In memory of the Pious and Virtuous*
> *Miss Mary Fisher*
> *whose Soul tooke her Flight to Heaven in ye*
> *Furious hurricane on*
> *November ye 27th 1703.*
> *This Monument of Respect is Dedicated by*
> *her true & faithfull lover.*
> *Anthony Drury*
> *of Mendham in Norfolk, Gent.*

FIRST WORLD WAR 1914–1918

On the 28th June 1914 the Archduke Ferdinand, heir to the throne of Austria-Hungary was assassinated at Sarajevo in Serbia.

A most severe ultimatum was delivered to Serbia by Austria on the 22nd of July at the instigation of the German Reich. The Serbians fully acceded to this in the most abject, submissive manner. The Kaiser, apparently sure of no war, went for a yachting holiday. Who started mobilisation I do not know – Germany said that Russia did and vice versa. Certainly their *Der Tag* had been toasted, prepared for, and desired for long by the imperial general staff and navy of Germany. In a day or two Russia, Germany and France mobilised. The Kaiser also felt sure that England would not fight. But when the British ambassador in Berlin was told that the treaty not to invade Belgium was 'only a scrap of paper', and the German troops accordingly seized Luxembourg and attacked Malines in Belgium, Britain declared war on the side of France, and sent her 'contemptible little army' to Flanders. Britons could hardly believe their senses, but were to a man furious at the treachery against Belgium. Haldane had started the territorial army, still in a fledgling state, but Winston Churchill, as First Lord of the Admiralty had kept the navy together – 'ready, aye ready' – after the summer naval review. Now it guarded the North Sea and the Straits of Dover; and the marines at the First Lord's instigation held up for precious days the Germans before Antwerp, and so helped the 'old contemptibles' falling back from Mons, and saved also Calais and the French channel ports.

In these first August days, when the sun shone from rise to

Bessie and Hector Wilson.

Red Cross Hospital, West Harling, March 1918.

Back row, L to R: Arthur Davis, ?, ?, ?, Walter Kerridge, Mr. Mitchell (Illington), James Davis, Mrs. Adams, Wilhelmina 'Granny' Coote, Mrs. Mourilyan (Eccles), Mabel Bussey, Mrs Elener, Agnes Davis, Mr. Elener, Mr. Bussey, Mr. Oakley, William Charles Davis, Charlie Petch, ?.

Front row, L to R: Lilian Pattinson, Rose Wilson, Mrs. Agnew (Eccles), Ann Garnier & Poppy Garnier (Quidenham), Dr. Adams, Evelyn Nugent, Lady Nugent, Sister Mitchell (Illington), Violet Nugent, Mabel Wiggett, Lizzie Riches, Miss Foured, Gertie Cross.

Tank Trial at Elveden.

WEST HARLING RED CROSS HOSPITAL.
ANNIVERSARY CELEBRATION—NOVEMBER 1915.

The completion of a year's successful work at the Red Cross Hospital in the park at West Harling was celebrated on Sunday, when Lady Nugent entertained at the Hall the present wounded soldier inmates, six in number, together with the entire staff of nurses and helpers. On the outbreak of war Sir Edmund and Lady Nugent at once placed their racquet court at the service of the local branch of the Red Cross Society, which with Miss Nugent as commandant, was at that time already a strongly established institution, and the building was transformed into a comfortable hospital ward, with complete equipment, the first patients being received on November 7th of last year. Since that date about 40 cases have been treated, the hospital accommodating six patients. Two of the former patients have since been killed in action. The soldiers had on Saturday very effectively decorated the ward with flags, bunting, and evergreens in suitable devices, and on Sunday morning each of the nurses received a card of greeting from the indefatigable commandant, Miss Nugent. Later in the day there was a large invited assembly at the Hall, where tea was served, and this was preceded in the saloon by an excellent programme of sacred music, both instrumental and vocal, to which Lady Nugent and the Misses Nugent contributed some very pleasing items on the organ, piano, and violin, in addition to choice vocal numbers. The company, which included the patients, the sister, Red Cross nurses, men night-nurses, boy scouts, and other helpers, was addressed by her ladyship, who in the name of the king heartily thanked all who had so kindly given their services during the year. The soldiers joined in the singing of special hymns, and, Lady Nugent having offered prayer, the proceedings closed with the singing of the National Anthem. The hospital staff is as follows:- Commandant, Miss Nugent; quartermaster, Miss Burroughes (Quidenham); sister, Mrs. St. John Mitchell (Illington): staff nurse, Miss Violet Nugent; nurses, Lady Albemarle (Quidenham), Mrs. Agnew (Eccles), Mrs.Mourilyan (Eccles), Mrs. Prue (Larling), Mrs. Adams (Kenninghall), Miss Hemsworth (Shropham), Miss Marshall (Bridgham), Miss Garnier (Quidenham), Miss Agnew (Eccles), Misses Wiggett, Beadle, and Wilson (West Harling), Misses Pattinson and Riches, and Mrs. Cross (East Harling); night-nurses, Messrs. Kerridge and Pollard (East Harling). Messrs. Davis, Petch, Beadle, Elener, and Oakley (West Harling); hospital doctor, Dr. W. Adams (Kenninghall); laundresses and cooks, Mrs. Nunn (Roudham), Mrs. Coote, and Mrs. Beadle (West Harling).

lovely setting in rosy clouds, it was hard to believe we were at war, and that the cornfields of France and Flanders, red with poppies, were also red with blood.

The camp of the Lincolnshire yeomanry, with their horses, was pitched on the green sward between the rectory and the lake. They overfilled the church at special services, and almost lifted the roof with great singing. They had no chaplain, but I did what I could. My man Barrett, with his friend Hector Wilson of Stonehouse farm volunteered. I still had a man, who with his wife lived in one of my Knettishall cottages. He was good in garden and stable, unable to bear arms, and after a year was tempted by impossible high wages to take service in J. Musker's racing stables. I had sold one of Kitty's foals, a lovely three year old that

Hector Wilson, Pte. Parker, Capt. Claxton, Fred Cole, Sam Bloomfield, Dick Cutter.

I had broken in myself, just before I left West Harling; and now I felt I must part with Kitty too, having no longer a groom, and no time to look after her properly myself. I also sold my motor-cycle, for it did not seem right to use the small ration of petrol allowed me. So I was down to a pedal cycle again for transport. For six months I had a Hopton boy in the garden, after which he had to go. I sold my last fat bullock, one of Polly's offspring, and had to sell her too. Except for poultry my little farmyard was now empty, and my glebe in the capable hands of the squire. For more than four years I carried on singlehanded all the work of the two big gardens, with an extra patch for potatoes. I kept on my bees, gathered the orchard and other fruits, maintaining drives, hedges, pruning and so forth. Though I say it myself the place looked as neat and workmanlike and as full of flowers, fruits and vegetables as before. I gardened from nine to six whenever parish duties did not call me away, and in summer was working out of doors often till nightfall.

Snare Hill Airfield.

The Lincolns went away, but Breckland and all around had camps for training troops. At Shadwell, hangars were erected to hold the little single or double seater airplanes of those days and stunt exhibitions, looping the loop and flying upside down, were given before amazed spectators – military and civil. At Elveden, it was freely spoken about that there were trials of strange monsters that pushed down walls, climbed over mounds and crossed ditches, carrying guns, and armoured like battle ships. Had these 'tanks' been kept secret and sent in great number at the onset to France, they might have ended the war at a blow. As it was, they easily broke through the previously impenetrable Hindenburg Line, and could have rolled it up if there had been more of them. All this clangour and traffic of war in our unpeopled Breckland was a horrible upset. Except for cavalry, because of rabbit holes, the great spaces of untilled Brecks were ideal for camps and training grounds.

BREAKING IN KITTY'S FOALS

The Wilson Family at Stonehouse Farm.

I missed the old quiet rides and it was hateful to have my stable empty. Kitty had gone to a good home to George Wilson of Stonehouse, who would not overwork her. I saw her again sometimes and she used to whicker, and nuzzle my shoulder. The filly 'went foreign' as they say in Norfolk. She had not given me the least trouble to break in. My method was to use a foal to a head-stall from the first, and at a year old to strap on a rolled rug and girth occasionally. A bridle with easy snaffle-bit followed in due course, and the foal would be lead about, proud of its trappings. When two-year old, collar, traces and rope reins would be added, and a very light bush-hurdle would be drawn over the brass by the novice. I always found, with Barrett at the head, and I at the reins, after a couple of kicks at nothing, the learner would go along as sweet as you please pulling steadily. From this it was only a step to a light two-wheeler and three-year-old light work. I did not need to lay a whip across one of my animals during breaking-in.

BISHOP POLLOCK

The Bishop of Norwich who followed Dr. Sheepshanks was Bertram Pollock, previously headmaster of Wellington College. I first met him when he instituted me to Riddlesworth. He was then a bachelor, middle-aged and rather ill for some years from an attack of phlebitis that unfortunately occurred just after he became bishop. Sallow, tallish and looking ill, he had nevertheless a dignified presence, and considerable charm of manner. On several occasions he showed me kindness. He ran the palace with manservants. It was rather a comfortless, dark, old pile of brick masonry, built on the north side of the cathedral, set in gloomy lawns surrounded by the high walls of the old monastery, with one of the great gates as its entry. He has a flock of geese as war-time lawnmowers, and the palace grounds, never very well kept, looked more untidy and mediæval than ever.

Bishop Pollock.

My friend Brocas Walters, wrote to ask me if I could go out to Harfleur where his cousins the two Misses Wood, whom I met at his wedding, were running the 'Woodbine Hut' that they had given to the Y.M.C.A. I took this letter to the bishop. He said that as I had only lately gone to Riddlesworth, was over forty five, and not strong and growing food, with church work, he thought I ought to stay at home. [Ed: Harper later married both Miss Woods, though not simultaneously!].

WAR TIME HARVESTING

We were short of labour at Riddlesworth, and I engaged to do the harvest with our men. The procedure of enlistment was the taking of one shilling hansel [i.e. deposit] by each man, after the election of the 'lord of the harvest' and the agreement of the lump sum to be paid to each of us on completion. James Bennett was our 'lord' – a relation I think of my West Harling parishioner friend. Jimmy, like Charles, was a short, broad, brown-bearded man, with a quiet blue eye and manner. Though I was nearly as old as he, I thought of him as old enough to be my father. He was a leading bellringer in the district, and also played a set of handbells. His only son enlisted in the first month of the war, and was killed in France directly he got out there. It was a terrible grief to Jimmy, his

Harvest Engraving

wife and three daughters. They lived in a good flint-built cottage against a covert just outside the park, with the hall laundry building adjoining carried on by his womenfolk. We harvest men were in the fields by 6 a.m. if the morning was dry enough for an early start. A 'hold-ye' boy was sent round by the lord at 5 a.m. to outliers to call them up and tell them of any change of plan. We had ten men in our gang, and two hold-ye boys for the wagon horses. So we could keep two wagons going from field to stack, two pitchers, two rakers, two loadmen on the wagon, and the four others; two on the stack and two on the ground. We would change over tasks as the day went on to give men a little relief. We started operations with the winter-sown oats. The scythemen first went in to cut around the headlands. After rakers had cleared this ground, the horses and reapers could cut, and we followed to set up the sheaves.

The smell of early morning was good as I went out to the harvest fields each day – some close to, and others not very distant from my rectory. A hare loped away down a hedge side. Families of partridges, already joining into coveys, whirred away in short flights, or merely ran as I approached them. Cock pheasants uttered angry protests at being disturbed at breakfast. Flights of pigeons, doves and lesser winged eaters of grain went back to the woods as the sun climbed higher. Our band of workers was blithe and merry after the night's rest and at the likelihood of fine weather continuance and so a quick prosperous harvest. This cheeriness would last nearly all day, though dying down somewhat from physical weariness towards evening. I got to know my fellow workers' ways and thoughts intimately. The oldest man, Curzon, was as tall and slim as his aristocratic namesake, erect, with closely clipped pointed white beard and well cut white hair. Notwithstanding years, his lean taut muscles apparently never tired. Like Jimmy, he knew the whole technique of the beautiful art of good husbandry according to the best traditions and customs. There was a competitive rivalry in speed and efficient neatness of work among the members of our team, that improved the quantity and quality of our daily output. Considerable skill and care are required to build up a wagon load or construct a stack. The tails of the sheaves must go to the ends and sides of the load or stack, which must be kept going straight up or sloping only very slightly inward.

Fourses in the harvest field.

The pitchers would try to throw up the sheaves faster than the load or stackmen could deal with them, and the latter attempted, on the other hand, to appear to be waiting for delayed supplies. "Yar fare t' be good tidily buried alive up thar bor, that yar wholly du, bor." "Nothen, bor, nothen. Yar kin wholly pitch 'm up double as quick ef yar kin, an' I kin take all yar kin pitch, that I wholly kin, bor." "Yar's as nigh heaven as yer'll ivver be, up thar, bor." "Ah, bor, them that's above sees all." Such pleasantries and little contests lightened labour. But in the fourth and fifth weeks when the weather broke, wet and windy, and the desired finish of harvest within six weeks seemed unlikely of fulfilment, tired men sometimes became a little fractious and despondent. 'Lord' Jimmy and Curzon showed the stuff they were made of at such times – always cheerful, patient and steady, they kept us all going.

Time after time the sheaves in the stooks of a whole field would have to be thrown out to dry and set up again. Our men went to piece work, hoeing and singling beet and turnips when work in the corn was impossible. There were fields of valuable clover seed to be turned over and over to dry, the ten of us in a line with forks, working round and about till all was turned. Then next day's wet made all to do again. But the sun came back, and a drying breeze, and hopes revived. The layer was now high in the barley, whose sheaves were thus heavier to pitch; and the wheat, that was carted last, was heaviest of all. The days and nights, just then, held no moisture. The barley came to a good malting colour. The wheat was plimmed and improved by the recent rain. The moon gave us light so that we could load sheaves till ten at night without harm from dews. We got harvest finished in capital good time, and everyone was well satisfied.

I think with pleasure of the many hours of labour that I spent with these men getting in the harvest during that great war. I do not think they were constrained by my presence, for they told the squire, "Our reverend is with us just like one of ourselves." We had our elevenses and fourses together seated on the ground, smoked our pipes, and I listened to much characteristic talk. I have set down elsewhere some of the rougher examples of East Anglian humour, but in my presence they never uttered an oath or a coarse expression, though perfectly natural and easy in the respectful way they treated me. Wartime rationing made traditional 'hawkeys' impossible, but we finished up with a little supper in my barn. Some hares and rabbits had to suffice for the scarcity of other meats, but Mary Ann Alderton surpassed herself in tasty preparations of these. Sugar for puddings and cakes had to be largely supplemented from my plentiful stores of honey. We had a barrel of beer, a few bottles of my home-made wine, and pipefuls from a canvas bag of Boer tobacco were all appreciated.

I had a lot of old briar pipes that were eagerly taken away as mementos of a happy evening. Old Mr. Cutter, our Riddlesworth blacksmith, a relation of the Bridgham Cutters, sang to us a few of his always applauded old-time songs – 'John Barleycorn', 'Little Brown Jug', 'The Girl Dressed in Blue' and others. He was a good six feet tall, brawny as a smith should be, and though now rather feeling his age his voice was rich and full as ever. Our hold ye boys were filled so full of good things that they were let off with only a brief exhibition of their vocal powers, The " 'tarn yar manny thanks" speech of the lord was a great success, finishing off with rounds of his handbells.

Though so remote from the scenes of war, in reality it was always in our thoughts – so many of our

*March 1918: German P.O.W. harvesting at Kenninghall.
The infant Daisy Bell (later Mrs. Martin) is seated on the right in black mourning clothes for her brother John, killed in the war on November 30th, 1917,*

cottage men were in France. On quiet nights I could hear the continuous roar of the guns in Flanders. Twice a Zeppelin came right over my house at night. I could hear the drone of its engines fifteen minutes before and after its arrival. I saw its long shape clearly overhead, blotting out and revealing stars in its progress. It dropped bombs at Bury St Edmunds, and one smashed the wall of Brocas's vicarage garden. I have a jagged fragment of steel from this bomb. We had a concentration camp of German prisoners in the old Guiltcross workhouse. My squire employed some of them to plant trees. These memories of the old war days in England, seem strange as I re-tell them now in Australia during this still greater war, nearly thirty years later.

My wife as amanuensis, writes them down for me.

Gaps and Changes

I have spoken of many gaps and changes among my friends and neighbours during those war years and after, in addition, my former old friend and parishioner Mrs Mann, who had gone to live at Brundall and afterwards at Thorpe, Norwich, was now dead, to the grief of her faithful companion Miss Frost. Sweeting, vicar of St. Cuthbert's Thetford, where I so often preached, was dead, his widow continuing to live in the pleasant house that belonged to her in the town. She was fond of books and music and foreign travel, a niece of my old London friend, Mrs Howlett. When Robinson of Rushford died he was succeeded by Adam, a young married parson, with a little son, a good fellow. I asked my squire to give Riddlesworth to him on my leaving, which he did. Two middle-aged clerical brothers with their sister were now at Garboldisham rectory. Soon after I left, they went to the living of Battle Abbey, where the younger man almost at once died, and his brother retired.

George Wilson in old age.

The Wood Sisters

Wilfred Blunt and I both missed our Sunday evening foregatherings when I left West Harling, though we met sometimes. On his seventy fifth birthday he walked over to Riddlesworth rectory and back in the snow to see me when I was ill - a feat he could justly be proud of. I had not given him or anyone else an inkling of the plans Agnes Wood and I had in mind when we cruised on the Broads. I was in my early fifties, she in her forties, and we wanted to be quite sure we would be good companions on a longer voyage.

She and her sister Grace were devoted to one another, and I doubted the rightness of breaking up their companionship, but Grace reassured me so warmly and whole-heartedly that I never could forget her wonderful self-sacrificing love for Agnes. Though he must have been indeed lonely sometime after her sister's marriage, she never showed other than complete content. I wanted to make quite sure too that Agnes should know truly everything about me that might be detrimental to our future happiness. I did not keep back from her a single thing. I would not hurry on our engagement, and she and I, with Grace and other friends spent number of weeks at various times at Hunstanton, Thorpeness, Cambridge, Dunster, and the two sisters had a final winter together in Italy and Sicily. All through this time, and even before the Broads cruise, Agnes was sure of her own wishes.

OUR MARRIAGE 1924

The Canon of Westminster was to have married us, but fell ill, and Frederick Appleton, took his place at St. Mary Abbots, Kensington Parish Church. Sir Robert Burton-Chadwick gave his cousin away and my brother Alan came from Bath to act as best man. Mary Ann Alderton helped to wait at the wedding breakfast in the great pomp of a silk dress and a real lace cap. We were married in the first week of December 1924.

[Ed: His happiness was not to last. Agnes died in Jerusalem, a few months after their third wedding anniversary. Harper subsequently married her sister, Grace. For a fuller account of their lives and the poetry they inspired Harper to write, the reader is referred to the companion, publication: A Breckland Time Piece].

> REMEMBERING THE SHINING AND MOST HAPPY LIFE OF
> **AGNES MARY HARPER**
> WHOSE EARTHLY TRAVELS ENDED AT JERUSALEM
> 24th MARCH 1928 AGED 53.
> WIFE OF CHARLES HUGH RICHARDSON HARPER
> AND SISTER OF GRACE BURTON WOOD.

[Ed: The title of this poem is also that of Harper's unpublished autobiography. By the time it was written, Grace had died following a fall].

BIRDS' EYE CASTLE

We said we would build a castle
On the edge of the sea of life,
A refuge of sight in blindness
Of peace amid war's bloody strife.

We could look out from the casements
Eastwards to our earliest years,
South to the joys and sunshine,
And north where lay sorrows and tears.

I'd tell for your pen my memories,
Yourself would record your own,
But the mighty present intruded
And I could not leave it alone.

I tried to hearten our fighters
Speak comfort to those who mourned,
Words, words, cast forth to the winds
With a prayer, and never returned.

Your scroll, dear wife, was unwritten,
You spent all your labours on mine,
Yet there is your story unfolded
Of love between every poor line.

We said if we'd life and strength left us
We'd look forth 'neath the westering Sun
To the future we'd like to see best
In a new better world here begun.

But you, my belovèd, have slipped
Away to the future alone.
I must try to keep tryst with our dreams,
And then in your footsteps I'll come.

> RECORDING ALSO THE SELFLESS AND
> MOST LOVING DEVOTION OF
> **GRACE BURTON HARPER**
> WHO DIED 16th AUGUST 1944 AGED 73.

[Ed. By the end of the war, Hugh, virtually blind and alone longed to return to England from Australia, but the journey was impossible.]

THE RETURN

England I long for thee;
All the miles of the world apart,
Set in another sphere thou art,
    And in another sea.

Long for the green hills and valleys,
Hamlets where time ever tarries
    For simple honest men.
The whole world is sick with cities,
Where man's wealth but not his wit is.
    I would return again –
To spring meadows filled with wild-flowers,
Offering incense thro' the long hours
    On the altar of God;
Plot again rich ploughland tillage,
Prate with gossips in the village,
    Pace slow the churchyard sod;

In mine own church I'd kneel and pray
And hear the Lord Christ kindly say
    Take heart. Lo, it is I!
I would return to the homeland,
And stand again on my own land,
    See it before I die.
How can I see who now am blind?
How can I hope my way to find?
    My soul at least shall fly,
When, far away, my clay is dust,
From mortal chains my spirit must
    Return to liberty.

CHARLES HUGH RICHARDSON HARPER
DIED 18th MAY 1947 AGED 78.

WE BELIEVE IN THE ETERNAL GOODNESS

West Harling Church.

INDEX

Adam, Rev., ... 75
Adams, Dr & Mrs, ... 41, 63, 70
Adams, Thirza, ... 11
Adlington, Capt., ... 60
Agnew, Mrs & Miss, ... 70
Airplanes, ... 39, 71
Albemarle family, ... see Keppel.
Alderton, Elizabeth, ... 44
    James, ... 44
       Jimmy, John & Sally, ... 20
          Mary Ann, ... 23, 45, 49, 74, 76
"America" Cottage, ... 47
Amherst, Lord of Hackney, ... 45
Antwerp, ... 69
Appleton, Frederick, ... 76
Arizona, ... 41
Association for the Employment of
    Discharged Soldiers, ... 64
Atkinson, Rev., ... 13, 56
Attleborough, ... 47, 63
Australia, ... 62, 77

Bacon, James, ... 60
Baghdad, ... 21
Baker, Agnes and Billy, ... 20
Baker, Elsie, ... 20
Balliol College, Oxford, ... 45
Banham, ... 23, 41, 55, 56, 63
Barbados, ... 12
Barker, Caleb, ... 1, 5, 60-1
Barker, Mrs Caleb, ... 60
Barker, N. J., ... 41, 63
Barnard, George, ... 52, 63
Barrett, Reggie, ... 23, 32, 35, 41, 67, 71-2
Barton, W. J., ... 41
Bath, ... 53, 63, 76
Battle Abbey, ... 75
Beadle, Mr, Mrs and Miss, ... 70
Beeches, The, East Harling, ... 1
Bees, ... 32-3, 35
Beeston Humber, ... 37, 53
Beevor, Edmund, ... 41
Beevor, Sir Hugh, ... 41

Belgium, ... 69
Bell, Daisy, ... 74
Bell, John, ... 4, 7
Bennett, Charles, ... 11, 12, 27-8, 32, 73
    James, ... 73-4
    Margaretta, ... (see Wilson)
    Mary, ... 11, 12, 27-8
Berlin, ... 69
Besthorpe, ... 56
Bethune, ... 62
Betts, Myrtle, ... 20
Biarritz, ... 55
Bishop of Durham, ... 5
Bishop Earle, ... 56
Bishop of Norwich:
    Pelham, ... 21
    Sheepshanks, ... 19, 21, 72
    Pollock, ... 72
Bismarck, ... 56
Bittern, ... 51-2
Blackburn, B&B&B, ... 34
Blo' Norton, ... 28, 41, 49
Bloomfield, Sam, ... 71
Blunt, Blanche, ... 19
Blunt, Rev. Henry Wilfrid, ... 17-20, 28, 37,
    . . . . 39, 42, 50, 52, 59
Bobs, (Harper's Dog), ... 22, 24, 25
Boer War, ... 7, 8
Boileau, Sir Francis and Lady, ... 9
    Margaret, ... 9, 63
    Maurice, ... 9, 63
Bolton Abbey, ... 19
Boulton and Paul's, ... 39
Boy Scouts, ... 63, 70
Bradenham, ... 60
Brandon, ... 26, 39, 47-8
Breckland, ... 14, 16, 26, 29, 31,
    . . . . 38-9, 47-9, 52, 56, 71
Breckland Time Piece, ... 76
Brettenham, ... 26, 42
Bridgham, ... 14, 16-20, 23-4, 26, 32-3, 39, 43-4,
    . . . . 47, 59, 63, 70, 74-5
Brighton, ... 38

Bristol,	38
British Museum,	45
Broads, The,	44-5, 52, 75-6
Browning, Robert,	34
Brundall,	75
Brundle/Brundell family,	11
(for Wilson-Brundle see Wilson)	
Brundle, Charles,	iv, 11, 14-16, 27, 29, 36, 37
Thirza,	11, 14-15, 27, 36
Buckenham, Mr.,	52
Bulwer, Sir Edward,	23
Bulwer family,	9
Bunyan, John,	37
Burlingham, Sidney,	20
Burlington Hotel Co.,	64
Burma,	41
Burnham,	66
Burroughes, Miss,	70
Burton-Chadwick, Sir Robert,	76
Burton, Mabel,	20
Bury St Edmunds,	75
Bussey, E. S. & Kate,	34
Bussey, Mabel,	34, 70
Bussey, Mr.,	7, 70
Butler, at W. Harling Hall,	1, 60
Buxton, Lady,	5, 31, 44,
Sir Robert,	31, 44, 60
Calais,	69
California,	41
Cambridge,	19, 53, 76
Cambridge, Duke of,	8
Canada,	64
Canterbury House of Laymen,	64
Carnegie, Andrew,	69
Cars: Benz,	38
De Dion Bouton,	38
Humberette,	39
Mercedes,	38
Minerva,	41
Rolls-Royce,	66
Rover,	39
Castle Hill, Thetford,	26, 32
Cavell, Rev. & Mrs,	7
Ceylon,	41
Champion, W. N. L.,	32, 35, 63, 66, 75
Champion, Mrs.,	66
Chapman, Marjorie,	20
Charity Commissioners,	15
Chaucer,	43
Chelsea,	18
Chelsea, Lady,	54
Chilcompton,	22, 24
Churchill, Winston,	69
Cirencester,	23
Clapton-in-Gordano,	56
Claxton, Capt.,	71
Clowes, Lawyer,	28
Coke of Holkham,	29
Colborne, Baron,	63
Lord,	6
Coldham, Mr.,	63
Mrs.,	41
Cole, Edith,	20
Fred,	71
Collins, Jesse,	29
Colman, Timothy,	27-8, 40
Coney Weston,	57, 66
Cook, at W. Harling Hall,	60
Cooper, Dr.,	15, 61
Coote, family,	8, 25, 35
Bob,	25, 49
Henry,	25, 34
Nellie,	25, 34
Percy Lake,	25
Reginald,	25, 34
Wilhelmina,	25, 70
William,	25, 34
Copeman, Bob,	20
Cotman,	44
Cowman, Mr.,	33
Crome,	44, 55
Cronshey, J. Henry,	41
Crook, Florrie,	20
Cross, E.,	41
Gertie,	70
Johnny,	4, 6, 34
Crowland Abbey,	66
Croxton,	29, 46
Crystal Palace,	38

Cuckoo,	9-10
Curtois, Rev. Hentley,	46
Curzon, Mr.,	73-4
Cutforth, Guy,	45
Cutter, Amos,	17
Dick,	71
Hattie,	20
Mr.,	74
Mrs.,	44
Damascus,	21
Davis, James, Agnes, William & Arthur,	70
Dennis, Rev. George,	46
Denny, Major,	41
Derby,	54
Derby, The,	66
Devon,	23
Dewhirst, Mr.,	63
Diss,	41
Dixon, W. D.,	41
Dover, Straits of,	69
Dreyfus case,	34
Drury, Anthony,	67
Duleep-Singh, Maharajah,	31
Prince Frederick,	28, 49
Dunster,	76
East Dereham,	41, 60
East Harling,	1, 2, 7, 17-8, 22-6, 35, 40, 45, 58, 60-4, 70
East Indies,	41
Eastwood, Rev. C. J.,	41
Eccles,	70
Ecclesiastical Commissioners,	61
Edale, Derbyshire,	66
Edgell, Mr.,	63
Edward VII,	see King
Edwards, Mr. & Mrs.,	41
Egerton, Lord of Tatton,	53
Einstein,	57
Elener, Mr.	63, 70
Mrs.,	70
Elveden,	31, 70, 71
Ely,	50
Encyclopaedia Britannica,	53
Endley, Charles,	52
W. & W.,	34
Eton College, Berkshire,	45-7, 63
Euston,	29, 31
Everett, Mrs.,	63
Exeter,	42
Exeter, Dean of,	23
Fellow, Rev.,	55
Fens, The,	26
Ferdinand, Archduke,	69
Fisher, Cecil,	29
Admiral Lord 'Jacky',	26, 29, 41, 54-5
Lord,	62
Fisher, Mary,	69
Fishing,	18, 19
Flanders,	69, 71, 75
Flatt, Lady,	44
Flint-Knapping,	47
Folkestone,	21
Follett, Col,	67
Forestry Commission,	61
Forman, Pearl,	20
Foster, Capt. T. H.,	41
Foured, Mrs.,	70
France,	60, 69, 71, 73, 75
Freeman, H.,	41
Frere family,	38
Frost, Miss.,	75
Fulloflove, Ralph,	6
Gainsborough,	4, 61
Gandhi,	57
Garboldisham,	28, 38, 41, 42, 61, 75
Garnham, Tom,	20
Garnier, Ann,	70
Canon Edward S.,	41, 54
Poppy,	70
Gascoigne family,	9
General E. F.,	63
Gasthorpe,	42, 65
Gawdy, Dame Dorothy's Charity,	14, 15
Philip,	45
George V & VI,	see King.
German P.O.W.,	74-5

Germany,	69
Gooding, Lacy,	35
Grafton, Duke of,	29, 31
Grand Canary,	37
Great Eastern Railway,	1, 34
Great Ouse, River:	see Ouse
Green, Mr., (Diocesan Architect),	65
Green, Rev. William Charles,	46
Grenadier Aunts,	iv
Grenadier Guards,	4, 8, 63, 64
Griffith-Williams, Delia,	66
Grigson, Rev. Baseley Hales,	40-2, 63
Mrs. B., Jack, Olive,	41
Mr. & Mrs. Pawlet,	41
Grimes' Graves,	47
Guiltcross Workhouse,	15, 28, 75
Guinness family,	31
Gypsies,	49
Haig-Brown, Alan,	39
Haldane, Lord,	54, 69
Halford, Sir George,	54
Hales, J. B. T. & R. T.,	41
Hall, John & Mrs.,	41
Halsbury, Lord Chancellor,	56
Hanton, Fred,	52
George,	24, 63
Jack,	8
M.,	34
Harbord, John,	5, 33-4
Harfleur,	72
Harling Rd. Station,	1, 35, 45, 63
Harper, Alan,	22, 24, 76
Geoffrey,	21
Helen,	22
Parents,	7
Roger,	21
Harvey, Di,	27, 78
Haywood,	41
Hemsworth, Miss,	70
Hepworth,	46
Hereward the Wake,	68
Herling, de,	7, 40
Hethersett,	45
Hewitt, Henry,	41, 63

Hindenburg line,	71
Holborn,	18
Hold-Ye, boys,	57-8, 73
Holkham,	29
Holme Hale,	60
Homburg,	55
Home & Colonial,	31
Hopton,	46
Horne, Rev.,	56
Howlett, Mrs.,	7, 75
Nellie,	7
Hunstanton,	76
Illington,	63, 70
India,	57
Irish Free State,	63
Italy,	76
Iveagh, Lord,	31
James, (Harper's groom-gardener),	23
Japan,	41
Jerusalem,	76
Jones, Rev. H.,	63
Jones, Rev. Robert & Mrs.,	41, 56
Kaiser Wilhelm,	55, 69
Kennaway, Rev. Charles L.,	42
Sir John,	42
Kenninghall,	15, 28, 56, 63, 70, 74
Kenninghall Workhouse,	see Guiltcross
Kenny, Doris & Stanley,	20
Kensington,	76
Kent, Mr.,	63
Keppel family	
Alice (Hon. Mrs. Geo.),	53-55
Countess of Albemarle,	53, 54, 70
Earl of Albemarle,	53, 54
Elizabeth, Lady,	54
George, Hon. Col.,	54
Harry, Admiral Sir,	55
Major,	55, 56
Viscount & Viscountess Bury,	54
Ker, Mr.,	61
Kerridge, Mrs.,	41
Kerridge, Walter,	41, 60, 61, 63, 70

Ketteringham,	9
Kilverstone,	26, 29, 38, 55
Kimberley,	8
King, D.,	34
King, G.,	34
King Edward VII,	31, 53-55
George V,	31
George VI,	62
William I, (The Conqueror),	40
King's House, Thetford,	26
Kipling, Rudyard,	8
Kitty, (Harper's horse),	22, 24, 26, 32, 35, 39, 41, 55, 67, 71, 72
Knettishall,	35, 41-2, 65, 68, 71
Knight, Rev. J. W.,	63
Knightsbridge,	63
Lake, Percy,	25
Lambert's, Thetford,	37
Lancashire,	66
Large, Lily,	20
Larling,	13, 26, 44, 56, 61, 62, 70
Lawrence, Mr.,	63
Lefroy, Dean,	21
Leicester, Earl & Countess of,	54
Lincolnshire Yeomanry,	71
Livermere Park,	46
Lloyd George,	29
Lock, John,	13
Lock, Miss,	63
London,	1, 15, 19, 21, 38, 41, 49, 50, 52, 67, 69, 75
Lophams, The,	41, 52
Lord Chancellor,	19
Luxembourg,	69
Mackenzie, Major,	29
Maeterlinck,	43
Malines, Belgium,	69
Mann, Mrs.,	57, 75
Martin, Daisy,	see Bell
Marshall Field Stores,	31
Marshall, Miss.,	63, 70
Mason, Harvey,	60
Maunder, Nanny,	iv
Meek, 'Happy',	44
Meek, Mrs.,	44
Mendham, Kent,	69
Merton,	29
Methuen, Lord,	8
Micklethwaite,	60
Middle Harling,	1, 5, 21, 23, 27, 57
Mitchell, Mr. & Sister,	70
Molyneux-Montgomerie, Sybil,	58
Squire, C. T.,	28, 38, 60
Mons,	69
Morgan, Rev. J. J.,	41
Mornement,	24
Major & Mrs. Edward,	41, 61
Morocco,	37
Motorcycles,	53
Mourilyan, Mrs.,	70
Munnings,	32
Murton-Webb,	41
Musker, Alice,	30
Boys,	45
Harold,	31
Herbert,	31
John,	30-32, 38, 42-43, 49, 50, 71
Percy,	31, 38
Nag's Head, East Harling,	22, 23
Nashe, Thomas,	45
National Patriotic Association,	64
Necton,	60
Nelson,	66
Newson, Ray,	20
Newspapers, Daily Mail,	19
Daily Telegraph,	33
Eastern Daily Press,	20
Guardian,	15
Pall Mall Gazette,	19
Times,	53
Westminster, Gazette,	19
New York,	31
New Zealand,	62
N. & N. Savings Bank,	64
N. & N. Soldiers' Institute,	64
Norfolk County Council,	64
Norfolk, Dukes of,	56
Norman & Beard,	69

Norris, Rev. C. L.,	41, 49
North Sea,	69
Norwich,	15, 21, 26, 39, 41, 45-6, 55-6, 58, 69
Norwich Diocesan Fund,	64
Norwich Castle Museum,	52
Nugent, Charles,	3, 61, 63
Claud,	3, 4, 61, 63
Dinah,	iv
Sir Edmund Bt,	1-6, 8, 9, 17, 21, 34, 49, 50, 52, 60-63, 70
Lady Evelyn Henrietta,	3-6, 60-63, 70
Evelyn Lilla,	iv 3, 4, 8, 34, 37, 41, 58, 61-63, 70
Rev. E. Frederick,	3, 4, 61, 63
Brig. George,	3, 4, 6, 8, 52, 61-3
Sir G. Guy, Bt,	3, 60, 63
Sir George, Bt,	63
Lord,	4
Maria Charlotte,	63
Sir Robin, Bt,	iv
Terence,	3, 58, 60, 62
Violet,	iv, 2, 3, 4, 8, 34, 37, 41, 61-63, 70
Nunn, Mrs.,	70
Nunnery, Thetford,	32
Oakden, Amy,	66, 67
Oakley, Mr.,	70
Oaks, The,	13
Old Buckenham,	55
Ouse, River Great,	16, 19, 26, 35, 42, 47, 49, 65
Oxford,	53, 59, 60
Pacific Ocean,	41
Paget, Mr.,	61
Paine, Tom,	26
Parker, Pte.	71
Pattinson, Lilian,	70
Peddars Way,	47
Peeks, Cyril,	20
Pelham, Canon,	63
Petch, Charlie,	70
Mr.,	63, 70
Pinner, John & Mrs.,	13
Pitt, Rev. R. W.,	41
Pole, Gertrude,	41
Pollard, Ellen,	23
Iron Mongers,	24
W. R.,	41, 63, 70
Poole, Rev. J. T.,	41
Popham,	31, 45
Porter, Nancy,	20
Portishead,	5, 53
Poultry,	32, 35
Prince Regent,	4
Privet Lodge,	25, 35
Prue, Rev., A. E.,	61, 62, 63
Mrs.,	63, 70
Queen, Alexandra,	55
Anne's Bounty,	5, 61
Elizabeth, I,	36, 45, 56
Victoria,	31, 55
Victoria Clergy Fund,	64
Quidenham,	53-6, 61, 70
Rand, The,	8
Ray, Mr. & Mrs. J. N. C,	41, 61, 63
Read, G. O.,	61
Red Cross Hospital, West Harling,	63, 70
Redgrave,	40, 41, 46
Reeve, John & William 'Peter',	20
Reeve, Mr. & Mrs.,	iv
Reynolds, Rev. Edgar,	62
Rhodes, Cecil,	8
Richardson, Ann & Cassie,	7
Riches, Charlie,	49, 52
Lizzie,	34, 70
H.,	34
Jack,	51, 52, 60
Jeremiah (Jerry),	49, 52
Riddlesworth,	13, 15, 32, 35, 42, 46, 47, 49, 51, 61, 63, 66-8, 71-75
Riddlesworth Hall,	65, 66
Ridley, Oliver,	36
Roberts, Lord,	24
Robinson, Rev. Thomas,	37, 42, 75
Rockland,	47
Rosebery, Lord,	45
Roudham,	24, 31, 43, 70
Roudham Heath,	15, 26, 47, 56

Rowley, Rev. H. S.,	41
Roxburgh Club,	45
Rudd, Kingston,	63
Rudham,	60
Rushford,	25, 26, 31, 42
Russia,	69
Samuel, Mr.,	60
Sarajevo,	69
Scoulton Mere,	47
Seaman, Jack,	44
Selfridge's Stores,	31, 50
Shadwell,	5, 25, 26, 31, 32, 44, 60, 61, 65, 71
Sawbridge, Rev. John Sikes,	46, 49, 50, 56, 67
his family,	46-7
Shakespeare,	43
Shaw, Nurse,	61
Shearme, Cmdr. & Olive,	41
Sheepshanks, Mr. & Mrs.,	19 (See Bishop)
Shropham,	41, 70
Sicily,	76
Smith, Ivy, Ethel & Jack,	20
Snarehill,	26, 31, 32, 71
Snetterton,	56
Soffe, Dr,	14, 15, 44
Solly, (the Butcher),	24
Somerset,	22, 25
South Africa,	24
Spellman, Miss,	41
Stammers, Evelyn & Mabel,	20
Stark,	44
Steggles, John,	44, 63
Stoat v. Rabbit,	50-1
Stonehouse Farm,	iv, 11-14, 71, 72
Streatham,	21
Sturgess-Jones, Rev. C. A.,	41
Suffield, Lord,	5
Suffolk,	16, 45-47, 49, 65
Sullivan, Sir Arthur,	63
Swaffham,	45, 47
Sweeting, Rev. & Mrs.,	75
Swift, Dean,	21
Switzerland,	41, 45
Tanks,	39, 70, 71
Tapper, Miss,	61
Taverham,	60
Thelnetham,	46-7, 57
Thet, River,	1, 5, 15-6, 18, 26, 31-33, 40, 47, 56, 59
Thetford,	17, 21, 25, 26, 29, 31, 32, 35, 37, 56, 63, 65, 75
Thetford Union Workhouse,	27-29
Thompson Water,	47
Thornhill, Sarah,	67
Squire,	67
Thorpe, W. H.,	5, 13, 26
Thorpe Farm,	25
Thorpe, Norwich,	75
Thorpeness,	76
Tourtel, Rev. W. E.,	41
Trent College,	45
Trent Expedition,	64
Trumpess, Fred,	20
Tucker,	45
Turner, Miss,	61
Tyler, Rev.,	56
U.S.A.,	31, 53
Upcher, Rev.,	56
Vavasseur (of Armstrong Vickers),	29
Velasquez,	2
Vicar of Wakefield,	5
Wake, Charles,	68
Hereward The,	68
Waller, Audrey,	20
Walters, Brocas,	72, 75
Walpole, Horace,	67
Mrs.,	7
Walsingham, Lord,	29
Walton, Izaak,	18
Warby,	63
Ward, Doris, Edna, Ivy & Olive,	20
Watson, Rev. G. W.,	41
Waveney, River,	44
Weaving,	52
Wellington College,	72
Wells, Rev. John Robinson & family,	42, 61

West, W., ... 41
West Africa, ... 47
Westminster, Canon of, ... 76
West Harling, ... 1-9, 15, 16, 21, 26, 27, 31,
    33-37, 40, 42, 45, 47, 50, 51, 53, 58-71, 73, 75,78
Wharfedale, ... 19
Whitehall, ... 15
Wiggett, Arthur, ... 63
    Mabel & May, ... iv, 34, 70
    Walter, ... 34
Wilby, ... 41
Willis, Sir George, ... 41
Wilson, Family of Stonehouse Farm, ... 11, 72
    Arthur, ... 13
    Bessie, ... 69
    Ella, ... 34
    George Brundle, ... 12-14, 63, 72, 75
    Hector, ... 12, 69, 71
    Jessie, ... 13
    Margaretta, ... 12, 13, 58
    Rose, ... 70
    Stella Wright, ... iv
Wilson, Rev. J. C., ... 41
Wilson, Rev. Leonard Holt, ... 41, 62

Wilson, Rowland, ... 40
Wilson, S., ... 34
Winchester School, ... 47
Wintle, ... 56
Wood, (Harper's sister-wives),
    Agnes Mary, ... 72, 75-6
    Grace Burton, ... 72, 75-77
Wood, Charles, ... 56
Woodbine Hut, ... 72
Woodhouse, ... 57
Workhouse, ... 15, 27, 28, 75
World War I, ... 33, 38, 39, 61, 69, 70-3, 75
World War II, ... 57, 75
Wretham, ... 41
Wright, Stella, ... iv
Wymondham, ... 58

Y.M.C.A., ... 72
Yare, River, ... 44
York, Duke of, ... 62
Yorkshire, ... 66

Zborowski, Count, ... 38
Zeppelins, ... 39, 75